Propaganda

BY THE SAME AUTHOR

FICTION
The Uniform
A Ball in Venice
The General's Summer-House
The Prophet's Carpet

WAR MEMOIRS AND HISTORY
Sword of Bone (The Dunkirk campaign)
Journey to Budapest 1956 (in Ten Years After)
The Vatican in the Age of the Dictators, 1922–1945

BIBLIOGRAPHY
The Poet as Superman—A Life of D'Annunzio
The Rise and Fall of Louis Renault

TRAVEL
A Sabine Journey
Where the Turk Trod
The Dalmatian Coast
Art Treasures of Eastern Europe
Princes of the Grape (the Great Wine Families)

BY THE SAME EDITOR

The American Poster Renaissance:
the Great Age of Poster Design, 1890–1900

Anthony Rhodes

EDITED BY
Victor Margolin

Angus & Robertson · Publishers

Angus & Robertson · Publishers ·
London · Sydney · Melbourne · Singapore · Manila

This book is copyright. Apart from any fair dealing
for the purposes of private study, research, criticism
or review, as permitted under the Copyright Act, no part
may be reproduced by any process without written permission.
Inquiries should be addressed to the publisher.

First published in the U.S.A. by Chelsea House Publishers 1976

This edition published by Angus & Robertson (U.K.) Ltd 1976
Copyright © Chelsea House Publishers 1975
ISBN 0 207 95719 3

Designed by Seymour Chwast

Made and printed in West Germany

Contents

Foreword by Victor Margolin
vii

CHAPTER ONE
The Propagation of the Reich, 1933–1945
9

CHAPTER TWO
Mussolini's New Rome, 1922–1945
65

CHAPTER THREE
Britain Improvises, 1936–1945
105

CHAPTER FOUR
United States: Isolation and Intervention, 1932–1945
137

CHAPTER FIVE
Rule and Resistance in "The New Order," 1936–1945
177

CHAPTER SIX
The Soviet Union: Propaganda for Peace, 1917–1945
209

CHAPTER SEVEN
The Rise and Fall of Japan, 1931–1945
241

Afterword by Daniel Lerner
283

Essay and Filmography by William Murphy
291

Notes on Color Plates by Victor Margolin
305

Bibliography
308

Index
311

Credits
319

Foreword

Though propaganda has never been a substitute for military strength, extensive resources, or skillful negotiation, it has often played an important role in wartime strategy. No one can deny the impact of German propaganda in softening up the French in 1940, nor the part played by Allied propaganda in preparing the German people for surrender after Normandy.

The term "propaganda" in this book covers a multiplicity of uses—from the posters, films, and comic strips which exposed the home front to images of the enemy, to the "psychological warfare" intended to directly influence the action of enemy troops and civilians. In its broadest sense, World War II propaganda was just about anything which affected or confirmed the feelings and behavior of all involved, both toward their own country's efforts and those of their enemies.

Within this broad definition, visual material was selected from public archives and private collections in the United States and Europe. The editor and the author wish to thank the many individuals and institutions who shared their knowledge and provided material from their collections. Washington D.C.: Michael Hardgrove and Jay Robbins of WETA/Channel 26, who made available a valuable collection of photographs; Dr. Edgar Breitenbach, former chief of the Prints and Photographs Division at the Library of Congress, Alan Fern, who presently holds that position, and the division's staff—Milt Kaplan, Elena Millie, Jerry Kerns, and Leroy Bellamy; Mrs. Seely, U.S. Army Photographic Agency; Mayfield Bray, National Archives; Charles McDonald and Joseph Ewing, U.S. Army Office of Military History. New York: Donald Richie and Mary Corliss, Museum of Modern Art Film Library; New York Public Library Theater Collection; Culver Pictures Corp.; Richard Merkin; Les Zeiger; David Stewart Hull; Maurice Horn; Edward R. Tannenbaum; Herb Friedman. Palo Alto: Dr. Franz Lassner and his staff at the Hoover Institution on War, Peace, and Revolution. San Francisco: Bill Blackbeard, director of the San Francisco Academy of Comic Art. London: Joseph Darracott, Barry Kitts, Mike Moody, Jeff Pavey, and Clive Coultass at the Imperial War Museum; Robson Lowe Ltd.; Victoria and Albert Museum; Reginald Aukland; Roger Bell; the Wiener Library. Paris: Mlle. Cécile Coutin, curator of the Musée des Deux Guerres Mondiales; Mme. Migliorini, Bibliothèque de Documentation Internationale Contemporaine, Nanterre; Michel Girard. Brussels: J. R. Leconte and M. Lorette, Musée Royal de l'Armée et d'Histoire Militaire. Amsterdam: Dr. Louis de Jong, director, and Jacob Zwann, archivist, Rijksinstituut voor Oorlogsdocumentatie. Koblenz: Mr. Haupt, Mr. Postupa, and Frau Loenartz, of the Bundesarchiv. Others who helped were Milton Cohen; Philip V. Cannistraro; Peter Robbs, hon. general secretary of the Psywar Society; and James Goodrich of the Missouri State Historical Society. Photographers included Simon Cherpitel, San Francisco; Teddy Schwartz, London; Mr. Bessam, Amsterdam; and Carmelo Catania, Rome.

Also to be thanked are the excellent production team of Harris Lewine, art director, and Seymour Chwast, designer, as well as David Sachs, copyeditor. Andy Norman and Harold Steinberg of Chelsea House showed great patience during the lengthy period necessary to prepare this book.

Victor Margolin
New York City, May 1975

CHAPTER ONE

THE PROPAGATION OF THE REICH
1933-1945

Nothing is easier than leading the people
on a leash. I just hold up a dazzling
campaign poster and they jump through it.
JOSEPH GOEBBELS

When on February 28, 1933, the Reichstag building in Berlin was set on fire, Chancellor Adolf Hitler obtained an emergency decree from President Paul von Hindenburg placing restrictions on personal liberty, including freedom of the press. Thirteen days later, on March 13, the Ministry for Popular Enlightenment and Propaganda was founded under the direction of Dr. Josef Goebbels, to control the press as well as all other means of expression—radio, film, art, and literature. It is most appropriate that propaganda in Nazi Germany should have been considered worthy of an entire government department. No "Ministry for Popular Enlightenment and Propaganda" had ever existed before, in Germany or in any other country. It was a sign of the age of the Common Man, of the hitherto apolitical and uneducated masses now awakening, and in whose manipulation, as the Nazis (and to a lesser extent the Soviets) were first to become aware, lay the secret of political success. Half a decade before they achieved that success, the Nazis were already skillfully using all the new 20th-century media—press, radio, film, and posters—to control, direct, and coordinate the masses. At the height of its power during the Second World War, the Propaganda Ministry was issuing daily directives to the editors of newspapers all over Germany about what to print, in such detail that the papers were virtually written for the editors.

Political propaganda had been used before in the 20th century, by the British in the First World War, but on a limited scale. It was left to Nazi Germany to employ it on such a scale, and with such effect, that by 1939 the German masses seemed completely indoctrinated. To the very end, most of them still believed that Adolf Hitler was a disinterested ruler, even a messiah, concerned above all with their welfare and, ultimately, that of the human race.

How did he acquire this spurious reputation? It is not enough to say that the Germans have always been responsive to patriotic slogans—"The call of duty," "The honor of the race," "The nobility of a soldier's death." There were a number of other factors: Hitler's own almost superhuman energy, his ruthlessness in crushing opposition, his craftiness in "dividing and ruling," and his manipulation of the armed forces. Hitler's use of propaganda, if not necessarily his most effective weapon (compared, say, to military victories), was certainly his most sinister, for it aimed at, and under Goebbels' masterly direction succeeded in, persuading the Germans that the Nazi system would restore their country's greatness.

Hitler had first become aware of propaganda and its uses before the First World War. In his early writings, he referred to the Austrian Marxists in Vienna, "who knew how to flatter the masses." During the war he saw the effect of British propaganda on the soldiers of the Central Powers; he later read Lord Northcliffe's words, "The bombardment of the German mind was almost as important as the bombardment by cannon." Northcliffe's aim was "to produce by propaganda a state of mind in the German army favorable to surrender—to enlighten it about

Sieg oder Unsieg ruht in Gottes Hand! Der Ehre sind wir selber Herr und König!

Two posters from the 1932 German
election. Though Hitler, the Nazi candidate, ran on a platform of economic
recovery and resurgent nationalism, he
was unable to defeat the 84 year old
Field Marshall Hindenburg, supported
by a coalition of Socialists, Centrists,
and liberals. (Top) "German women,
think of your children. Vote Hitler."
(Bottom) "Our last hope, Hitler," a
poster by Mjölnir (Hans Schweitzer).

the hopelessness of its military situation."

Of this Hitler wrote, "What we failed to do in propaganda
was done by the enemy with great skill and ingenious delibera-
tion." It is significant that Hitler's first appearance on the political scene was in the role of military propagandist at the end of
the war. The officers of the 1st Bavarian Rifle Regiment, in which
he was serving, recognized in the voluble corporal a committed
nationalist whose oratory might counter the revolutionary Marx-
ism now making headway among the demoralized troops. They
made him "regimental political education officer." He was remarkably successful.

A few years later, when he was writing *Mein Kampf* (*My
Struggle*), he devoted two chapters to the study and practice of
propaganda. Although he said that in the future the man who
controlled the masses would control the state, he made no attempt to hide his contempt for the masses. "The psyche of the
masses," he wrote, "is not receptive to anything that is weak.
They are like a woman, whose psychic state is determined less
by abstract reason than by an emotional longing for a strong
force which will complement her nature. Likewise, the masses
love a commander, and despise a petitioner."

To his friend Rauschnigg he said, "Haven't you ever seen a
crowd collecting to watch a street brawl? Brutality and physical
strength is what they respect. The man in the street respects
nothing more than strength and ruthlessness—women too for
that matter. The masses need something that will give them a
thrill of horror." For the next fifteen years, Hitler was to give
them just that, in ever increasing measure.

He started from the premise that propaganda must be addressed to the emotions and not to the intelligence; and it must
concentrate on a few simple themes, presented in black and
white. "Propaganda," he wrote, "consists in attracting the
crowd, and not in educating those who are already educated."
He had no use for the intelligentsia or the upper classes.

He first put his theories into practice in 1925, in the Nazi party
newspaper, the *Völkischer Beobachter (People's Observer)*.
It contained none of the long, rambling articles and academic
discussions which characterized the liberal bourgeois, socialist,
and communist presses, but instead short, sharp hyperboles on
"patriotic" themes—The Infamy of Versailles, the Nobility of
the Teutons, The Weakness of Weimar, The Virus of Jewry, The
Evil of Bolshevism, and the ringing slogan *"Ein Volk, Ein
Reich, Ein Führer"* (one people, one nation, one leader).

This paper, and others which the Party subsequently acquired
(such as the anti-Semitic *Der Stürmer*), were all characterized
by Hitler's statement about the masses' admiration of violence.
Their propaganda was vicious and gruesome, with lurid photographs of the atrocities, sexual and physical, alleged to have
been committed by Jews and communists on unsuspecting German women.

As leader of the Party, Hitler was too busy to devote much
time to propaganda, important though he recognized it to be. It
required a full-time expert. In Josef Goebbels he found his man.

Goebbels was to become one of history's greatest political propagandists. A Rhinelander of humble origins, he had obtained a number of scholarships to universities and became a doctor of philosophy. Hitler met him in 1926 and, quickly appreciating his oratorical power of persuasion, made him head of the party propaganda department. It is probable that Goebbels—a cynic in most matters—genuinely admired, even hero-worshipped, Hitler. Goebbels and many like him had suffered from the political and economic chaos in Germany in the early 1920s; in Hitler he saw the savior of his country from both chaos and communism. He immediately set about creating the Führer legend which was to carry Hitler and his Party to power, and to make Hitler revered throughout Germany.

Goebbels had studied the methods employed by the Fascists in Italy to create the heroic image of Mussolini; and he applied them a fortiori to Hitler. He realized that to impress the masses, the modern dictator must be at once a superman and a man of the people, remote yet accessible, wise yet simple, lonely on his Olympian height, yet ready to mix with the crowd. This is seen in two articles which Goebbels wrote in his paper *Der Angriff* (*The Attack*)—"Adolf Hitler, Statesman," and "Adolf Hitler, Human Being." In the first, he showed the Führer as infallible in his political judgments, which were beyond human acumen; yet he was, as the second article showed, surprisingly human and kind. "The simplest people," Goebbels wrote, "approach him with confidence, because they feel he is their friend and protector."

Hitler was, he argued, really an artist, an architect and painter, who had forsaken his muse to help the German people in their darkest hour. When he had completed his political work, he would return to his calling. For Germany's sake he had learned to negotiate with all the statesmen of Europe, in polished dialogue and with a masterly command of diplomacy, for days on end, sometimes in fifteen-hour sessions.

In his many public speeches and articles in *Der Angriff* before the Party attained power, Goebbels was also careful to depict the Führer as a man of the people, who had shared their plight and knew their problems. He described, for instance, how Hitler once visited his native land at Oberammergau and mingled with the Austrian crowd, speaking to one or two of them. So moved were they by his kind and understanding words that they were unable to answer because "their tears choked them." Goebbels described how the goodness of the man shone out in his face: "His eyes are bright with unimpaired radiance, his high forehead is noble and bold. Only his hair reveals a light silver touch, the sign of countless days of work and worry and nights in which he is awake and lonely. Never does one word of falsehood or baseness pass his lips."

Goebbels occasionally introduced a religious note about this paragon of virtues. Of a speech Hitler made in Cologne he wrote, "One had the feeling as if all Germany had been transformed into one vast church embracing all classes and creeds, in which its spokesman appeared before the high altar of the Almighty to

The Illustrierter Beobachter *was a popular tabloid newspaper filled with photographs of meetings, demonstrations, and processions. Reporting was confined almost exclusively to glorifying the Nazi movement. Articles on all topics were heavily slanted. (Top) "They fought and bled for Germany's freedom," 1942. (Bottom) "Russia arms! . . . and Germany?," 1933.*

Sie kämpften und bluteten für Deutschlands Freiheit

Russland rüstet! ...und Deutschland?

Sowjetrussische Schulkinder beim Waffenunterricht

Posters, photomontages, and magazine covers by John Heartfield, a Communist designer who attacked the Nazis until the party was banned after Hitler became Chancellor. (Bottom, left) "6 million Nazi voters; fodder for a huge mouth." (Top, right) Stamps for a 1932 peace congress. (Bottom, right) A play on the proverb, "Lies have short legs." Opposite page. (Top row, left) "Adolf—the superman; swallows gold and talks nonsense." (Top row, middle) "Have no fear; he's a vegetarian." (Top row, right) Hitler as a Prussian officer. (Middle row, left) "Göring the hangman." (Middle row, middle) "The bishop of the Reich inspects the Christian ranks." (Middle row, right) "The cross wasn't heavy enough." (Bottom row, left) "Blood and Iron, the old election slogan in the new Reich." (Bottom row, middle) "New chair in the German universities." (Bottom row, right) A Christmas tree in the shape of a swastika.

6 Millionen Naziwähler: Futter für ein großes Maul

"Und den Fisch hab ich gewählt!"

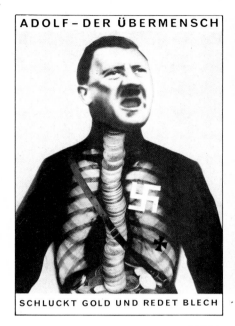

ADOLF – DER ÜBERMENSCH

SCHLUCKT GOLD UND REDET BLECH

NUR KEINE ANGST – ER IST VEGETARIER

S.M. ADOLF

Ich führe Euch herrlichen Pleiten entgegen!

GÖRING, DER HENKER

DER REICHSBISCHOF RICHTET DAS CHRISTENTUM AUS

„He, der Mann da, das Kruzifix etwas weiter nach rechts!"

ZUR GRÜNDUNG DER STAATSKIRCHE

Das Kreuz war noch nicht schwer genug

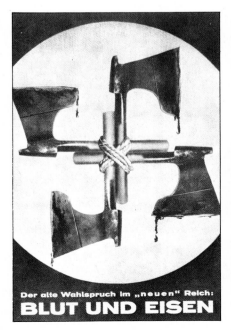

Der alte Wahlspruch im „neuen" Reich:

BLUT UND EISEN

Neuer Lehrstuhl an den deutschen Universitäten

Ein Professor Witlawopsky von der Universität Heidelberg hat festgestellt, daß das menschliche Hühnerauge, allerdings nur das germanische, befähigt ist, in die Zukunft zu schauen. Hitler hat sogleich nach Bekanntwerden der Entdeckung des genialen Forschers die Überführung von 1300 Hühneraugen-Operateuren ins Konzentrationslager angeordnet.

Originalaufnahme aus dem teutonischen Busch von J. H.

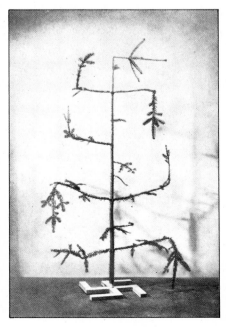

(Below) "The Field Marshall and the Corporal," a 1933 poster which showed Hitler and Hindenburg as partners in shaping Germany's future. In March 1933, the Nazis pushed through legislation enabling Hitler to rule unsupervised. (Opposite page, top and middle, left) Medals commemorating the Nuremberg rallies in 1935 and 1936. (Bottom, left) National Socialist Party songbook. (Top, right) Burial ceremony for Horst Wessel, an S.A. tough who was killed by the Communists in 1930 and martyred by Goebbels. A song he wrote, the Horst Wessel Lied *became the official song of the Nazi party and the second national anthem after* Deutschland über Alles. *(Middle, right) Nazi troops hold a banner at a Party Day rally in Nuremberg. (Bottom, right) Hitler was a supreme orator who could play on the emotions of a crowd. He was at his best before a mass audience and, unlike Roosevelt, was ineffective in a broadcast studio.*

render an account of his achievements, and to implore His mercy and protection for the uncertain future. In Cologne that morning, we saw hard and strong men who had overcome many a danger burst into tears at the closing words of the Führer. This was religion in the most mysterious and deepest sense of the word."

Goebbels even went so far on one occasion as to introduce a mother image of this essentially masculine man. "And so, the whole nation loves him because it feels safe in his hands, like a child in the arms of its mother."

How did Goebbels explain the Führer's role in the events of June 30, 1934, "The Night of the Long Knives"? On that occasion, Hitler ordered, and personally supervised, the butchery of some 150 of his former comrades, whom he suspected of plotting to take over the army. The morning after the slaughter, Goebbels printed a photograph of the Führer in which he stressed "the tragic loneliness in his face"; for the Führer had become "another Siegfried who has been forced to shed blood so that Germany might live." His face reflected "grief and sorrow over the deaths of his Old Comrades who had been misled."

Had not the Führer himself said that all his actions were dictated by a higher power? "I go," he said, "with the assurance of a sleepwalker in the path which providence dictates." He was the rock in the ocean of peoples' lives, as well as Atlas bearing on his shoulders the cares of Germany and the whole world, which he alone could save from the Jews and communists.

Another photograph of the Führer which Goebbels continually reproduced was of Hitler with the universally loved but moribund President von Hindenburg. "The Führer's face," wrote Goebbels, "here reflects grief and sadness over the merciless death about to take away his fatherly friend." (In fact, far from being a "fatherly friend," Hindenburg could not bear the sight of Hitler, whom he always referred to as "the Bohemian corporal." Hitler, for his part, was longing for Hindenburg to die, so that he could take over his job.)

For his creation of the Führer legend, Goebbels made great use of the mass demonstrations which became a regular feature of Nazi Germany after Hitler's assumption of power. Emotional manipulation, he found, was most effective at these mammoth gatherings, when both participants and onlookers became part of the Führer intoxication, when each single individual underwent, in his words, "a kind of metamorphosis from a little worm into part of a big dragon." These demonstrations generally took place at night, after 8 P.M., when people's resistance was at its lowest ebb, and their minds most open to persuasion. At the annual rally in Nuremberg, the Nazis' holy city, half a million people on the tribunes watched 200,000 banner-carrying uniformed men belonging to a plethora of Nazi organizations march past the Führer, who stood on a dais for all to see.

Albert Speer, Hitler's favorite architect, was the "chief decorator" of the rallies. He devised the idea of placing 130 anti-aircraft searchlights around the rally field at intervals of forty feet. He called the ring of vertical beams a "cathedral of light."

(Top and bottom) Leni Riefenstahl, whose film of the 1934 Nuremberg rally, Triumph of the Will, *became a classic of film propaganda. Heavy-handed in its symbolism and tedious in its endless shots of marching troops,* Triumph of the Will *was nevertheless used to create the impression of Nazi strength and discipline. Though the film appears to be a documentary, the rally was as carefully staged for the camera's sake as a Cecil B. DeMille epic.*

At the 1936 rally, after a torchlight procession 150 searchlights converged in a vast cupola in the sky above the multitude. Speer also designed a huge eagle over 100 feet in wingspread to crown the stands. Fanfares sounded and bands played the Führer's favorite march, the *Badenweiler,* as erect, grim-faced, jackbooted, he trod the podium. His personal standard was unfurled and suddenly, at a shrill command, 30,000 flags dipped in salute. The entire ceremony centered around the Führer's podium, where the Man of Destiny stood alone with upraised arm. He then addressed the multitude over the loudspeaker network in a harangue which sometimes lasted an hour, and which rose at the end to a crescendo of hysteria. It dealt with the old hackneyed patriotic themes—the heroic struggle of the Party to restore Germany's greatness, the pollution of the Jews, the beastliness of the Bolsheviks, the decadence of the democracies. When he had finished, the flags were dipped again and half a million people sang the national anthem, *Deutschland über Alles,* and Goebbel's Party hymn, the *Horst Wessel Lied.* In the silence that then fell, he shrieked, "Hail, my men!", and the multitude bayed back, "Hail my Führer!" (The use of *my* instead of *our* gave each individual the feeling that it was *his* Führer, to whom he belonged.)

The Führer then consecrated the new Party colors by touching them with one hand, while the other grasped the cloth of the bullet-riddled *Blutfahne,* the flag drenched in the gore of the Nazi martyrs who had carried it to their death in the abortive putsch of 1923. The whole parade finished in a welter of fanfares, drum beats, flaring pylons, massed choruses, and banner-waving marching columns passing before the Führer, beneath triumphal arches adorned with stylized eagles clutching wreathed swastikas.

Hitler had likened these emotional masses to a woman, and it was the women of Germany who were most fanatical and hysterical on these occasions. He was always receiving letters from female admirers imploring him to father their children. It was even said that mothers-to-be in labor often called out his name to ease the pain.

By the outbreak of the Second World War, Goebbels' Propaganda Ministry had complete control of the press, radio, theater, cinema, the creative arts, music, writing, art exhibitions. When every contemporary book people read, every newspaper, every film they see, every broadcast they hear for years on end is permeated with the same spirit, the same propaganda, they are no longer able to relate what they see and hear to alternative reports; they lose their judgment. By 1939 no one thought it odd, let alone funny, that a Nazi sports leader proclaimed to the cycling clubs of Germany, "The Führer demands the unity of the whole German cycling movement"; or that bowlers were informed that their sport now enjoyed its high position in the public esteem entirely due to the Führer.

Goebbels openly admitted that propaganda had little to do with the truth. "Historical truth," he said at a mass meeting in Berlin, "may be discovered by a professor of history. *We* however are serving historical necessity. It is not its task, any more than it is the task of art, to be objectively true." The sole aim of propaganda, he said, was success. Here he was claiming for propaganda what Machiavelli had proclaimed 500 years before as the sole aim of statesmanship.

All the same, Goebbels was careful not to tell whole lies; he was a master at distorting the truth. In the words of Schwerin von Krosig, "He hid the nucleus of truth with all the veils of interpretation. He always had a channel of escape when anyone questioned the truth of his statement."

The cinema was Goebbel's special foster child. He not only had a personal weakness for female screen idols (a number of whom became his mistresses), but he was quick to realize that this new art form could reach a far wider audience than books or theater. The notion of thousands of adult men and women all cooped up in the dark, staring at the same image on the silver screen appealed to his sense of uniformity. Also, the film with its well-worn cliches—suspense, adventure, love, crime, murder —could be addressed to the lowest common denominator of the human intellect. Thanks to governmental stimulus, cinema attendance quadrupled in the ten-year period from 1933 to 1942.

Because the Nazis considered the cinema such a powerful medium, its personnel—actors, directors, electricians, cameramen, etc.—were immediately made to take the oath of loyalty to the Führer. As early as May 1, 1934, five thousand employees of the UFA studios took it, without apparent demur. The old Motion Picture Law of 1920 was replaced by the Reich Motion Picture Law, which enacted that the subject of every proposed film must be "handed in before the making of the film to the Reich Film Drama Advisor in outline and scenario form for examination." Paragraph 2, Section 5 stated that the censor's aim must be "to hinder such subject matter as runs counter to the spirit of the times."

Goebbels took a personal interest in all the films made during the Third Reich, and he often intervened personally to make a change or an addition. His known addiction to the cinema sometimes caused unexpected, even embarassing situations. Once, he had seen a preview of a film about hospital life—the usual love story of doctors and nurses—and he was on his way to another appointment. In his hurry, he said in passing to his adjutant, "Now, we've had enough of these *Arztefilms* (doctor films) to last us a long time. Tell them—no more!" But the adjutant thought he said "*Ernstefilms*" (serious films). He dutifully transmitted the instructions to the screen writers, with the result that for months after the Propaganda Ministry was flooded with quantities of light comedies—and this at a time (1943) when the Nazi leaders wanted people to be fortified by serious and heroic films, of the Frederick the Great type.

The best-known films of the Nazi period are Leni Riefenstahl's *Triumph of the Will*, about the 1934 Nuremberg Rally, in the documentary form she perfected, and her *Olympia*, another documentary about the 1936 Olympic Games in Berlin. Both are Nazi propaganda, but of a relatively subtle kind. The former

(Top) A scene from Leni Riefenstahl's Triumph of the Will. *The three huge banners behind the podium were designed by Albert Speer, Hitler's chief architect. Riefenstahl's second full-length propaganda film was* Olympia, *the subject of which was the 1936 Olympic games in Berlin. (Below) A Dutch poster protesting the 1936 Olympics.*

(Top) A page from a Nazi textbook. (Bottom) A scene from Eduard von Borsody's film, The Trial of Binnie Casilla *(1939), a mockery of American press and court procedures. A man is tried for kidnapping his own daughter from her foster parents. The child becomes a film star and the foster parents, not wishing to lose her income, regularly inject her with a serum to prevent her growth. The father's German origin raises antipathy in court but he finally wins the case.*

Mein Führer!

(Das Kind spricht:)

Ich kenne dich wohl und habe dich lieb
　　　　　　　　wie Vater und Mutter.
Ich will dir immer gehorsam sein
　　　　　　　　wie Vater und Mutter.
Und wenn ich groß bin, helfe ich dir
　　　　　　　　wie Vater und Mutter,
Und freuen sollst du dich an mir
　　　　　　　　wie Vater und Mutter!

opens on the heavens with magnificent shots of cloud formations behind which the threatening sound of Hitler's bombers can be heard. The Führer is seen alighting from an airplane, and then the whole Nuremberg Rally is filmed. With her technical skill, Riefenstahl was able to present the Party and its leaders in a heroic light for Germans, and a respectable one for foreigners. The film also fostered the feeling of the participation of the masses in the ceremony. "The preparations for the rally" wrote Riefenstahl, "were made in concert with the preparations for the camera work." That is, the rally was planned not only as a spectacle, but as spectacular film propaganda. The arenas and approaches for the Olympic Games were designed and constructed in the same way, as much for Riefenstahl's army of cameramen as for the athletes.

The Olympic Games proved an ideal vehicle for Nazi propaganda to foreign countries. At the previous games, in Amsterdam in 1928 and Los Angeles in 1932, no arrangements had been made for simultaneous broadcasting of the events as they took place. At Berlin in 1936, during the sixteen days of the games, 2,500 reports were broadcast in twenty-eight languages by German and foreign reporters. Afterwards, the foreign press and radio correspondents sent congratulatory telegrams to Goebbels on this admirable organization. Goebbels personally supervised the propaganda arrangements and produced an image of a smiling, jovial people filled with vitality. The result was that many of the foreign dignitaries, suitably wined and dined, came away deeply impressed by the New Germany. For the benefit of these visitors, the Nazis soft-pedaled much of their propaganda. All anti-Semitic regulations, such as "Jews not admitted," were removed from hotels and restaurants. Julius Streicher's anti-Semitic *Der Stürmer* could not be bought on the streets, and other aggressive propaganda measures were suspended or abated. The only discordant note—from the Nazi point of view —was the success of the black American sprinter, Jesse Owens, who received more international attention than any other athlete. But Leni Riefenstahl was careful not to show Hitler petulantly leaving the stadium when Owens ran.

Jüd Süss (*Jew Süss*) was a different form of propaganda, a nauseating anti-Semitic film. Set in the Middle Ages, it depicts a repulsive, crooked-nosed Jew who threatens a German maiden: if she does not let him ravish her, he will have her fiancé broken on the wheel. After the rape the heroine, like a good German, commits suicide. The hanging of the Jew at the end was described by a German critic as a "joyous crescendo." The actress in this film was one of the Nazi screen favorites, Kristina Söderbaum, a snub-nosed Nordic blond who was often cast in roles of this kind. In another film, from Billinger's novel *Gigant*, she plays a Sudeten German peasant's daughter who becomes bewitched by the lure of a big city and forsakes her father's hearth for Prague. She pays for worshipping this false (Czech) idol by first being made pregnant and then deserted by her Czech seducer. She returns home, where her old father is so ashamed of her behavior that he commits suicide. In the film version however, the ending is different, because the Propaganda Ministry insisted that the disgraced daughter, not the guiltless father, should suffer for the racial pollution. In her films, Kristina Söderbaum generally committed suicide by drowning. This became such a convention that the end always showed her—whether she had suffered rape, seduction, or desertion—floating Ophelia-like on the water. For this she became popularly known as the *Reichswasserleiche* (the national floating corpse).

Another way in which the Propaganda Ministry interfered was in the censorship of foreign films. It banned the French film *Nana*, based on Zola's novel, because of a scene between a soldier and a prostitute. Since the army is the foundation of the state, ran the argument, to depict a soldier cohabitating with a prostitute undermines the state's authority.

One of the most important uses of the cinema was for the indoctrination of the young. In April 1934, the first "Film Hour for the Young" was opened in Cologne. Two months later Goebbels' film administrator, Dr. Rust, ordered the showing of "politically valuable films" in all schools throughout the Reich. In his directive he said, "To disseminate our National Socialist ideology we know of no better medium than the film—above all for the youngest of our citizens, the schoolchildren. The National Socialist state deliberately makes the film the transmitter of its ideology."

Within two years Rust had equipped 70,000 schools with motion picture projectors. The cinema attendance in schools increased from 650,000 children in 1934 to 3 million in 1939. Two hundred and twenty-seven films were produced for schools. They dealt with "the great problems of our epoch," which were nothing less than the preparations, mental and emotional, for war.

The theme of nearly all these school films was *Wehrerziehung* (military education), and their protagonist was the UFA film director, Karl Ritter, a fanatical Nazi. His films glorified death in battle; films like *A Pass in Promise* in which a young composer prefers to die in November 1918 fighting for an already conquered Germany, rather than live on for the première of his symphony. As Ritter himself said, "My films all deal with the unimportance of the individual. . . . all that is personal is as nothing compared with the Cause." His film *Traitors and Patriots*, which romanticized fifth column activities in foreign countries, was shown to some 6 million schoolboys.

The effect of these films was inordinate. Many of the Hitler Youth who had been herded by the thousands into the cinemas to see them were taken prisoner during the war. Under Allied interrogation, they revealed the influence these films had had on them. Arrogant in victory, cold and unperturbed in defeat, they openly confessed that they were, as individuals, utterly unimportant, and that in war their sole function was to be instruments.

Nazi society was completely male dominated, and some of these films, such as *Hitlerjunge Quex*, have overtones of homosexuality. Writers like Ernst Jünger had advocated the substitution of male comradeship for love. The Nazis had no particular

Scenes from three films on Nazi youth. (Top) A film on the Hitlerjugend *(Hitler Youth Movement). (Middle) Hans Steinhoff's* Hitlerjunge Quex, *one of several feature films on party themes made in 1933. (Bottom)* S.A. Mann Brandt *(1933), directed by Franz Seitz. After these initial party films, Goebbels encouraged features that were more entertaining or less overtly propagandistic.*

Nazi propagandists had enough faith in Hitler's charisma to print this 1932 election poster of his disembodied head floating on a black background. Erwin Schockel wrote of this poster in Das Politische Plakat *(1938), "Peace, strength, and goodness radiate from Hitler's face and are communicated to the viewer. The effect on men with uncorrupted souls must be good." The heavy square lettering reflects the ponderous Nazi taste in graphic design. (Opposite, full page) Hitler in the pose of a Renaissance prince. The slogan on the poster,* One people, one nation, one leader, *was often used in the Reich. (Opposite, inset) The single word* Ja *(Yes) combined with the forceful image of Hitler expresses confidence in his leadership.*

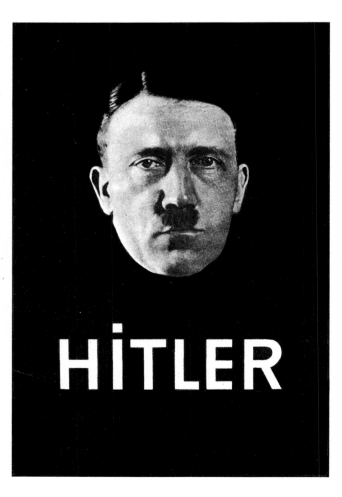

moral objection to homosexuality as a physical act. Why then was homosexuality so savagely punished in the Third Reich? Because, quite simply, it was sabotage—sabotage of the nation's future manpower.

A feature peculiar to 20th-century dictatorships is their concern with reaching the juvenile mind. Youth is to be courted by the state, trained, educated, organized, and finally marshaled. Already in the Weimar period the Nazis had been successfully wooing the youth of Germany, who, during the 1920s, had been much neglected by the Weimar government; they had become aimless, skeptical and pseudoromantic, waiting for something to fill the void and give them what they wanted—a sense of importance and some emotional involvement.

Goebbels' propagandists found the youth an easy prey. With unlimited appeal to the emotions and ruthless exploitation of their readiness to believe and follow, the Nazis had won the German youth several years before they assumed power. During these years the principal attraction for the young people was the "new comradeship of the Hitler Youth"—the Hitler parade of uniforms, in marked contrast to the drabness of everyday life in the Weimar Republic.

Until as late as 1936 a number of youth organizations, such as the Catholic Youth and the Boy Scouts, existed in Germany alongside the Hitler Youth. In that year Baldur von Schirach, leader of the Hitler Youth, gave an order that all these organizations were henceforth forbidden to take part in any form of organized sport. Now, if a young man belonged to the Catholic Youth or any other of the organizations apart from the Hitler Youth, all forms of organized sport—athletics, hiking, skiing, gymnastics, even camping—were denied him. In addition, Schirach forbade all members of youth movements (apart from the Hitler Youth) to wear uniforms, together with badges, shoulder straps, lanyards, etc. They were also forbidden to march in formation, have their own bands, carry flags, banners, and pennants. These measures reveal the Nazis' understanding of the juvenile mind.

The *Bund deutscher Mädchen* (German Girls' League) was the female counterpart of the Hitler Youth. It too had a monopoly of all sport for girls. They attended Youth Hostel weekends, where they learned to run 60 meters in 12 seconds, swim 100 meters, throw a ball over a distance of 20 meters. Like the boys, they had to learn all the facts about the Führer and his "days of struggle," as well as the names of Hitler Youth "martyrs." The girls wore white blouses, almost ankle-length skirts, and sturdy shoes.

Concurrently with the cinema as a means of visual propaganda appeared the poster. This apparently simple form of advertisement played a greater part in the Nazis' rise to power than is generally realized. Goebbels' propagandists knew that visual impressions are extremely strong, that people may forget a newspaper article, but not a picture—if they see it often and its message is obvious. In this respect the poster had certain advan-

Ein Volk, ein Reich, ein Führer!

Two versions of a poster by Mjölnir (Hans Schweitzer) who perfected the image of the iron-jawed Storm Trooper. (Top) " The organized will of the nation," the later version of Mjölnir's 1932 election poster. (Bottom) The earlier cruder version of the same poster from the late 1920s. Nazi troopers of this period were shown as tough revolutionaries. Mjölnir was the graphic artist most closely associated with the Nazi party.

tages over the other forms of propaganda. A pamphlet or a newspaper could be thrown away, unread; the radio turned off; political meetings not attended; likewise the cinema. But everyone at some time or other walked in the streets. The poster could not be avoided. It was one thing to hear about Hitler's strength of character, sincerity, honesty, simplicity, etc.; it was quite another to see these qualities glaring down from a huge head-and-shoulders portrait, ten times life-size. If the passerby averted his eyes, he ran into Hitler again around the corner. No inhabited place in Germany was without him, nor "the heroic German male" about whom the Nazis were always boasting. Suddenly in the street on the opposite wall he stood—lantern-jawed, erect, determined, puissant, girding himself to defend Germany from "the Red Terror" or "the Jewish Bacillus."

The master of these political posters, on whom was bestowed the title of "Reich Plenipotentiary for Artistic Formulation," was the artist Mjölnir (Hans Schweitzer). As a Nazi leader once said, "What lengthy speeches failed to do, Mjölnir did in a second through the glowing fanaticism of his powerful art." Mjölnir's poster of the three Storm Troopers' heads is quintessential Nazi propaganda—simple, emotional, powerful. Hitler had said, "by the masses, brutality and physical force are admired." Here they are. These are three Nazi "fighters," one young, the second middle-aged, the third an older man, who have all clearly passed through the fires of combat, in the trenches or the streets, and whose faces have a male strength verging on brutality. Done in 1932, one poster depicts the "Aryan" fighting to bring the Nazi movement to power. The other prominent poster designer of the Third Reich was Ludwig Hohlwein, one of Germany's leading commercial artists. Unlike Mjölnir, he idealized the fair-haired youth so admired by the Nazis.

The same principles of propaganda posters held good for postage stamps. The stamp reaches an even larger public than the poster. Stamps on envelopes referring to the Saar referendum in 1935 brought the subject to the attention of the entire German people. There were Party rally stamps; Hitler's birthday stamps; stamps referring to the return of Eupen and Malmedy to the fatherland; to the union of Germany and Austria. In all German post offices stamped postcards were sold bearing slogans and quotations from Hitler's speeches. There were Hitler Youth stamps and a Hitler stamp souvenir sheet with the slogan, "He who wants to serve a people can think only in heroic terms." That the Nazis appreciated this form of propaganda is seen in their prohibition of the sale of Soviet stamps to collectors in Germany between 1933 and 1939, and between 1941 and 1945.

In the other visual arts, the Nazis were not as successful as they were with the poster; more intellectual forms of art could not be made to serve their purposes as effectively. However, if only for foreign consumption, they had to show some concern for it.

They used pictorial art in two ways: as an illustration of what they called the moral and material decay of their predecessors, the men of Weimar with their "decadent Expressionism," and to propagate their own "Aryan" policies. For the first, many who could not understand modern art could be convinced that it was indeed degenerate and rotten. The Nazis simply selected the least successful works of the Expressionist artists—and their more abstract and extreme experiments—and displayed them all over the country in a series of elaborate exhibitions entitled "Degenerate Art." The exhibits were so displayed as to shock people, hung with the intention of making the artists appear at their worst. The public which came in thousands were told that their money, in taxes, had been spent by the Weimar government on these abominations. They could see for themselves how cynically the Expressionist artists treated such sacred themes as love, "the German woman," heroes, and the fatherland. All had been mocked and reviled. They were told that Jewish dealers had made fortunes out of peddling this "trash."

The "Nazi art" which replaced this was also used as an instrument of propaganda. It is significant that Nazi painting can easily be described in words because the subject matter is more important than the form. For the Nazis, the range of these subjects was limited: peasants with large families, emphasizing the importance of the German soil and fertility; allegories of the Muses, an opportunity to depict nubile nudes of pure Aryan descent; fair-haired, uniformed marching boys with banners and swastika flags; lantern-jawed Storm Troopers in steel helmets, with clenched fists, in action or participating in some national ceremony; and then the Führer himself in heroic pose, sometimes wearing medieval armor in the role of the new St. George slaying the Jewish-Bolshevik dragon. The titles are self-explanatory: *The Last Hand Grenade, The New Youth, The Guardian of the Race, Make Room for the SA, The Pilot, The Day of Potsdam 1933.*

Many of the paintings took the form of murals. The revival of the mural was in fact one of the most important features of Nazi art. The Nazis postulated coordination of all the arts in their public buildings, particularly of architecture and mural decoration. The proportions of mural and fresco paintings suited their grandiloquence, as well as providing work for thousands of artists on vast surfaces. The propaganda value of these huge paintings, which forced themselves on the eye of every visitor to the ministries, Party buildings, public halls, and schools which housed them, was considerable. Even those who never entered the Haus der Deutschen Kunst (House of German Art) in Munich could not escape them, because they were reproduced in newspapers and magazines all over the country. Well-produced art publications were also devoted to Nazi Art. The most elaborate of these, *Die Kunst im Dritten Reich* (*Art in the Third Reich*), was beautifully laid out, with paper and color plates of the highest quality.

It was not the artistic influence of these paintings which mattered, for there was little artistic about them; it was the content. To the impressionable youth of Germany, these pictures reinforced what they were being taught in school—the supremacy of the Teutons, the injustices to which they had been subjected

(Top) A massive relief figure by Arno Brecker, one of the Third Reich's official sculptors. (Bottom) Jacob Epstein with an example of his "degenerate" sculpture. Works by Epstein and other modern artists were displayed at a 1937 exhibition of "degenerate art," which backfired as propaganda by becoming the most popular exhibit ever mounted in the Reich.

Albert Speer, the chief architect of the Third Reich, envisioned Berlin as the capital of a world empire. The buildings he designed according to gigantic proportions were "to tower up like the cathedrals of our past into the millennia to come." Architecture as propaganda was intended to impress people with the power and solidity of the Reich. (Top, middle, and bottom) Three sections of Speer's model of Berlin: the Great Basin, Tempelhof Airport, and the German Plaza.

GROSSES BECKEN - JUNI 1938

DEUTSCHER PLATZ   JANUAR 1937

since 1919, the romance of war, the superiority of the physical over the intellectual.

Even in the sports grounds where the Germans sought recreation, in the parks and forests around their towns, the new art was prominent, generally in the form of vast statues, representing the vigor of Germany's manhood, with bulging muscles and energetic attitudes. The sculptors Arno Brecker and Josef Thorak were responsible for many of these gargantuan monuments. When on one occasion a visitor to Thorak's studio asked, "Where is the sculptor?" an assistant replied, "Up in the left ear of the horse."

The very streets of the cities were transformed into propaganda. Trees were uprooted and houses pulled down to make room for the great mass demonstrations. The ponderous new buildings in the various cities, particularly in Berlin, Munich, and Nuremberg, with their huge squares and courtyards and rows of neoclassical columns, were conceived as a background for the marching SS. Albert Speer, the great architect of the Third Reich, built Hitler's pompous chancellery in Berlin, a combination of ancient Greece and Prussian classicism, decorated with Nazi symbols. He also planned the reconstruction of the capital on a grand scale, as befitted the metropolis of the Nazi empire.

As the Party owed its success in propaganda more to the spoken than to the printed word, it is understandable that the other 20th-century discovery of which Goebbels made good use was the radio. He once said that radio would do for the 20th century what newspapers had done for the 19th. He regarded it, he said, "as an important means toward the uniformity of the German people—in north and south, east and west, of Catholic and Protestant, or bourgeois, workers, and peasants." (Significantly he made no reference to the upper classes whom he, like Hitler, regarded as of no importance.) "With this instrument," he told the heads of his radio stations, "you can make public opinion." Hitler, too, was well aware of this; in his first year as chancellor he made over fifty major broadcasts. These were speeches at meetings and rallies rather than studio broadcasts. Hitler attempted one studio broadcast, but felt uncomfortable without the presence of a visible audience.

Before 1933, the big German cities all had their radio stations emitting their own programs. In contrast to this decentralization, Goebbels concentrated the control of all broadcasting in Berlin, under his Propaganda Ministry, which was, significantly, sometimes referred to as the *Befehlszentrale*, the center for issuing orders.

To increase the number of listeners, the Nazis put on the market one of the cheapest wireless sets in Europe. It was heavily subsidized so that it cost no more than a worker's weekly salary; it was appropriately known as the VE (*Volksempfänger*, peoples' radio). The aim was to install a set in every home in Germany. As that goal would not be reached for some time, communal listening was also encouraged, in the factories, offices, restaurants, cafes, even at street corners. When a speech by a Nazi leader or an important announcement was to be made, factories and offices had to stop work so that everyone could listen. In 10,000 restaurants throughout the Reich, when the announcement "*Der Führer spricht*" was made over the radio, diners felt embarrassed to go on masticating while the harsh and familiar sounds reverberated around the room.

Another technique used was the "radio warden" for each block of houses or apartment buildings. This Party member would encourage his neighbors who did not own a radio to buy one (sometimes he would lend them the money to do so); otherwise, to listen to important speeches in his or a friend's home. He sent in regular reports on their reactions to the broadcasts. Thus, when a program on the importance of having large families was greeted by a listener with the jocular "Not for me! Grandpa had diabetes," he was reported and taken severely to task. The radio warden became of special importance during the war when he reported those listening to foreign broadcasts.

Listeners soon learned to recognize the signature tunes associated with the various Party leaders. Hitler's imminent arrival at any gathering was invariably preceded by his favorite march, the *Badenweiler*. Goebbels' annual eulogy on the Führer's birthday was always preceded by Wagner's *Meistersinger* Overture, and Hitler's speech on Heroes Day by the second movement of Beethoven's *Eroica* Symphony.

Between 1933 and 1939 the number of private radio sets in Germany quadrupled. The radio was also important for influencing foreign opinion. Other nations could prohibit the import of Nazi written propaganda, but it was much harder to interfere with a radio broadcast. The radio played a great part in both the Saar plebiscite and the Anschluss (union) with Austria.

The rich industrial area of the Saar valley had been occupied by France since the end of the First World War; the region's status was to be decided by a plebiscite in 1935. The Nazi propaganda campaign for the Saar plebiscite was begun over a year earlier. In January 1934, Goebbels set up an office for radio transmission to the Saar. Every Wednesday a series, "The Saar —the Way to Understanding is Clear" was broadcast. Between January 1934 and April 1935, some 4,000 *Volksempfänger* radio sets were distributed in the Saarland. The French made only a last-minute attempt to influence the Saarlanders by broadcasting. Undoubtedly the Saar plebiscite would have returned the territory to Germany, but not with the large majority—over 90 percent—which Goebbels' radio campaign insured.

In planning the enforced Anschluss with Austria, the big Nazi transmitter in Munich played an important part. The Austrian transmitters were not as powerful, and for three or four years before the Anschluss, the Austrian people were bombarded aurally each night with propaganda about the great German Führer, about what he had done for Germany—and what, if invited, he would do for Austria. It is significant, too, that at the time of the abortive 1934 putsch in Austria, the Nazis' first goal was the Vienna radio station.

(Top and middle) A commemorative stamp and poster for the Volkswagen campaign. Germans were asked to pay out five marks a week for a "People's Car" which was never delivered. (Bottom) Goebbels regarded broadcasting as the most effective means of propaganda. "All Germany listens to the Führer with the People's Radio;" a poster advertising the cheap wireless set produced by the Nazis.

(Below) *Anti-British and anti-American cartoons by Seppla (Josef Plank) appeared in* Die Brennessel, *the official humor magazine of the Nazi party, which Hitler called "the dreariest rag imaginable." Other cartoons appeared in weekly humor magazines such as* Kladderdatsch *and* Simplicimus. *Both Roosevelt and Churchill were portrayed within Germany as agents of the Jewish-Bolshevik conspiracy.*

The Nazis made good use of short-wave transmissions to the Americas. Here a different technique was required from the blustering methods and language employed for Austria. The aim was to impress the North and South Americans with the good fellowship of Nazi Germany, and the speakers contrived an atmosphere of cozy chumminess with the listeners. They often addressed a local town or school and sent greetings to individual listeners. Intimacy was also fostered by reading these listeners' letters and answering their questions about the New Germany. Later, the globe was, for foreign broadcasting, divided into six "culture areas": North America, South America, Africa, East Asia, South Asia, and Australia. From 14 hours weekly in 1933, foreign broadcasts rose to 58 hours in 1939. Daily, 130 German transmitters broadcast 180 foreign news programs in 53 languages.

The radio, which Nazi fuglemen had early described as "the towering herald of National Socialism," soon came to be regarded as the principal propaganda medium. Neither Italy nor the Soviet Union, the other totalitarian countries, used it to such a degree on their less literate populations.

That the Party knew it owed its success to the spoken rather than the written word was neatly summed up in a directive by Goebbels to the German newspapers on how to write: "The reader should feel that you are in reality a speaker standing beside him." The pages of the Nazi newspapers therefore exuded the atmosphere of mass meetings, sweat, leather, and bloodlust; and the Party newspaper, the *Völkischer Beobachter*, became virtually no more than a glorified poster masquerading as a newspaper.

It was originally owned by Hitler's crony and wartime sergeant, Max Amman, and edited by the drunken, drug-addicted Nazi poet, Dietrich Eckart. In those days it had only 127,000 readers; but after 1933 its circulation leapt at the rate of 100,000 annually until, in 1942, it became the first German newspaper to top the million mark. That it was compulsory reading for Party members was partly responsible for this phenomenal growth. But also, civil servants, schoolteachers and the like could not obtain preferment unless they knew what was in it. A university professor got into serious trouble for giving a low grade to the essay of a student who had lifted it entirely from the columns of the *Völkischer Beobachter*. Hitler once said that the *Völkischer Beobachter* was nothing more than a humor sheet. Conversely, he called *Die Brennessel (The Nettle)*, the Party humor magazine published in Munich, "the dreariest rag imaginable." *Die Brennessel* featured the cartoons of Seppla (Josef Plank), which were vitriolic attacks on the British, Americans, and Russians.

For controlling the press, *Sprachregelungen* (language rulings) were issued daily by Goebbels' ministry to editors all over the country. When they had read them, they were instructed to destroy them and sign an affidavit to that effect. By 1939, these directives had become so detailed that the papers were virtually written for the editors, who by then offered no opposition. In a moment of candor, Goebbels admitted in his journal (April 14, 1943), "Any man with the slightest spark of honor left in him will take good care in the future not to become a journalist."

The *Sprachregelungen* dealt with almost every aspect of German life. To take a few at random: Thomas Mann was not to be written about, because his name had "been removed from the national consciousness." The same for Charles Chaplin. On the other hand, Greta Garbo and the Duke of Windsor, who had shown certain positive sentiments, were to be treated in a sympathetic manner. Photographs of ministers of the Third Reich and high Party officials attending sumptuous banquets were forbidden. No reference was to be made to a case of cattle poisoning due to excess potassium in cattle fodder; nor to an auto accident in which Ribbentrop and his daughter had been hurt; nor was Frau Hess to be shown at the Berlin dog show.

Quantitatively as well as qualitatively, the national press declined. When the Nazis came to power, there were 4,500 newspapers reflecting a variety of political persuasions. By 1939, the number had been reduced to 1,000, all of which were following the Party line.

About literature and theater as forms of propaganda in Germany there is less to say. Literature is addressed primarily to the intellect and has little mass appeal. In the words of the Nazi writer Schunzel, "In this land we do not read books. We swim, we wrestle, we lift weights." Theater too is addressed to a relatively small audience. These art forms took a minor place in the Nazi scheme of propaganda.

Most writers and dramatists of any merit had left the country or were proscribed when the Nazis came to power; men like Thomas Mann, Remarque, Zweig, Reinhardt, Toller, Brecht, Franz Werfel. The place of these "degenerates and racial undesirables" was taken by writers who turned out books and plays on the prescribed Nazi themes. Most of what has been said about the cinema applied to them. Plays had to be submitted for approval to the Reich Theater Chamber, whose task, according to the Theater Law of 1934, was "to watch the production from the point of view of conformity of its spiritual content with National Socialism." Even the German classics, plays by Goethe and Schiller, were given a nationalist flavor and their universal or humanist values attenuated. Of foreign writers, those like Bernard Shaw were approved, not for any literary merit, but because they pilloried what were regarded as the vices of English hypocrisy and "plutocracy." Hanns Johst, president of the Reich Theater Chamber, had once publicly boasted that whenever someone mentioned the word "culture" to him he wanted to reach for his revolver.

During the twelve years of Nazi rule not a single playwright of any consequence emerged. It was the heyday of the third- and fourth-rate writer; and the principal themes for books and plays were historical, the favorite subjects being medieval Germany and the rise of Prussia. A popular theme in literature was the *Fronterlebnis* (life at the front), as in the novels of Beumelberg;

(Below) Seppla (Josef Plank) mocked Churchill in this cartoon for Die Brennessel. *During the victorious phase of the war, Goebbels made Chruchill his personal enemy and heaped scorn on him. After the German defeat at Stalingrad, Goebbels paid an indirect compliment to Churchill by basing his 'total war' speech on the Prime Minister's "blood, sweat, and tears" address of 1940.*

(Top) Der Angriff (The Attack) *was the weekly newspaper launched by Goebbels in 1927 when he was Gauleiter of Berlin. Goebbels used the paper to attack his enemies in the Weimar government. After 1930,* Der Angriff *became the daily vehicle for Goebbels' propaganda. (Bottom)* Der Stürmer, *edited by Julius Streicher, first appeared in Nuremberg in 1923 shortly after the Munich putsch. It was the most viciously anti-Semitic of the Nazi papers.*

scenes alternate between brutal descriptions of trench warfare and bathetic "comradeship" in the Teutonic sentimental style. Among other popular fictional themes was the *Heimatroman* or regional novel. Typical of these was Kunkel's *Ein Arzt sucht seinen Weg* (*A Doctor Seeks His Way*), in which a restless undergraduate forsakes the medical school in the great city where he is studying to return to the hearth of his shepherd grandfather, whose life he attempts to imitate. He finishes as an herbalist effecting miraculous cures.

Another literary favorite was the Führer-type biography. It did not deal directly with Hitler, but with historical characters whose careers were made to resemble his. Thus, the biographies of the poet Schiller, the alchemist Paracelsus and the inventor Diesel, illustrate the triumph of untutored genius over formal learning, of intuition over intelligence.

All creative artists had to belong to the appropriate department of the Reich Chamber of Culture, which was founded in September, 1933. The chamber could expel or refuse entry for "political unreliability," which meant in practice that even artists who were lukewarm about National Socialism could be prevented from practicing their art. On May 10, 1933, in Berlin's Franz Jozef Platz, the notorious "burning of the books" occurred. The works of the "decadent" writers—Freud, Marx, and Zweig among them—were thrown on a ceremonial bonfire and Goebbels made a speech relayed by all German radio stations, in which he referred to the authors as "the evil spirit of the past" and declared that "the age of intellectualism" was now over.

To conclude, what lessons can be learned from the Nazi use of propaganda during the period 1933–1939? The most important, if not the most conspicuous, concerns its influence over youth. If after only six years of power Goebbels' propaganda could convince the adult masses to believe in their Führer as they did, what effect would it have had on the next generation, the youth of Germany? Had Germany won the Second World War, these young people could have spent their entire lives under the spell of a system invented and perfected by Goebbels. Fortunately, the other nations, who had fallen behind both militarily and in the practice of propaganda, quickly gained ground as soon as Hitler sprang his war on them. Because their propaganda, both to their own people and to the Germans, was based on the truth, it gradually became, as the long and testing years of war unrolled, more credible, more effective, and finally more successful, than that of Dr. Goebbels.

It is no small measure of Goebbels' skill that in 1939 he could manipulate German public opinion like a seesaw. One day in August of that year, the Germans were dutifully acknowledging that Soviet Russia was the enemy of mankind; the next day (August 24, 1939), that it was their friend and ally. Goebbels maintained this image of friendship while the Soviets were swallowing large tracts of Eastern Europe—half of Poland, the Baltic states, Bessarabia, and northern Bukovina. This he did as long as it suited Hitler's strategic requirements. When these changed with the Nazi invasion of the Soviet Union in June 1941, he switched back; bolshevism again became the bogeyman of Europe. All the anti-Soviet literature which had vanished from the German book shops in August 1939 appeared on the shelves again. This manipulation is of course relatively easy in a dictatorship. All the same, even Stalin—himself no mean propagandist—thought the Nazis went too far when they wanted to include in the nonaggression pact of August 1939 a passage about "Russo-German friendship," after, as Stalin said, they had for fifteen years been covering him with "pails of manure."

In 1939 the German people did not want war, but they had been so conditioned to the idea since 1933, and to that of their own military and racial superiority, that they accepted it without demur. When war was declared, Goebbels could proudly boast that the situation was quite different from 1914. Then, the German leadership had no idea of how to influence public opinion. But today, on September 1, 1939, "Germany knows," he wrote, "how to handle the weapon of truth with sovereign certainty."

Until the war, Goebbels' handling of "the weapon of truth" about England and France had been somewhat ambivalent. While despising "the decadent democracies" and satirizing them in such humorous papers as *Simplicissimus* and *Die Brennessel* he had, following his leader's directions, also attempted from time to time to court them. He had even referred to some of England's empire-building virtues in his papers. At the Olympic Games in 1936, he had instructed his department to treat important British visitors with respect. But now that was all over. In the winter of 1939–40, he told the Germans by press, radio, and film how perfidious and Machiavellian were the countries which had declared war on Germany. England was depicted as a citadel of "plutocracy," where a handful of corrupt financiers, most of them Jews, encouraged international warfare, because it increased their wealth, as well as their hold over the poor workingman. The Germans had no quarrel with the English masses, he said, only with their rulers. He instructed his ministry: "Our aim must be the separation of people and government in England." It was relatively easy for him to show the Germans who was responsible for the war. Britain and France had encouraged Polish "intransigence," for their own ends; it was they who had declared war on Germany, not vice versa. Germany had no alternative but to defend herself. Goebbels was even able to convince the public in April and May of 1940 that the German occupations of Denmark, Norway, Holland, and Belgium were defensive measures, taken in time to forestall the invasion of those countries by England and France, whose plans to use them as pawns had, fortunately, fallen into German hands.

The principal aim of Goebbels' propaganda in the first two years of the war, when Germany was everywhere victorious, was to convince the people that the Greater Reich which the Führer was building would benefit them all, and in the long run all of Europe. For this he had plenty of material. By the autumn of 1941, the rich corn lands of the Ukraine were in German hands;

(Top) Emil Jannings played a Boer hero in Hans Steinhoff's anti-British film, Ohm Krüger *(1941). The English are depicted as greedy expansionists, anxious to possess the Transvaal gold fields. They trick Krüger when he visits London and is presented to the queen who is portrayed as a clever old harridan addicted to whisky. Krüger, on the other hand, has the mystique of a great national leader. (Bottom) Erich Waschruck's* Die Rothschilds *was one of several virulent anti-Semitic films which appeared in 1940. It flopped at the box office.*

(Below) Nazi propagandists perpetrated racial stereotypes such as the Soviet Untermensch, *the Jewish Bolshevik, and the American black man. Goebbels singled out the black American G.I. as a symbol of cultural barbarism. This theme was often used later in the war when Allied planes were bombing German cities. In this cartoon, one soldier says "We're fighting for culture, Jimmy" and the other replies, "But what is culture?"*

BEFREIER

*„Wir kämpfen für das Kultur, Jimmy."
„Ja – aber was ist Kultur eigentlich?"*

it was self-evident that German farmers and settlers would make two blades grow where the Slav could produce only one. Russia and its great steppes could feed a continent, if the land were "properly" cultivated and exploited. The Propaganda Ministry was inundated with requests from soldiers about how to obtain land in the Crimea or Caucasus, and settle there when the war was over. Then there was the overgorged British Empire, also ripe for plucking. With German troops nearing the Suez canal, the vast British territories in Africa, as well as the Indian subcontinent itself, beckoned.

In those early days of the war, the documentary campaign films, made in Poland, Norway, and the Low Countries, played an important part in exalting German morale. Cameramen were attached to the fighting units and accompanied them into battle, of which they gave a factual, if slanted, picture. This bias was described in 1940 by a Nazi journalist, Hans-Joachim Giese, whose comments about newsreels also held true for the campaign documentaries: "The newsreel does not, in its fulfillment of the precept of propaganda, represent truth in itself—for that would be senseless and not even within its power—but rather, with proper expedients, the newsreel represents just that aspect of the truth which of necessity ought to be spread in the interest of the German nation." Although Goebbels would have put it more succinctly, this sums up the essence of Nazi propaganda.

Baptism of Fire, a documentary about the Polish campaign, was shown simultaneously in 55 movie houses in Berlin, and throughout the Reich. Mobile film vans took it to remote villages which lacked movie theaters. In this and other films, the horrors of war were always shown as being visited on the resisting army, never on the German troops. So important were these films considered that in 1940, a law was passed forbidding anyone from leaving or entering a theater during the showing of a war documentary.

In this period of military victories, the task of the Propaganda Ministry was relatively easy. Victories are the best form of propaganda, and the army communiqués did most of Goebbels' work for him. This did not entirely please him, because the Supreme Command of the Wehrmacht took over, as it were, a part of his traditional role. In war, the demands of military secrecy hampered the use of propaganda as he understood it. He even said, "Hitler will soon be listening to his generals only, and it will be very difficult for me." However, it at least enabled him to turn his attention for a while to propaganda for the enemy.

Already in the "phony war" of 1939–40 the Propaganda Ministry was organizing broadcasts to France, sowing discord between the Western Allies. The French were told that the British had sent only six divisions, and that the eighty French divisions would have to bear the brunt of the fighting. The British, as usual, would fight "to the last Frenchman." Leaflets, such as the famous "Falling Leaf," were dropped by air on the French troops in the Maginot line, describing how the British army in the Lille area was ravishing their wives and sweethearts. From Stuttgart a French traitor, Ferdonnet, broadcast to France lurid accounts of corruption in the French government and Jewish high finance. There was always an element of truth in these allegations; for as Charles Roetter, the English expert on war-time propaganda, says, "It must strike a chord that is always there." To his own people, Goebbels depicted the French as "a dying nation," a highly talented but unfortunate people at the end of their political tether, "becoming more and more negroidal."

To sow dissension in the British camp, Goebbels set up the so-called "Scottish transmitter," with dialect broadcasts on the English iniquities in Scotland and Ireland, and the English habit throughout history of enlisting Scottish and Irish regiments to fight their battles for them. The heartlessness of the "pluto-cratic" English upper classes was also proved, he said, during the Battle of France. Thousands of Frenchmen were dying daily, but the British aristocrats went on the first Wednesday of June to watch their horses racing in the Derby. Just how much effect this propaganda had is uncertain. It undoubtedly had some in-fluence on the collapse of the French army, but the broadcasts of traitors like William Joyce, "Lord Haw-Haw," were never taken seriously in England.

A month after the German invasion of the Soviet Union, Goeb-bels set up a secret radio station broadcasting to the Soviets, calling itself "Leninist" and purporting to be from within Rus-sia. Its speaker was one Albrecht, a Russian of German origin who had fled to Germany after Stalin's 1936 purges. He voiced the popular discontent in Russia with the Stalinist regime. Goeb-bels established a similar operation for North America. When it seemed that America's sympathies were inclining more and more toward England, a "black" radio station purporting to be in America was set up in Germany broadcasting isolationist pro-paganda to the United States.

Both Goebbels and Hitler believed that their anti-Semitic and anti-Bolshevik propaganda, as served up for home consumption, had only to be repeated abroad to have the same effect. Here they were wrong. Neither before nor during the war did anti-Semitism prove a good article of export. The endless tirades against the Jews in Germany lost the sympathies of many English and Americans who were not particularly pro-Jewish. This can be explained in part by the Nazis' ignorance of foreign countries. Neither Hitler nor Goebbels had traveled much out-side Germany, and they knew no foreign languages. For rulers of the most powerful military nation in the world, now at war, their ignorance about their adversaries is truly staggering. In the winter of 1940 they believed that their anti-Churchill pro-paganda to Britain would soon make the British realize that Churchill was responsible for their sufferings, and that they would dismiss him. In his "Table Talk" Hitler reveals this. "Churchill," he said, "is a typical big mouth, and an incom-petent drunkard—in his private life not a gentleman either." Goebbels was equally preposterous about Anthony Eden. "The perfumed British foreign secretary," he wrote in his diary, "cuts a good figure among these characters from the synagogue. His

(Top) William Joyce, known as Lord Haw-Haw, was a turncoat Englishman who broadcast Nazi propaganda to his countrymen from Germany. After war was declared, Britons ceased to take him seriously. (Bottom) As part of Goebbels' anti-Semitic campaign, photographs of Eastern European ghetto Jews were distributed to news-papers by the Propaganda Ministry.

(Top) A British photograph of
Churchill inspecting a new machine
gun. (Bottom) "Churchill, a sniper;"
a 1941 German poster which used the
same photograph of the Prime Minister
with his head cocked at an angle.

whole education and his entire bearing can be characterized as thoroughly Jewish." These comments are revealing of the inferiority complex and jealous hatred by the upstart, whose power has gone to his head, for the aristocrat.

Once the power of the German army had been established in the Polish campaign, Goebbels did not bother much about the susceptibilities of any foreigners he wished to influence. On April 5, 1940, a number of important Danes and Norwegians, politicians and businessmen, were invited to the German embassy in Oslo, where they were shown the film *Baptism of Fire*, in which the futility of the Polish resistance to the German army is graphically depicted. Five days later, the German army invaded Denmark and Norway.

Baptism of Fire, Feldzug im Polen (*Campaign in Poland*), and later those films of the campaigns in Scandinavia, the Low Countries, and France, such as *Sieg im Westen* (*Victory in the West*), were sent to German embassies all over the world for distribution to local movie houses. The public in Ankara, Sofia, the South American countries, even China, were to become aware of the invincibility of the Wehrmacht. Why, the films seemed to ask, should other cities have to suffer the fate of Warsaw? Why should so many young men be killed to no purpose? It was better not to be an enemy of Germany. As the Germans invaded country after country, these propaganda techniques were extended to occupied territories. Occupied Europe became a monopoly market for Goebbels' films and traveling exhibitions.

In those years of victory, when Goebbels had less work at the ministry, he threw himself hecticly into every other form of war work. He toured armament factories in the Ruhr and gave pep talks to dockers in Hamburg; he received delegations of Japanese Youth leaders, Spanish publishers, Dutch poets. Everything interested him, from the price of potatoes to the sexual needs of the foreign workers in Germany. He personally directed the publication of a fictional diary recording the pornographic experiences of a British soldier in France, for distribution in that country. And in a particularly brilliant propaganda coup, Goebbels had the same *wagon-lit* in which Germany had surrendered to France in 1918 brought to Compiègne in 1940 for the French surrender to Hitler.

One element of home propaganda which remained completely in his hands was the Führer legend. Before the war, he had shown Hitler as the wise and sober statesman; now, the Führer was presented as the great strategist and military genius who, in spite of the pessimistic warnings of his generals, had shattered the entire French army in a month. He was a clairvoyant with the prophetic gift of a seer—a universal man, an expert in all military techniques, intimately familiar with the workings of every tank and machine gun. Films were shown of him in his Field Headquarters. The camera would catch a group of deliberating generals, then move slowly to a table where the Führer stood alone poring over the map of Russia, his face charged with worry and the burden of his thoughts. "There he stands!" wrote Goebbels in his paper, "Planning the future. Utterly great and utterly lonely!"

However this "universal genius," for whom nothing went wrong between 1933 and 1941, suddenly ran into trouble. Although in 1942 still in possession of most of Europe—from the Don to the Spanish frontier, from Norway to the Greek isles—he found he had, as Napoleon had 140 years before, brought into existence against him one of the greatest coalitions the world has ever seen. His run of successes was halted. It was now that propaganda in the sense that Goebbels understood it—influencing public opinion—came into its own again. Between 1939 and 1941, German public opinion had needed no influencing. The roar of the tanks at Sedan, the scream of the diving Stukas at Dunkirk, had muffled the voice of Goebbels. But now as the blows of the Allies began to fall on Germany, all those skills were called upon again. Propaganda came into its own with the first German defeats. Goebbels had to compensate for the failure of the German army. And this he did in the greatest propaganda exercise of his life.

He addressed himself first to the unfortunate German troops who by the winter of 1941–42 were not victorious, as expected, in Muscovite billets, but sitting in the snow and ice outside the Soviet capital in the worst winter for fifty years. No provision had been made for this; in fact, the overconfident troops were wearing summer uniforms. Goebbels immediately inaugurated his *Winterhilfesspende,* a collection throughout the Reich of winter clothing for the troops. For the first time he had to admit that the estimate of a short campaign had proved incorrect. He could no longer continue the line of infallibility. The Nazis, like other human beings, he admitted, could make mistakes. But for that very reason, everyone must now work harder for victory. The Russian soldier, he explained, had proved to be a tougher fighter than expected (he was careful to add that it was purely animal toughness, in this blunted human material, and should not be confused with valor). There was an immediate response to his appeal for warm clothing from all over Germany. For weeks, the collections took first place in the public mind. Athletes and film stars were engaged to make patriotic speeches at them. All Germany contributed, both men and women offering everything from their mink coats to their woolen underwear. In fact, the collection came a little late for the troops in Russia, when most of the winter was over; but it proved an excellent means of strengthening the links between the home and the fighting fronts which—Goebbels had noted in his diary—were, after the run of constant successes, not as close as they should be.

In the summer and autumn of 1942 German forces had one more victorious spell, advancing as far as the Caucasus and Stalingrad. Again the communiqués told their joyous tale. But it was the last time. In October of that year came defeat at El Alamein, immediately followed by the Anglo-American landings in North Africa, and the great Soviet victory at Stalingrad.

Goebbels was instantly at work. When the German army was expelled from Africa in 1943, he explained it in his paper *Das Reich* as a peripheral affair. "What happens in North Africa,"

(Top) On May 23, 1944, British and American troops launched a successful offensive against the Germans from the Anzio beachhead in Italy. This leaflet was intended by German propagandists to lower Allied morale. (Middle) Another leaflet showered on the Allied forces in Italy as they advanced northward in 1944. (Bottom) "To the Honorary Headhunter in the White House," a cartoon from the humor magazine Kladderdatsch.

Dem Ehrenkopfjäger im Weißen Haus

(Top) An advertisement encouraging Germans to observe the weekly "one pot" meal to conserve food, especially meat. The text reads, "the meal of sacrifice for the Reich." (Bottom) "The correct mask position protects your health;" a poster exhorting people to wear their gas masks during bombing raids.

he scoffed, "is absolutely unimportant. It is on the rim of Europe. The war will be decided in Europe." Even when the Allies invaded Sicily and established a foothold on the Italian mainland, the news was given little prominence in the German press and radio, compared with the battles in Russia.

To explain away Stalingrad was a harder task; but Goebbels made a brave attempt. The 300,000 dead there were all now heroes in Valhalla; their action had not been in vain. For several months they had held up the assault of six Soviet armies who would otherwise now be rampaging across the Don. On February 18, 1943, he summoned an enormous rally at the Sportpalast in Berlin to explain this. He worked up the thousands who had been specially selected to be present—by virtue of their sure "spontaneous" reactions—into a frenzy of patriotic hysteria. "The Germans," he shrieked, "have been inwardly purified by the blow of fate that fell on them at Stalingrad. It has given them the new strength they require for victory." The vast audience bayed their approval. His two-hour harangue was relayed over all the radio stations so that it, and the vociferous mob, might influence unseen millions both at home and abroad. The doubters and waverers, hearing the audience's reaction to Stalingrad and imagining it to be representative of all Germany, were to be reassured, as were foreigners, by the impression of a nation united as never before. This meeting, in which Goebbels demanded "Total War," was one of his masterpieces of mass propaganda.

But nothing he said could hold up the Soviet tide. By now the Red armies had taken the initiative, and all along the 1000-mile front the Germans were in retreat. A new note now sounded in Goebbels' propaganda. Until Stalingrad, he had always represented Nazi Germany as "The New Order" in Europe, young and vital, supplanting the old, effete, reactionary European systems which had been governing it for too long. The pre-1933 Europe, Goebbels had constantly proclaimed, was finished, tired out. Good riddance to it! No mention was made of Europe's glorious past, of the works of art and literature which had made this "effete system" for centuries the wonder of the world. Now with "the barbarian hordes advancing from the East," Goebbels depicted Nazi Germany as the defender of all that was sacred and traditional in Europe, the sole bastion of Western civilization against "the Slavonic flood"; in his own words, "Always Prusso-Germany has been the wall against which the Eastern hordes were crushed. Today, Germany stands guard for the whole of Europe." The Russians were depicted as subhumans to whom a Gothic cathedral was a place for stabling horses. To show what these barbarians looked like, he published photographs of Russian prisoners of war taken after long forced marches or days in suffocating cattle trucks, arriving in Germany in such a state of emaciation that they indeed looked subhuman. In 1942 a traveling exhibition entitled "Europa gegen den Bolshewismus" (Europe against Bolshevism) was sent around all occupied Europe. Anti-Bolshevik films such as Village in the Red Storm revealed the alleged inhumanity of the

Soviets to their own people.

Here Goebbels played on the Germans' traditional feelings about the Russians, which had been strong in Germany long before the name Hitler had ever been heard—a mixture of superiority complex and fear. If the Russians penetrated into Germany, he warned, the young German manhood would be carried off to Siberia, while her womanhood would be delivered to the lust of savages from the steppes. All German males would be sterilized, the children separated from their mothers and deported. He was much helped in this propaganda at the time by the Allies' unconditional surrender demand, which convinced the Germans that they would obtain no mercy from the Allies. He quoted foreign newspaper reports that Soviet Russia would immediately take 10 million German males to rebuild their country. Every German was aware of the centuries of conflict between Teuton and Slav, an awareness most favorable to the propagandist. Similar apprehension about the West, Britain and France, could not be stimulated because there was no national tradition to nourish them. The theme "Europe as a Russian slave camp," which Goebbels played on right up to the end, was undoubtedly effective in keeping the Germans fighting. "Strength through Fear" he called it.

It was now that Allied propaganda to Germany presented Goebbels with a new difficulty. As long as the Wehrmacht was triumphant, Allied propaganda could have little effect. In the first years of the war, the BBC could do no more than repeat, "We will be back," a slogan regarded by most Germans in 1940 and 1941 as ludicrous. Allied propaganda was a late starter, but when the German defeats began in October 1942, it was quick to take advantage of them. Goebbels had said that the expulsion of the Germans from Africa was of "the smallest importance because it is peripheral," and he had naturally not mentioned how many German troops were taken prisoner in Tunisia. The BBC quoted this back and then asked, was it of small importance to lose a quarter of a million men? And then there were the *Sondermeldungen*, the special announcements which had made such a stir at the time of the German victories. With a fanfare, the latest victory would be proudly announced over the radio, the fall of each capital of Europe: Paris, Belgrade, Athens, Kiev, etc., and all the victorious battles. The German people would remember the broadcasts, said the BBC. There had been 65 *Sondermeldungen* in 1941. In 1942, there had been 19. In 1943, only two. What did this mean?

The BBC also began to play back the speeches made by the German leaders in their hours of victory. On October 25, 1940, Goebbels had made a great speech claiming that England was already beaten. This speech was played back verbatim on the German service of the BBC, with the comment that three years later England seemed to be alive and kicking—witness the holocaust the RAF had just caused in Hamburg. Goering's speech in 1940 was also replayed: "We shall not allow a single enemy bomb to fall on the Ruhr." Three nights prior, Essen had been almost obliterated by British bombs. Hitler's speech in 1941,

(Top, left and right) British "black" propaganda parodies of the Winter Relief charity stamps issued by the German Post Office. Himmler solicits contributions at gunpoint and a German soldier is shown with his face shot off while Nazi officers offer a toast in the background. (Bottom) British "black" parody of a German stamp. 30 January 1933 was the day Hitler became Chancellor. Himmler is placing leg cuffs on a manacled civilian who represents the German people.

(Below and opposite page) Several pages from the British book Truffle Eater, *by Oistros, published in 1940. The book was a sophisticated form of propaganda for an audience who could joke about the Nazis even in the midst of war.*

Shock-Troop Headed Adolf

Look at Adolf where he stands
With his Nazi hair and hands,
Murmuring beneath his breath
Like the lady of Macbeth,
As he seeks in vain to blot,
What he sees: "Out damnéd spot."
But though rather like a tweeny
In the clothes of Mussolini,
Adolf, you can shelter when in
Doubt, behind your uncle Lenin.

"the Soviet Union is already destroyed and will never rise again," was also played back; it was immediately followed with detailed figures about the German casualties at Stalingrad. Incidentally, asked the BBC, what had happened to Hitler? He had never stopped speechifying in 1940 and 1941. Now he had become silent. He had not made a public speech for over a year. Could it be that he was ashamed of something?

Goebbels was equal to this last one. He answered haughtily and with a hypocrisy which was exceptional even for him, "The Führer stands in contrast to the commonplace figures on the other side, who lose no opportunity of displaying themselves before the footlights of the world stage." Men of true historic caliber, he said, did not need the unstable approval of publicity. Their strength sprang from the demon of their historic mission, which they fulfilled according to a higher law.

That the BBC broadcasts were based on the truth soon became apparent to listeners all over the continent. In Germany itself, as the military situation deteriorated the clandestine audience grew so large that severe penalties were imposed for listening to Allied radio; in Goebbels' words; "it is for a civilian as despicable as for the soldier who commits self-mutilation." The *Volksempfänger* was so constructed that it could tune in to only one or two German stations. Yet though lacking short wave, it could tune in to the powerful BBC transmitter on medium wave. At one point, when listening to the BBC in the occupied countries had also increased alarmingly, the Nazis considered confiscating all wireless sets; but the plan was abandoned (except in Holland), because the Germans would thereby lose a valuable instrument for their own propaganda. The radio, which Goebbels had used in such masterly fashion during the '30s, was now being turned against him.

In the last years of the war, Josef Goebbels continued his activities relentlessly. While the other Nazi leaders gradually realized the hopelessness of the situation, and withdrew into silence or secret negotiations with the enemy, the little doctor became more belligerent and chauvinistic. Every instrument of propaganda which came to hand he eagerly seized. When the V-1 and V-2 secret weapons were being constructed, he organized a "whispering campaign" about them. The public morale was to be lifted by stories that the new V weapons were unanswerable and that when they were put to use London would be entirely destroyed in 48 hours. He encouraged rumors about a new U-boat which could travel submerged at such speeds that it could chase the British battle squadrons around the Atlantic, sinking them one by one; and about a special anti-aircraft cannon whose missiles were magnetically drawn to the aircraft in the sky. All this made people feel better.

After the 1944 invasion of Normandy, the German people were shown films which undeniably revealed British troops being driven back into the sea, leaving quantities of dead and wounded. In fact, the films were of the British failure in Dieppe two years earlier. Then there was the Katyn incident, where some 2,000 corpses of Polish officers murdered by the Russians

The Story of Adolf Head-in-Air

As he trudged along to be
Europe's Man of Destiny,
Adolf always kept his eye
Vaguely fixed upon the sky,
Far too much preoccupied
To decide
In what streets he walked about,
Or to hear the children shout :
"Look at little Adolf there—
Little Adolf Head-in-Air."

First, when walking on a wharf,
He encountered Ludendorff,
Adolf's gaze was souf and norf,
Floating high
In the sky.
And he did not hear the cry
"You'll be sorry bye and bye."
Ouch !
Putsch !

With his head as high as ever,
Much too clever to be clever,
Adolf watched the eagle's eyries,
For the wings of the Valkyries,
Having guessed
That it may be cleverest
Just to dream and not to look
(*Vide* Joseph in the Book),
Leaving lads like Roehm and Goebbels
To attend to daily troubles,
While Big Business and the Yunkers
Picked his ball out of the bunkers,
And then laid it
On the green, and swore they'd played it,
With no shame or that or thisness,
Trust the Junkers and Big Business.

Like a picture etched by Dürer,

The Story of Baby Goering

Baby, Baby Goering !
Mother's simply purring.
Father's gone to shoot a Yid
To make a supper for his kid.

The Story of Goering who would not have the Jews

Goering, looking like a cherry
In a glass of grocer's sherry,
From his fingers to his frown,
All synthetically brown
Used to spend his time in Sweden
For his private reasons hidden.
But, returning home one day,
Screamed "O, take the Jews away,
Take the nasty Jews away,
I won't have any Jews to-day."

Kind Mama, discreetly purring,
Thus addresses bully Goering :
"Child, in the all seeing plan
For the chosen Aryan,
Jews exist to give the Teuton
Something he can wipe his boot on.
There, no doubt, are other toys
Suitable for German boys,
Such as soldiers and guns
And the history of the Huns.
But the Jews so beautifully
Fit the purpose of the bully,
That to banish all the vermin
Positively is un-German."

Will he listen ? He will not,
"If I were the lieber Gott
(As cocaine suggests I am),
I would smear the tribe like jam,

The Story of the Boy who went out to Burn the Books

This is the boy who burns the books,
This is the way he always looks,
As though his mind were made of suet,
And this is the way he went to do it.

He washed his eyes with yellow soap,
He stole his father's microscope,
For books are books and the law is law,
And he had to be sure of what he saw.

(And meantime mild angelic eyes
Smiled amiably in Paradise
At this attempt to change the plans
Of Heaven's own librarians).

Then, like a spaniel in a fog,
He snuffles through a catalogue,
Slowly, because he has to spell
It syllable by syllable.

Theology, of course, is banned,
With metaphysics out of hand,
Because all these are merely views
Of Social Democrats and Jews.

Next he destroys what seems to him in
The worst of taste—all books by women,
Who actually write as if
Thought weren't man's prerogative.

But when he contemplates the novel
He needs an automatic shovel,
To clear a path through the abysm
Of post-armistice pacificism.

(Top) An illustration from The Ordeal of Oliver Airedale/*D. T. Carlisle. (Middle) a caricature of Hitler by the American cartoonist Broder. (Bottom, left) As German defeats piled up, Goebbels' propaganda strategy based on the "big lie" collapsed. (Bottom, right) A cartoon by Clifford Berryman from the* Washington Star.

in 1940 were discovered by the Germans in a trench in east Poland. By giving this great publicity, Goebbels managed to cause the first rift in the Grand Alliance, between the Polish government-in-exile in London and Soviet Russia. "How clever we are," he boasted, "to have converted the Katyn affair into a highly political question." To the end, he believed that this rift would result in England and America dissociating themselves from the alliance with the Soviet Union because, in his words, it was "so unnatural."

His active part in crushing the Officers' Plot of July 20, 1944 to assassinate Hitler is well enough known. His propaganda about it afterwards was most ingenious. By insisting on the incompetence and cowardice of these brave men, he successfully diminished their stature in the eyes of their countrymen. He was even able to persuade the German people that the whole episode was beneficial, evidence that the hand of providence was behind the Führer. After it, he coined the slogan *"Hitler ist der Sieg"* (Hitler is Victory). Then late in 1944, when it was clear that the war was lost, he made his last attempt to stimulate the flagging morale by producing a film about the Napoleonic wars in which the besieged Prussian city of Kolberg fought to the last man, and was saved by a military miracle. The lesson was clear. But no military lessons, nor miracles, could now save "the New Germany." On April 30, 1945, after naming Goebbels chancellor, Hitler committed suicide in his Berlin bunker. After an unsuccessful attempt to negotiate with the Soviets, Goebbels shot his wife, six children, and himself on the next day, May 1, 1945, exactly one week before the Allied victory in Europe.

Most nations will stop fighting when they have given up all hope of victory. It is Goebbels' supreme achievement that, by his sinister art, he persuaded the Germans to continue fighting long after they had abandoned all hope.

"Who is the most important man in the world?"
National Socialist election poster, 1932/Germany/Artist unknown.

National Socialist election poster, 1932/
Germany/Photomontage by Heinrich Hoffman.

"The flag bearer," 1930s/Germany/
Hubert Lanzinger.

"Germany lives," 1930s/
Germany/K. Stauber.

Hitler had no use for intellectuals like Einstein,
c. 1933/Germany/Seppla (Josef Plank).

The Nazis sweep out alien elements, early 1930s/
Germany/Seppla (Josef Plank).

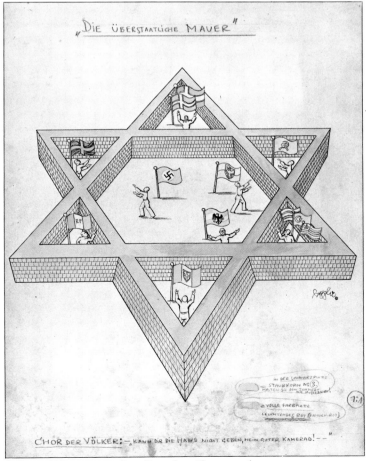

"The wall between nations," no date/Germany/
Seppla (Josef Plank).

"Germany, your colonies," c. 1935/Germany/
E. Glintzer.

"World Meeting of Hitler Youth," 1935/
Germany/Ludwig Hohlwein.

Hitler Youth postcard, no date/Germany/
H. Bargher.

SA cutout toys, 1930s/Germany/
Artist unknown.

*"And You?" (Poster for the Stalhelm Soldier's League),
1932/Germany/Ludwig Hohlwein.*

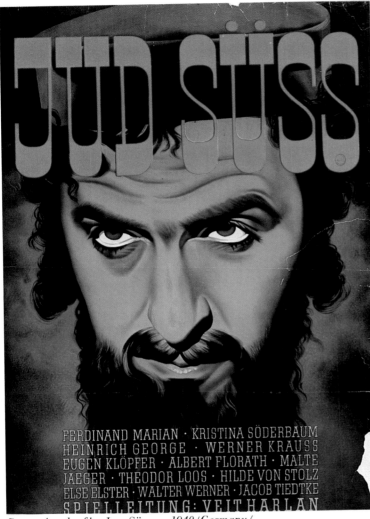

Poster for the film Jew Süss, c. 1940/Germany/
Artist unknown.

Churchill as a greedy octopus, c. 1940/Germany/
Seppla (Josef Plank).

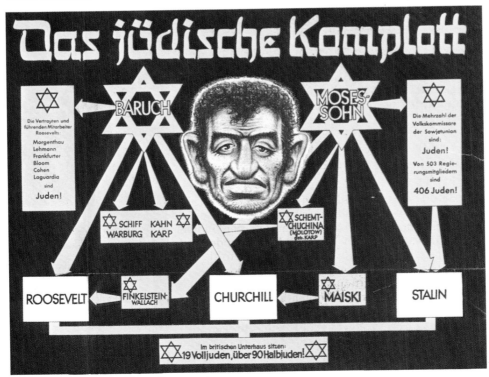

"The Jewish Plot," no date/Germany/
Artist unknown.

Poster for The Eternal Jew *exhibition, 1937/Germany/Artist unknown.*

"The German Student Fights for the Führer and the People,"
1930's/Germany/Ludwig Hohlwein.

(Top) Issued to mark the Saar Plebiscite, 1934. (Middle, left)
In commemoration of the 10th anniversary of the Lufthansa
air service, 1936. (Middle, right) Commemoration of the 1935
Nazi Congress at Nuremberg. (Bottom, left) Issued to commemorate
the 12th anniversary of the first Hitler "putsch" at Munich,
1923. (Bottom, right) Issued to commemorate War Hero's Day,
1935/Germany/Artists unknown.

Winter Olympics, 1936/Germany/
Ludwig Hohlwein.

(Top) Issued in commemoration of the fifth anniversary
of the assumption of power by the Nazis, January 28, 1938/
Germany/Artist unknown. (Above) Issued in commemoration of
the Winter and Summer Olympic Games, 1936/Germany/Artist unknown.

Ein Volk, ein Reich, ein Führer!

"One people, one nation, one leader," 1938/
Germany/Artist unknown.

*"Help Hitler build. Buy German goods," 1930s/
Germany/Gunther Nagel.*

*"Build youth hostels and homes," 1938 or 1939/
Germany/Hermann Witte.*

*"Strength Through Joy Folk Festival," 1930s/
Germany/Artist unknown.*

*Issued to commemorate the union of Austria with
Germany, April 10, 1938/Germany/Artist unknown.*

Issued to commemorate Grand Prix racing triumphs.
International Automobile Show, Berlin, 1939/Germany/
Artist unknown.

Issued as a reminder of Hitler's "People's Car" (the Volkswagen).
International Automobile Show, Berlin, 1939/Germany/Artist unknown.

Anti-Russian cartoon before the short-lived
peace pact, 1937/Germany/Seppla (Josef Plank).

"Bolshevism threatens when we let up; fight to victory!" c. 1942,/Germany/Artist unknown.

"Big Antibolshevik Exhibit," 1930s/Germany/ Artist unknown.

«¡Se adapta perfectamente a nuestra bandera!»

"Perfectly adapted for our flag (postcard)," c. 1942/ Germany/Artist unknown.

*"Uncle Sam's economic platform," c. 1941/
Germany/Seppla (Josef Plank).*

*England is threatened by a Jewish Bolshevik
conspiracy, no date/Germany/Seppla (Josef Plank).*

Schach dem King!

*"Check to the king!" 1940/Germany/
Artist unknown.*

Recruiting poster for the Waffen SS, 1941/
Germany/Anton.

Recruiting poster for the Hermann Göring
Division, 1943/Germany/Apportin.

"Victory will be ours," c. 1942/Germany/
Artist unknown.

"One struggle, one victory," 1943/Germany/
Mjölnir (Hans Schweitzer).

"Just as we fight, work for victory," c. 1942/
Germany/Rothgaengel.

"Adolf Hitler is Victory," 1943/Germany/
R. Gerhard Zill.

Issued to commemorate the Day of Youth Obligation,
March 26, 1943/Germany/Artist unknown.

"SA service develops comradeship, toughness,
strength," 1941/Germany/Otto Flechtner.

"Germany's victory, Europe's freedom," c. 1942/
Germany/Artist unknown.

Germans were warned that anyone might
spy, no date/Germany/Artist unknown.

"Traitor!" 1944/Germany/
Max Spielmanns.

Model for "black" parody stamp (page 64)
1944/Germany/Artist unknown.

"Blackout! The enemy sees your light," c. 1940/
Germany/Herweg.

12 12

FUTSCHES REICH

British "black" parody of a German stamp, no date/
England/Artist unknown.

MUSSOLINI'S NEW ROME
1922-1945

"Books are good, but muskets are better."
FASCIST SLOGAN

The first modern Italian propagandist was Gabriele D'Annunzio (1863–1938), the flamboyant poet and nationalist. As early as 1912 in his patriotic play *La Nave* (*The Ship*), he called for a revival of the Roman Empire. He despised the Italy he lived in, the parliamentary Italy with its unadventurous, security-seeking, property-worshipping bourgeois society. "In Latin days," he cried, "the Italian was king of all the seas, ruler of all domains to the distant horizon and the limits of empire." Like Hitler and Goebbels in Germany twenty years later, he was among the first propagandists to recognize the latent power of the masses. In *La Nave* he depicts a crowd being worked up by a skilled orator from relative apathy to collective curiosity, and thence to patriotic frenzy. A natural orator as well as a poet, D'Annunzio made impassioned speeches in 1915, inflaming the Roman masses and helping to bring Italy into the war. Later in 1919, having seized the disputed city of Fiume for Italy by a daring *coup de main*, he held it for over a year with his oratory, in face of all international opposition—including that of the Italian government.

It was his avowed intention to revive the Mediterranean past in Italy; he proclaimed, "I glory in the fact that I am a Latin, and I recognize a barbarian in every man of non-Latin blood." He thus sowed the seeds of Fascism, which Mussolini was later to reap. When the dictator came to power in 1922, the example of D'Annunzio in Fiume was still before him, and he took over all the poet's rabble-raising paraphernalia—the mob oratory, the cult of ancient Rome, the uniforms, the gun at the belt, the violence, the dialogue between orator and audience.

During the D'Annunzian occupation of Fiume, the people and the *arditi* (D'Annunzio's troops) would gather daily in the piazza before the Commandatura. The poet would come out on the balcony in his bemedalled uniform and deliver a harangue about the iniquities of the Versailles treaty, the treachery of the Allies, and the resurrection of poor, mutilated Italy under a new Roman Empire.

This was to be repeated even more theatrically in the years to come by Benito Mussolini, from the balcony of the Palazzo Venezia in Rome. He too revived the power of the piazza and enlisted the spontaneous voice of the mob. He too liked to palaver with them, and they would shout back *"Salutiamo il Duce! Fondatore dell'Impero!"* ("We salute the Duce! Founder of Empire!")—cries which reverberated across the piazza, and then over the radio to every city, town, and hamlet in Italy.

Mussolini shared D'Annunzio's scorn for the liberal Italy of the late 19th and early 20th centuries, as well as his nostalgia for the glories of ancient Rome, whose resurrection he calculated could be a powerful factor in achieving power for his party, as well as the only way of saving Italy in the modern technical world. Long before Hitler came to power, Mussolini was proclaiming that some time between 1936 and 1940, a turning point would come in European history, when a new era would be ushered in. This was remarkably prescient. He deduced that if Italy was to take advantage of this change, she must be fully

(Below) The knitted brow and pursed lips in this early-1930s caricature of the Duce express his intensity and determination. A former journalist, Mussolini knew the value of propaganda; the Fascist party continually sought affirmations of approval from the public for its policies. One leader called propaganda an instrument for the continual conquest of the masses.

armed. Armaments alone, he believed, could compensate for Italy's natural economic weakness.

To the Italian people, disillusioned by the peace treaties of 1919 and uninspired by their parliamentary leaders (men like Giolitti and Nitti who lacked entirely that bravura so dear to the Italian soul), Mussolini offered something new, as well as old— a return to the military virtues which had made Rome great. In the social and political chaos left by the First World War, with its permanent strikes and political upheaval on the left which the Italian bourgeois politicians seemed powerless to prevent, Mussolini offered hope and glory. He intended that Fascism should be not only a party, but a way of life, based on courage, discipline and self-sacrifice, such as had not been seen in Italy since the days of the elder Cato. This was later codified in the *Enciclopedia Italiana*: "The Fascist conception of the State is all-embracing. Outside it, no human or spiritual values can exist, much less have value." And Mussolini invented the graceless word *fascistizzare*, "to fascisticize," which meant applying the Fascist doctrine to all spheres of human life. To recall the modern heroic past, he used the name of Goffredo Mamelli, a patriot who fought and died for Garibaldi. This also established a link between Garibaldi's red shirts and the black ones with which Mussolini clothed his followers.

Like Hitler a man of the people, he understood the masses, particularly their admiration for violence which, as an approved weapon for the Fascists, was revealed in the symbols on the letterheads of their newspapers and pamphlets—a clenched fist, a club, a provocative jutting chin. Mussolini's use of violence between 1919 and 1922 for dealing with the communist riots was certainly effective, and brought many waverers into the Fascist camp. All over the peninsula, he organized his men into well-armed *squadristi* who simply exterminated the communists physically. Any town or village with a socialist municipality was their target. In the province of Ferrara, for example, there were twenty-one socialist councils in November 1920. By the end of 1921, all but four had disappeared, liquidated by the *squadristi* under Italo Balbo, one of Mussolini's most active lieutenants. The supine liberal governments, changing every few months, could no more curb the Fascist terror than they could control the communist-led riots. On October 28, 1922, Facta's government capitulated to Mussolini.

The absolutist regime which he now instituted was based on the theory of an elite of forceful men, not elected but in power by merit, led by a single heroic figure inspired by destiny—the Duce. One of the slogans Mussolini employed to implant this image in the Italian mind was "Caesar has come to life again in the Duce!" He had also chosen the name Fascist for its classical associations. The *fasces* were bundles of elm or birch rods from whose end projected an axe, carried in ancient Rome by the *lictors* (attendants of a magistrate); they were the insignia of official authority, symbolizing the magistrate's power to scourge and decapitate. Mussolini adopted the term in 1919, not yet as Fascist but as *fasci di combattimento*, literally "bundles for com-

(Opposite page) "Read The Fascist Worker." *All professional groups in Fascist Italy were organized, and propaganda programs were produced for each group. The swirling lines of the figure show that the Fascists, unlike the Nazis, could tolerate contemporary design. (Below) An early Fascist election poster. The young squadrista sounds a trumpet to awaken the sleeping conscience of the public.*

VI APRILE   SVEGLIA per le coscienze che dormono

VOTATE LA LISTA NAZIONALE

(Below) Schoolbooks, which had to be approved by the state, were rewritten to stress militaristic themes. School-children were told that "A book and a rifle make a perfect Fascist." The government created a secular rite of passage for young boys through a succession of youth groups, beginning with the "Sons of the She-Wolf" at age four and ending in the army in their late teens. The lurking shadow of a soldier behind the Balilla youth in this textbook illustration leaves little doubt that the lesson was war.

bat." These bundles became the *squadristi* who mowed down communists and other opponents.

Other devices he employed for identifying his party with ancient Rome were: the Roman salute instead of the bourgeois handshake; the use of Roman numerals for counting the years from 1922, and the initials E.F. (*Era Fascista*) instead of A.D. (thus 1929 A.D. became VII E.F.) The standards of the various Fascist leagues and organizations were modeled on the Roman *labarum* surmounted by the Imperial eagle. The ranks of the Youth Movement, the *Balilla*, bore the titles of units of the classical Roman army. The anniversaries of famous Roman political and literary figures—Caesar, Augustus, Virgil, Horace—were celebrated with great pomp. Postage stamps were issued to recall the memory of these famous men, together with other great Italians of the past: Dante, Ariosto, Tasso, da Vinci. Stamps also depicted ancient and modern ships, the former in the background, the latter in the foreground, with the motto "*Il nostro destino è stato, è sarà, sempre sul mare*" ("Our destiny has been, and will be, always on the sea"). This last was to remind Italians of their ancient Mediterranean supremacy (*mare nostrum*, "our sea"), as well as of the old Roman colonies of the North African shore, which must return to Italy. The vast monuments erected during the fascist period also contributed to the atmosphere of ancient Rome reborn—in particular the great Foro Mussolini, an imitation of the Roman forum. In a series of impassioned speeches, Mussolini informed his countrymen that the Italians were about to rule Western civilization again, after a lapse of 1500 years; and that they must discipline themselves for the conquests ahead. The Second Rome, the period of decadence, was over, to be replaced by the Third Rome, which would be as glorious as the First.

This cult of a revived Rome may be compared in contemporary Germany with the Nazi cult of the Teutonic past. The broad lines of propaganda in the two dictatorships, Italian and German, were the same—the mob oratory, the early domination of the juvenile mind, the cult of violence, exaggerated nationalism, and the scorn for democracy and the League of Nations. It is noteworthy that the advent of the dictator states coincided with the new mass communication techniques such as film and radio, which were suited to their needs. But in Italy, due principally to the different temperaments of the two peoples, the best use was not made of all the modern media of persuasion.

During the first decade of Fascist power, from 1922 to about 1933, the various forms of propaganda were not coordinated; nor was there anything like the Nazi Ministry of Propaganda. At the outset films, radio, and all the more modern media were lumped together under Mussolini's press office. Mussolini had been a journalist before he entered politics, and right up to the end of the Fascist era the press was still regarded as the most effective way of influencing public opinion. The Duce referred to it as "an orchestra played in concert, though on different kinds of instruments." By the Press Decree of 1924, prefects were empowered to confiscate issues of newspapers which contained "false information, calculated to inspire class hatred, or to bring the government into contempt." The liberal-minded editors of great newspapers like the *Corriere della Sera* of Milan, or *Il Messaggero* of Rome, were dismissed, and the papers ceased all criticism of the regime. Meanwhile Fascist journals such as Mussolini's *Popolo d'Italia* and the *Regime Fascista* were granted additional subsidies and government aid. By 1926, every paper in Italy had to obtain government permission to publish.

It was not until the 1930s that the regime realized that the press office could not possibly handle all the propaganda media, and in 1933 an Undersecretariat for Press and Propaganda was created. It was not until 1937—after Goebbels' ministry had already been systematically regimenting the German mind for several years—that the German example was followed, and a full-scale Ministry of Propaganda, called the Ministry of Popular Culture (Minculpop), was founded. On June 1 of that year, all the previous offices in the press department—for radio, cinema, theater, literature—were abolished, and those media passed under the control of the new propaganda ministry. From now on, the regime abandoned its purely negative role of censorship, and adopted a more positive approach, issuing directives aimed at indoctrination of Fascist principles in all fields. The ministry was managed by party extremists and had the closest links with the leadership. The three men who followed one another as heads of propaganda, from the undersecretariat days to the ministry, were Count Ciano (Mussolini's son-in-law), Alfieri, and Pavolini. Though their methods became increasingly effective, none of them could be compared with a propaganda genius like Goebbels.

Italy also differed from Germany in the role played by the Catholic church. Because of the church's special position in Italy, and its power over the masses (whether they were devout or not), the regime made no attempt to transform the Fascist doctrines into an alternative religion, as the Nazis had in Germany. The Italian heaven was not to become a Valhalla. This was to have a considerable moderating effect on Fascist policy and propaganda.

In one aspect of propaganda, however, the Fascists always remained the equal of, if not superior to, the Nazis—the indoctrination of the young. Here, the Nazis themselves admitted that in their first years of power they had learned much from Fascist Italy. When Mussolini took office in 1922, he immediately instructed his Education Minister, Giovanni Gentile, to reform the school and university curricula. He understood the importance of youth for the future, and he wanted much more time devoted in the schools to patriotic subjects, with history and geography interpreted in terms of the Roman past. Very soon, at least 20 percent of the curriculum in the elementary schools had been revised in this sense, teaching the adolescent from very early days his duties as a Fascist citizen.

The school day started with the singing of *"Giovinezza"* ("Youth"), the official Fascist hymn. Before beginning their

The Fascist government wanted to teach schoolchildren the qualities of obedience, sacrifice, and intense devotion to the Duce. Mussolini was shown in schoolbooks as a stern but kindly father figure. The text for beginning readers says "Benito Mussolini loves children very much. The children of Italy love the Duce very much. Long live the Duce. I salute the Duce: To us!"

BENITO MUSSOLINI ama molto i bambini. I bimbi d'Italia amano molto il Duce.

VIVA IL DUCE!

Saluto al Duce:

A noi!

Even the comic strips in the youth newspapers were used to instill the virtues of a military caste. (Top) Grillo, from the pages of Il Corriere dei Piccoli, *was already building airplanes in 1934. (Middle) As soon as war was declared in 1940, Romolino and Remoletto were helping the Italian army to fight the British. (Bottom) "Il Balilla Moschettino" (The Balilla Youth "Little Rifle") appeared in the boys' paper* Mastro Remo.

studies, the boys and girls would march past the national flag, giving the ceremonial Roman salute. For the older ones, a series of "Conversations on Fascist Culture" were arranged, conducted by party officials and youth leaders, with subjects such as the History of the Fascist Revolution, Imperialism and Italian Foreign Policy, and the Economic Institutions of Fascism. In higher education at the universities, *Gruppi Universitari Fascisti* were formed, which students had to join if they wished to succeed. At Perugia University, a faculty of political sciences was founded to develop Fascism on doctrinal lines; and a summer school was opened to spread Fascist ideas among foreign students. For the intellectual and professional classes, the Instituto Nazionale Fascista di Cultura was founded by Giovanni Gentile in 1925; its function was to recruit the educated classes into the service of the regime. It had chapters throughout the country and a membership of 100,000. As well as sponsoring lectures and publishing Fascist political theory, the Institute conducted seminars and maintained reading rooms. Similar to this was the Italian Academy, founded in 1927, as "the organ of the Fascist Revolution in the field of Art." But owing to its repressive and stifling atmosphere, it exerted little influence. The regime did, however, succeed in enlisting the support of a few cultural luminaries— Giacomo Puccini, who was rewarded with a seat in the Senate; D'Annunzio, who was given a fine property above the lake of Garda; Luigi Pirandello, and Guglielmo Marconi. Benedetto Croce, Italy's leading intellectual, always remained aloof. Arturo Toscanini was a Fascist in the early days, but when he refused to include the *"Giovinezza"* in his programs he was beaten up by thugs. He resigned from the party, moved permanently to the United States, and refused to conduct in Italy for the duration of the Fascist regime.

Meanwhile in the schools and universities, all the textbooks had been revised; of 317 history books in use in the elementary schools in 1926, 100 were banned. A government decree stated, "In the fields of history, economics and law, all books must be in accord with the historical, juridical and economic requirements established on October 28, 1922." Teachers were required to take an oath of loyalty to the regime, or risk dismissal.

Concurrently with these educational reforms went the creation of the various extramural youth organizations. The Fascists took possesion of the child even earlier than the Nazis did. At the age of four the young boy had to enlist in the "Sons of the She-Wolf," another significant Roman allusion, and don his little black shirt. At eight he graduated into the *Balilla*, where he remained until the age of fourteen, in a continuous atmosphere of uniforms, songs, banners, badges, salutes. (The *Balilla* was named after a Genovese youth who, in 1746, had given the signal for the uprising against the Austrian overlords.)

Children's magazines such as *Il Corriere dei Piccoli* or *Giornale dei Balilla* give some idea of the indoctrination the child underwent. In their comic strips the young hero, aged anywhere between four and ten, wearing a uniform, was depicted instructing other admiring non-*Balilla* children in various sporting activities—yachting, riding, hunting—as well as learning about airplanes, and even how to fire a machine gun. Later, when war came in 1940, the comic strips derided Italy's enemies. Thus, George VI of England and Winston Churchill were shown as being so terrified of the heroic Italian soldiers that they were reduced to hiring an orangutang to protect themselves.

The instruction given in the *Balilla* after school hours and on weekends was essentially physical. The Fascists were well aware of the fascination of sports for the growing boy—football, athletics, swimming, boxing, riding, miniature-range shooting; no expense was spared to provide facilities for these. The Duce set the example himself. He gloried in his own physical fitness, and described boxing as a typically Fascist method of self-expression. Passages were read in school from journalists who had visited him at the Villa Torlonia describing how, while dictating his orders for the day, he would suddenly break off to swim six lengths in his pool, or play a violent set of tennis, or ride his horse over a dozen fences in the paddock. The newspapers were strictly forbidden from reporting that he had a cold or stomach cramps; nor even that he had become a grandfather. The Duce must be 100 percent fit; 100 percent virile.

After the *Balilla* the youth, aged fourteen, joined the *Avant-guardisti*, where to these sports were added sham battles and marching in formation with rifles. He lived in a permanent round of political indoctrination sessions, rallies, military parades, drills, and athletic events. At eighteen he was ready for the *Giovani Fascisti* which, after two more years, would judge whether he was a suitable candidate for the party—whether he was imbued with the necessary virtues of toughness, obedience, blind courage, and self-sacrifice. If so, he was eligible to become a member of the new ruling class of Italy. Each of the graduation ceremonies, from one group to the higher one, was accompanied by an elaborate ritual, the *Leva Fascisti*, again recalling ancient Rome.

During the whole indoctrination, the youth were kept constantly aware of the personality of the Duce. His portrait hung in every school and lecture room, beside smaller ones of the king and the pope. With his jaw thrust out, his fists clenched, his arms akimbo and legs apart, he seemed the living image of his own slogans: "Better to live one day like a lion than a hundred years as a sheep"; "A minute on the battlefield is worth a lifetime of peace"; *"Credere! Obbedire! Combattere!"* (Believe! Obey! Fight!")

Thus a boy who started in 1923 as a Son of the She-Wolf would, by the outbreak of war in 1940, have passed through the whole gamut of Fascist education, at four levels. It would take an exceptionally refractory youth to withstand all these impulsions and blandishments.

Parallel youth groups were organized for girls. The *Piccole Italiane* was their counterpart of the Sons of the She-Wolf. Then came the female *Balilla*, with final graduation into the *Giovani Italiane*. Under the auspices of the *Fasci Femminili*, for adults, a set of lectures propagating Fascist principles for women was

(Below) Mussolini, with his bombastic rhetoric, spread before his countrymen the splendor of Imperial Rome. He promised them a share in the Axis hegemony of the Western world. After the decadence of the Second Rome, he heralded the arrival of the Third Rome in which Mussolini himself would perpetuate the glorious ruling tradition of the Caesars. Jack Oakie as Napaloni in Chaplin's The Great Dictator (1940) portrayed the Duce as a buffoon who played second fiddle to Hitler while Rome burned.

(Below) Paul Muni as "Scarface" Carmante in Howard Hawks' Scarface: The Shame of a Nation *(1932). The film was banned in Rome because it portrayed Italians as gangsters. (Opposite, top) Mussolini was a master of theatrics and overblown oratory. He spoke barechested to show his machismo. (Opposite, bottom) The film industry was not as tightly controlled in Italy as it was in Germany, where Goebbels had the aspirations of a Cecil B. De Mille.* L'Uomo del Croce (The Man of the Cross, *1940) was one of the more overtly propagandistic films of the Fascist period. The central character was an Italian priest on the Russian front who took up arms against the Soviets.*

given regularly. The older girls were also required to take part in physical training, athletics, even in paramilitary exercises. It was here—and over youth education in general—that the Fascists had their only real dispute with the Catholic church.

The church had always regarded the education of youth as its own special preserve. Pope Pius XI in his encyclical *Non abbiamo bisogno* of 1926 showed that he was fully aware of Fascist pretensions in this area. He wrote: "The undoubted resolve to monopolize completely the young, from their tenderest years up to manhood and womanhood, for the full and exclusive advantages of a party or regime is no less in full conflict with the natural rights of the family than with the supernatural rights of the church." In the view of the Catholic church, youth should be educated by three "societies": the family, the church, and lastly the state. First comes the family, which has a natural God-given right to bring up its offspring, to nourish it, love it, and teach it the elements of civic behavior. Should the family not have the financial means to do this, the state must step in—but only to help. The church possesses all the means for the eternal salvation of the human being. The education, therefore, of that human being, which means the inculcation of moral as well as intellectual values, is the responsibility of the church.

Matters came to a head on May 4, 1928, when a mammoth demonstration took place in the Roman Stadium, where thousands of *Balilla* girls clad in gym clothes gave a physical-training display, and hurled javelins. They then marched in ranks through Rome with rifles at arms-length, chanting Fascist slogans. On May 11, the *Osservatore Romano*, the Vatican newspaper, expressed the Vatican's disapproval of "these groups of Fascist womanhood departing from the principle of modesty and reserve which should govern the education of girls and young women." It was not in keeping with Christian ideals of feminine education for girls, the paper said, to be taught violent physical exercises and to carry firearms; nor for scantily dressed young women to disport themselves in front of predominantly male audiences; nor "to raise their rifles to heaven." "When female hands are raised to heaven," said the pope in a public allocution, "they should be in prayer, not holding rifles."

To this the secretary of the Fascist party, Turati, replied in *Il Tevere* that physical exercise had a beneficial effect on the mind. It was better for young girls to take part in such displays than to spend the day covering their faces with makeup. As for rifles, the regime had no intention of turning the girls into auxiliary troops; it merely wanted to train them not to faint at the sight of a loaded weapon, or when they heard a shot fired in war. The *Osservatore Romano* replied that the girls could perfectly well undergo physical training in the privacy of their school. The paper recalled a speech by Mussolini on May 18, 1927, in which he said he wanted the modern female youth of Italy to remain essentially "Latin," and not allow themselves, "under the influence of the cinema and other forms of modernism, to become Americanized." Well, said the *Osservatore Romano*, that was

(Below) "Keep quiet, the enemy is listening." The British Tommy, used to personify the enemy on this 1943 poster by Gino Boccasile, cocks an ear to pick up military secrets. One of the most common home-front propaganda themes of the war was the threat of "fifth column" activity. Posters linked casual remarks to the sinking of ships and the derailing of trains. Different countries had their own variants of the "careless talk" theme. The British, using puns and cartoons, took a lighter approach. German posters had a cloak-and-dagger quality. To Americans, the connection was often made between a careless comment and its consequences.

IL NEMICO VI ASCOLTA

TACETE!

precisely what the government was doing with these immodest public displays. The notion of females taking part in sporting competitions was essentially Anglo-Saxon. The argument rumbled on for months. It is some measure of the church's power in Italy that the Vatican continued to speak up in this way—to an absolutist regime which had stifled every other voice of criticism. Finally, as a concession to Catholic sensibilities, the Fascists agreed that in the future the girls would not carry rifles at these ceremonies, but bows and arrows.

The Catholic church showed its teeth again on another occasion, in 1928, when the *Balilla* youth introduced a political note into an open-air mass which was being celebrated in the Campo Dux. They began it with the singing of the *"Giovinezza,"* followed by an invocation to the Divine Being to help Mussolini in his empire building. Worst of all, when the host was elevated, 15,000 youths drew their daggers from the scabbards and pointed them dramatically to the sky. This was severely reprehended in the *Osservatore Romano.*

These propaganda attempts by the regime to give the impression that the church was on its side were often clumsy. Once, when commemorating the dead Fascist heroes, it evidently thought the church would be flattered by the use of hagiographic language. It described an exhibition of the "Fascist Revolution" as "Fascism's Holy Year," and referred to "the blood of our martyrs, which will one day liquify as does that of Saint Januarius in Naples." A Fascist newspaper in the Trento region wrote of the Italian irredentists, Battisti and Sanro, who had been executed by the Austrians, "There is a halo round the brow of Battisti, whose journey through Trento on the hangman's wagon recalls the journey to Golgotha of the flagellated Christ"; while Sanro's mother "wept before her son's body as did Mary under the Cross." The fertile imagination of one journalist became almost evangelical over a Fascist who had been murdered by communists. "His martyrdom was perhaps greater than that of the blond Nazarene, for the Nazarene was accompanied to his execution by his mother and Mary Magdalene; but our man had no one to support him." The *Osservatore Romano* commented tartly on all this that such attempts to glorify earthly things had in fact the reverse effect. To bring godly and human things together in this way did not of course damage the godly; it only rendered the wordly ridiculous.

The use of recreation and sport as vehicles for propaganda was not confined to the youth of Fascist Italy. To monopolize the leisure time of the working classes on behalf of the regime, an organization entitled *Dopolavoro* ("after working hours") was formed. It offered many attractive and free services and facilities. Besides sport, it provided inexpensive vacations and excursions—as did the *Kraft durch Freude* organization in Nazi Germany—and also films and theatrical performances. Sporting contests among its members were often elaborate spectacles, and the victorious athletes were given personal publicity as examples of the new regime's manliness. *Dopolavoro* was also careful to give lectures and instruction on the party organization, the Fascist Revolution and the Fascist syndicates (trade unions). Its avowed purpose was "the healthy and profitable occupation of workers' leisure hours through institutions for developing their physical, intellectual, and moral capacities."

To outlying provinces, the party sent mobile theater groups to present Fascist morality plays, usually followed by political commentaries from local party leaders. In Milan, the brashness of the leadership was revealed in a set of lectures it arranged called *Lectura Ducis*, modeled on the *Lectura Dantis*, a famous set of lectures on Dante Alighieri given by renowned scholars in the Florentine church of Orsanmichele. In the series *Lectura Ducis* a party leader read from Mussolini's speeches, and then commented on them in Dantesque phraseology. The Duce was to be not only the new Caesar but, in political thought, the new Dante as well.

As a propaganda vehicle, the cinema was never exploited as extensively in Italy as in Nazi Germany. Up to the end of the Fascist era, the Italian film companies still remained largely in private hands. This was due primarily to the Italian public's lack of interest in serious films about politics, such as the government-made *Battle of the Grain*, incorporating shots of Mussolini driving about on a tractor surrounded by vociferating peasants. The public preferred American-type films about glamorous couples eating caviar in chic hotels, or driving Cadillacs. Deplorable as this was, the regime knew there was not much to be done about it. When in the thirties someone suggested to Mussolini that he should take a leaf out of Goebbels' book and nationalize the film companies, he refused. The attitude of his regime towards the cinema, at least in the first decade of Fascist rule, was that of a censor. The concern was with what could *not* be shown, rather than what should be shown. Thus, a "decadent" Hollywood film such as *Wings over Honolulu* was banned, because it dealt with the immoral goings-on of a group of divorcees. Although this ban may have been in part to ingratiate the church, divorce conflicted with Fascist principles about the sanctity of marriage and the rearing of large families. The film *Scarface* was banned for other reasons. It was about gangster life in Chicago, and its protagonist was the Sicilian mobster Al Capone; it might give wrong ideas to his countrymen at home.

In spite of this, Mussolini knew perfectly well that the cinema had propaganda value. In 1925, he founded *L'Unione Cinematografica Educativa* (LUCE), a purely governmental body which produced documentaries about Fascist achievements. To counteract the influence of the American-type "high life" film, all cinemas were required to include at least one LUCE film in every program. Thus, if the public wanted to watch Cary Grant making love to Mae West, they also had to look at an old peasant in the Pontine Marshes, on the horns of a dilemma about whether he should adopt modern farming methods or remain true to those of his fathers. This was the LUCE film *Il Sole* (*The Sun*). Another LUCE film, *I ragazzi di Mussolini* (*Mussolini's Youth*), showed what the Duce was doing for the youth of Italy.

(Below) "To the army, to the army, youth of Italy, for the salvation of the country." This recruiting poster was one of a series seen on the streets of Rome in late 1943. As Italy's military fortunes declined, the "New Rome" became an extended family; the matriarch replaced the Duce in the appeal for more soldiers. *(Following spread)* Mussolini's ability to spellbind an audience equaled that of the greatest Italian actors. His use of gesture, voice modulation, and emotional extremes were exceptional. This flamboyance, enshrined in bronze and stone, adorned public plazas throughout Italy.

(Below) The Duce was an easy target for the mockery of cartoonists abroad. This 1937 cartoon by the Soviet artists, the Kukriniksi, lampoons the pretension of Mussolini's "New Rome," where vast monuments were erected in the Foro Mussolini, modeled on the ancient Roman Forum. The Kukriniksi showed Mussolini as an oppressive dictator whose pedestal was a prison.

In the LUCE films, army maneuvers, battleships, and bombing planes were also given a prominent place, which may have made them a little more palatable to the Italian public.

It was not until 1937 that anything to compare with the Nazi film *Triumph of the Will* was produced. It was called *Credere, Obbedire, Combattere (Believe, Obey, Fight)*, and it showed the achievements of Fascism, accompanied by selected excerpts from Mussolini's speeches. This was followed by other patriotic films, expensive productions such as *Scipio Africanus* (1937), which drew the parallel between ancient Rome's conqueror of Carthage and Mussolini, who had just conquered another part of Africa, Ethiopia. It was made in Rome, and when it was shown the carping Italian critics pointed to the anachronism of telegraph poles sprouting on the hills and wrist watches on the arms of the Roman legionaries.

The Italian invasion of Ethiopia was also the subject of *Luciano Serra Pilota* (1938), about the instinctive passion for flying which passes from father to son. It told of a father who lost his life flying in Ethiopia to save his son. In 1940 came *The Siege of Alcazar*, proudly relating Italy's part in the Spanish Civil War. Later in the Second World War, when things were going badly, a film was made to appeal to Italian nationalist rather than Fascist sentiment: *L'Uomo della Croce (The Man of the Cross*, 1943). This was about an Italian priest on the Russian front who exchanges his cross for a rifle, and fights with the black shirts against the Soviets.

Radio as a propaganda instrument was better handled. It could be centrally controlled and made to broadcast the bulletins of the government press agency, Stefani, which alone could dispense news abroad, because it had the monopoly of contracts with all foreign press associations, such as Reuters and Associated Press. Although Mussolini hardly used the radio for studio talks himself, preferring like Hitler the balcony approach, he realized that thanks to this new medium his open-air speeches could be heard all over Italy. His aim was, he proclaimed, "to see a radio in every home." To this end, a cheap set, significantly named the *Balilla*, was put on the market at 430 lire, which was payable in 18 monthly installments. As the figures reveal, it had some success. Whereas in 1927 there were 40,000 subscribers to the *Ente Italiano Audizione Radiofonica*, by 1939 there were 1,170,000. But for a population of 43 million this could hardly compare with the 12,500,000 sets which Germany had in the same year. It was not until 1937 that the Inspectorate for Radio Broadcasting was made part of the Ministry of Popular Culture. From Germany the Fascists borrowed the habit of installing a communal radio set in the halls and recreation rooms where the peasants gathered in the evenings, and where they could listen to government announcements. Loudspeakers were also placed in the piazzas and outside the offices of local authorities.

The Fascists also used the radio extensively in youth education. The program *"Giornalino del Fanciullo"* ("Children's Little Newspaper") broadcast stories, poems, songs, and religious

Project for a standard monument in the Italian "empire."

services, interspersed with tales of fabulous exploits by Mussolini and other Italian heroes. Special attention was also paid to the countryside through the *Ente Radio Rurale,* providing regular agricultural news and advice to the peasantry.

The regime's greatest radio achievement was in support of the invasion of Ethiopia. Just before it began, in October 1935, the Fascist party organized huge assemblies all over Italy, in every town and village, with songs, bands, sirens, and patriotic speeches by fiery local party leaders. Then, when an estimated 20 million people were gathered, the voice of the Duce came announcing that Italy, too, was about to take her "place in the sun." On a thousand piazzas, his booming voice infected the mob with collective hysteria, and they shrieked their approval—just as fifteen years earlier in Fiume, D'Annunzio had worked up the population of a small and modest town to a state of insensate frenzy. After this, the Fascists could claim that these unanimous cries of approval for the Ethiopian invasion were tantamount to a national plebiscite, and that the Duce was only carrying out the people's will.

On May 9, 1936, after the Italian army's triumph in Ethiopia, Mussolini appeared on the balcony of the Palazzo Venezio to announce the foundation of the new Italian Empire under Vittorio Emmanuele III, who would henceforth assume the style and dignity of the king-emperor. Rome had been born again. Radio sets and loudspeakers throughout Italy blared out the Duce's words. "The Italian people," he cried, "have created the empire with their own blood. They will nourish it with their own labor, and defend it against all comers with their own arms. Supremely confident of this, lift up your mansards, my legionaries, your weapons and your hearts, to salute after fifteen centuries, the reappearance of our empire on the fateful hills of Rome! Are you not worthy of it?"

Another form of propaganda during the Fascist period was the holding of immense exhibitions. The greatest of these was the *Mostra della Rivoluzione Fascista* (Exhibition of the Fascist Revolution) in Rome on the tenth anniversary of the seizure of power. Under one large roof were gathered exhibits from the years 1914–22, among which were the bloody uniforms and medals of the martyrs who died during the March on Rome. The exhibition also included a "sacrarium," or votive chapel to the Fascist fallen. The quasireligious atmosphere was further enhanced by the great cross in the center of a semicircle bearing the illuminated words, *"Per la Patria Immortale"* and *"Presente! Presente!"* (that is, our dead are still with us), and "To us! To us!" Millions of country dwellers were attracted to Rome for this exhibition by reduced fares and free excursions organized by the local Fascist authorities.

Posters were created for the Duce by Italy's leading graphic artists. Foremost among them was Gino Boccasile, whose posters epitomized the Fascist themes: the courage of the black shirts against the Allies, anti-Semitism, and the portrayal of the enemy soldiers as barbarians.

The Fascists excelled in the concoction of slogans, surpassing

(Below) Few observers outside Italy were fooled by the propaganda of the Rome-Berlin axis, which Mussolini, in a 1936 speech in Milan, said was "not a diaphragm but an axis, around which can resolve all those European states with a will to collaboration and peace." Abroad, Mussolini's bombast was disregarded and he was portrayed as Hitler's lackey, as in this 1936 Soviet cartoon by Boris Efimov.

(Top) A British "black" parody stamp paraphrased Mussolini's slogan, "Two nations, one war," as "Two nations, one Führer." (Bottom) Like two actors, the Führer and the Duce rode through the streets of Berlin, which were decorated by Germany's outstanding stage designer, Benno von Arendt. (Opposite page, top) Hitler and Mussolini greet crowds in Rome. (Bottom) Art mirrors life in this scene from Chaplin's The Great Dictator.

even the Nazis. Mussolini the ex-journalist knew the power of the written word, and he personally was a great coiner of slogans. They were to be found scrawled on half the walls and wayside buildings of Italy: "He who has steel has bread!"; "War is to the male what childbearing is to the female!"; "All within the State, nothing outside the State, nothing against the State!"; "The Fascist man does not believe in everlasting peace"; "Nothing has been won in history without bloodshed"; "Right without might is vain"; "The plough makes the furrow, but the sword defends it!" And the most famous of all, *"Mussolini ha sempre ragione!"* ("Mussolini is always right!").

An acid comment on this slogan mania was made by Hitler himself on his ceremonial visit to Italy in May, 1938. Albert Speer, who was with him, writes in his memoirs that Hitler was not at all impressed by the walls he saw everywhere daubed with these phrases. *"We* don't need that," he said. "The German people are tough enough, if it comes to war. This kind of propaganda may be all right in Italy. Whether it does any good is another matter." Hitler knew little of foreign countries and peoples, and his comment is of more value about himself, and his overweening conceit, than about the Italian slogans. They were devised by leaders who knew their countrymen.

It was during Hitler's visit that Mussolini fell completely under the spell of his more powerful fellow dictator. He had first met Hitler in Venice in 1934, and had not been impressed by him; of *Mein Kampf* he had said, "that boring book which I have never been able to read." But by 1936, as Hitler consolidated his power and supported Italy's aggression in Ethiopia, Mussolini began to change his opinion. In Milan in that year he referred to the "axis" for Italo-German collaboration. "The Berlin-Rome line is not a diaphragm," he said, "but rather an axis around which can revolve all those European states with a will to collaboration and peace."

On an earlier visit he had made to Germany, in September, 1937, Mussolini had been much impressed by the German army, at whose magnificent parades he had been the guest of honor. It was then that he told Ciano, "We must make the Italians harder, nastier, more hateful, more Prussian." With this in mind, he introduced the German goose step into the Italian army, because "it is strong, secure, inexorable, making every march into a conquest," and is "so difficult that a lazy or weak person cannot perform it." This did not please the Italian king, who was far from pro-German. But Mussolini brushed his criticism aside with the explanation, "The goose is after all a Roman bird. Did it not save the Capitol?" He ordered that the goose step was to be known in the Italian army as *il passo Romano* (the Roman step).

On the Führer's return visit to Italy, Mussolini was determined that it should be as impressive as his own to Germany. Planning began six months before, and Mussolini spent hours supervising the arrangements of the military parades, and checking the details of every march. Particular care was paid to the decoration of the streets, to give Hitler a splendid welcome. Al-

After Mussolini's visit to Germany in 1937, the Italian army was ordered to adopt the goose step, renamed the "passo romano" (Roman step). Mussolini claimed that it symbolized the will and energy of youth. The step, he said, was difficult; lazy and weak people couldn't do it. Nevertheless, the Italian soldier was ridiculed as a coward in such films as Billy Wilder's Five Graves to Cairo.

though some of the Roman shopkeepers refused to display Hitler's photograph in their windows, the German dictator was suitably impressed. He felt that even if Italy was not particularly strong militarily, here was an ally he dare not lose.

Much more serious and sinister was the anti-Semitism which Mussolini, again aping his German mentor, introduced into Italy at the end of the thirties. Before 1938, he had emphatically rejected anti-Semitism. Now, after entering into the "Pact of Steel" with Hitler, he made it an official tenet of the regime. There were only about 50,000 Jews in Italy, and anti-Semitism hardly existed. But the dictatorship issued manifestos on the German lines, stating that the Italian race was pure, and that the Jews did not belong to it, however long their families had lived there. Racist magazines such as *La Difensa della Razza (The Defense of the Race)* were published. Courses were held on such topics as "Preserving Racial Integrity"; "The Danger of Mixed Marriages"; "The Purity of the Italian Race since Roman Times"; and "The Jews and Modern Culture." These lectures received wide press and radio publicity, and some were published in book form for use in the schools. Decrees were issued forbidding the entry of foreign Jews into schools, and preventing them from settling in Italy. Italians were later forbidden from marrying Jews, and Jews were excluded from the army. But no amount of propaganda could stir up much feeling in a country where there was probably less anti-Semitism than anywhere else in Europe. When the war came, much energy which could have been employed elsewhere had been wasted in this unprofitable field.

Together with the Fascist propaganda to transform Italy into a race of warriors as valiant as the legionaries of ancient Rome went a campaign to represent her enemies as unmilitary and decadent. By the late thirties, Mussolini had become convinced that the main opponent to his expansionist plans would be Great Britain. In 1936, Britain had done everything short of war to impede his invasion of Ethiopia, sponsoring the League of Nations' economic sanctions against Italy. The failure of these gave Mussolini the excuse he required for exacerbating Italian nationalism still further. Italy's success in Ethiopia proved, he said, that the British navy's domination of the Mediterranean was over. Gone were the high colonial days when men like Rhodes, Kitchener, and Lord Roberts made the British Empire great. Britain was now governed by a pusillanimous businessman armed with nothing more than an umbrella. Italy would supplant Britain in North Africa and the Mediterranean.

An excerpt from an article in the Fascist magazine *Gerarchia* illustrates the scorn which was being fostered for Great Britain (January 1938): "Englishmen are incapable of understanding great ideas, and they have a profound dislike of anything theoretical or abstract . . . They lack any real intelligence . . . but are moved solely by material ambitions and immediate interests . . . In the pursuit of personal advantage, they assume attitudes which are often contradictory and absurd . . . Their's is a country without literature and without art or music . . . Serious scholarship is derided in England and intellectual subjects are never discussed . . . Only the sheer ignorance of John Bull and the docile attitude of official writers could ever have suggested that such a chaotic agglomeration as the British Empire could resemble the empire of ancient Rome . . ."

In addition to journalists, eminent professors of biology and anthropology were enlisted to show that the Anglo-Saxon race was effete and degenerate. In the years immediately before the Second World War, the Fascists created an image of an Anglo-Saxon society based entirely on wealth—or "gold," as they preferred to call it. Their slogans referred to the coming struggle between gold (the bourgeois democracies) and work (the "proletarian" axis nations). The Western plutocracies, they asserted, could maintain their domination in the world only by gold, for in all other spheres they were inferior. With gold, however, they intended to strangle the new, young, and vigorous societies surging in Italy and Germany, whose strength lay not in gold but in work. The Duce was "the creator of the civilization of work." When the struggle came, victory would go to the work nations, for work was the highest, noblest, most spiritual expression of life.

All this anti-British propaganda the Italian public was forced to swallow in increasing quantities as the international tensions grew. The journalist Ermanno Amicucci went so far as to say, "Thanks to the heroism of our soldiers, gold will prove incapable of subjugating work—in a holy war against the slave-master, gold, and the ferocious egotism of our hereditary enemy, the British Empire, the profiteer for centuries of the blood and sweat of others . . ." The British were accused of every form of vice and foppery. Their energy, it was said, was sapped not only by their worship of Mammon, but by such crankish addictions as psychonalysis and spiritualism, five-o'clock tea, golf (the "anti-Mediterranean sport"), even by the unmasculine habit of shaving once a day. The Italian public was told that in English secondary schools, young girls were bought and sold, their principal purchasers being Anglican bishops and members of Parliament. The historian Alessandro Luzzio said that the English were a race of drunkards, drug addicts, and homosexuals, being encouraged in the latter vice by "the many thickets conveniently placed in Hyde Park," and by the ugliness of English women. There were seven million spinsters in England, whose sexual frustration could be relieved only by a royal decree permitting polygamy.

As for the British fighting qualities, their army was composed largely of Indian mercenaries and Australian ex-convicts; it would mutiny rather than parade in the rain, and it always broke off action at five o'clock for tea. Even the usually well-informed Italian ambassador in London, Count Grandi, subscribed to this rubbish. He informed his government that the British Brigade of Guards could not stand up for a moment to their Italian counterparts. The British were, he said, "a people entirely without the military virtues."

It might appear from all this that the Fascist propagandists

(Below) The text of Boccasile's poster reads "Germany is your friend." In 1940 Mussolini said, "If the Germans ever get here they will never go home." Immediately after Mussolini's fall in 1943, Hitler sent German troops to Italy to occupy the country. After a bitter struggle, the Germans were defeated in May 1945 by the Allies, whom the disillusioned and weary Italians welcomed as liberators.

LA GERMANIA E VERAMENTE VOSTRA AMICA

had gone off their heads, and that their charges were not worthy of rebuttal. But these are only a few of the accusations about British decadence which are listed, in all seriousness, by the eminent British historian and expert on Fascist Italy, Professor Dennis Mack Smith, in his study of anti-British propaganda, *Inghilterra e Italia nel' 900.*

Great Britain's potential allies, France and later the United States, came in for a similar, if less virulent, treatment. France with her popular front government was, the Fascists deduced, clearly under the domination of a foreign power, the Soviets, and therefore not fit to call herself a sovereign state. She too was corrupted by innumerable modern vices—contraception and the low birth rate, gambling, the immoral writings of Marcel Proust and André Gide, Pernod, bathing shorts, permanent waves. France would collapse like a pack of cards at the first cannonade. Nor was she fit to administer North African territories like Tunisia which was, in any case, "an Italian province governed by French bureaucrats."

The United States did not come in for this sort of abuse until the spring of 1940, when her sympathies were clearly veering towards the Western Allies. Short-wave broadcasts from Radio Roma were now addressed to the large Italian community in the United States, fostering an isolationist feeling. The broadcasts condemned President Roosevelt for plotting to involve his country in a war which could bring only suffering and disaster to all Americans.

This sort of propaganda was relatively successful in peacetime when the Anglo-Saxon powers, busy with their commercial affairs, could not be bothered to counter it. But in war, when they revealed that they could not only defend themselves but could go on the offensive with an avalanche of ad hoc armaments, the decadence propaganda began to ring hollow. The Italians are more cynical than the Germans, and they had no Goebbels to make up their minds for them. In the first weeks after the Italian entry into the war, the Italian newspapers made ludicrous claims, announcing that Italy now had complete mastery of the Mediterranean. In three days, they said, the Italian air force had sunk half the British fleet; it was now turning its attention to the Battle of Britain and destroying the RAF in its own skies. The first claim was quickly disposed of by the Battle of Cape Matapan, where the British navy gave the Italian fleet such a mauling that it hardly dared show its nose again outside territorial waters for the rest of the war. Fascist claims about the Battle of Britain and their part in the bombing of London were soon seen to be equally absurd. *Il Tempo* wrote on January 16, 1941, "The city of London, the citadel of British commerce, is burning down. Soon the whole of England will burn down to its last house, its last tree, its last man." The verb *coventrizzare* —derived from the city of Coventry, whose cathedral had been destroyed by German bombs—was delightedly coined to describe the nemesis which would shortly overtake all the cities of Great Britain. Nevertheless, all this ruin did not appear to affect the RAF, which began visiting the cities of northern Italy

(Bottom) The Kukriniksi, who had earlier drawn Hitler goose-stepping in an Italian boot, now showed him trying to extricate his foot from that same boot. Actually, Hitler was prepared to fight to the end. In January 1944, German troops established the Gustav Line to defend Rome, which Hitler said "must be held at all costs for the sake of the political consequences which would follow a completely successful defense." This was another tactical error which ended in defeat.

nightly, peppering them with high explosives in ever increasing quantities.

The finest propaganda in the world cannot make up for military defeats. Probably Hitler's greatest propaganda mistake was, in a moment of euphoria in late 1941, to announce that the Soviet Union had been beaten and the war won. Even Goebbels could not afterwards fully repair the damage done to the public mind. In the same way, as the Italian defeats multiplied and the Italian army was ejected by the "decadent" British and American troops from one place after another, and the African empire crumbled before the people's eyes, they began to lose faith in the words of their leaders. Just as Mussolini had, as the war continued, announced his increasing belief in the German alliance, so the Italian people began to withdraw theirs. They began to hate the Germans more than the Allies.

Here, Allied propaganda in the form of pamphlets from the air proved particularly effective. The British had the brilliant idea of invoking the sacred name of Garibaldi in their pamphlets. Garibaldi had once said in a famous speech that Italy's future after unification would remain always linked with England's. The pamphlets read:

> ### THE CURSE OF GARIBALDI!
> Giuseppe Garibaldi, whose name is revered wherever free men live, said in 1854, "Should England ever call for help to an ally, cursed be that Italian who fails to answer the call!" Benito Mussolini, by leading you under the yoke of your secular enemy, the Teuton, has brought down that curse upon you!
> ### THE CURSE OF GARIBALDI HAS COME HOME TO ROOST!
> Benito Mussolini, obedient to the commands of Hitler, informed you that the defeat of France signified the defeat of England. But Hitler has not defeated England. He therefore brought you into the war on his side, so that the English bombs destined for Germany might rain down on you!
> ### THE CURSE OF GARIBALDI IS NOW COMING TO YOU IN THE FORM OF BOMBS!

To this the Italian propagandists retaliated with posters depicting a far greater curse than bombs which would descend on Italy if the Anglo-Saxons won the war—barbarism. Their propaganda about barbarian mercenaries in the British army was supplemented when the United States came into the war by Boccasile's famous poster of an American black G.I. carrying off the marble statue of the Venus de Milo with a $2 price ticket attached to its neck. The Americans would plunder and destroy the cultural treasures of the more civilized continent. Another poster depicted a brutalized British Tommy leering out from under a tin hat. The well-known Italian "mamma" cult was exploited in a sentimental poster of an elderly peasant woman of great dignity, in bombazine black, proudly wearing on her bosom the medal for gallantry won by her son, who was killed in action. "Do not betray my son!" she solemnly warns.

A caricature of Mussolini by the Brazilian artist José Ozon, 1944. The Duce had already fallen from power. Before his death at the hands of Italian partisans he was propped up by the Germans as a puppet ruler in northern Italy. The wind had gone out of his sails and he remained only the shell of his former self.

(Below) The Kukriniksi in this 1943
caricature caught the essence of the
sagging dictator who was ousted from
power in July 1943. Mussolini told a
friend a few months later that the
Italian people hated him as much in
defeat as they had loved him in victory.
Though one Fascist committed suicide
when he heard of Mussolini's removal,
it generally caused little stir other
than a sense of relief; not a single voice
was raised in his defense.

For propaganda to the United States, the Fascists employed the American auricular poet Ezra Pound, an admirer of Mussolini and a rabid anti-Semite. He broadcast twice weekly from Radio Roma via short wave to the United States, and also wrote scripts in English for Italian propagandists. Sometimes he attacked President Roosevelt as a "warmonger"; sometimes, when he was for some curious reason announced as "Ezra Pound, the poet and economist," he expatiated on the monetary reforms necessary to save the United States from disaster. Sometimes, he read his own poetry or talked about his literary friends (which caused most of the listeners to switch off). He claimed to be protesting less against present conditions than against "a system which creates one war after another." He remained in Italy ranting against the Allies until the end of the war, when the American army picked him up and indicted him for treason. He was found insane, and confined to a mental institution. He was released after a decent interval, to die in his adopted land, Italy. Of all the propaganda episodes of the Second World War, his was one of the most sordid.

Against Soviet Russia, Fascist propaganda aimed at persuading Italians to fight beside the German Waffen SS on the Eastern front. This worked well enough when the Germans were advancing in the hot summer months; but the first defeats in the Russian snows quickly disillusioned the Italian volunteers. A number of them were also attracted by the good pay in Germany, to go there and work in the Todt Organization which required their technical skill. They too were soon disillusioned when they found that they were treated by their allies as members of an inferior race.

With the fall of Mussolini in the autumn of 1943, Badoglio and a number of other Fascist renegades acted as an interim government. For some months, they attempted to maintain the fiction of a German alliance, and continued to brand the Allies as "barbarian invaders." But the Italian people had had enough; they welcomed the Allies not as barbarians, because that propaganda word had been overdone, but as liberators, and Badoglio was forced to adopt their viewpoint.

In the period of Fascist propaganda examined here, 1922–1945, comparisons between the Fascist and Nazi methods are inevitable, owing to the similar state structures. Although the Fascists were in the propaganda business twice as long—twenty-three years to the Nazis' twelve—it cannot be said that they were as successful. In the field of mob oratory there was probably little to choose, but on the whole the cynical Italians proved harder to delude. Compared with the ominous workings of Dr. Goebbels, Italian propaganda methods proved to be dilettantish, surprisingly ill-informed about other nations, and frequently ludicrous.

Cover of the magazine Fascist Youth, *late 1920s/Italy/A. Canevari.*

Issued to commemorate the Summer Exhibition for Child Welfare, June 28, 1937/Italy/Artist unknown.

(Top and bottom, left) More Child Welfare commemoratives. (Bottom, right) Fascist Legionary issue on the founding of Italian East Africa, 1938/ Italy/Artist unknown.

Hitler and Mussolini. ("Two Peoples, One War").
Issued in commemoration of the Rome-Berlin Axis,
1940, 1941/Italy/Artist unknown.

Allied "black" parody of Italian stamp,
c. 1944/Allied propaganda for Italy/
Artist unknown.

*"Enlist in the Auxiliary Service of the
X Flotilla MAS," no date/Italy/Artist unknown.*

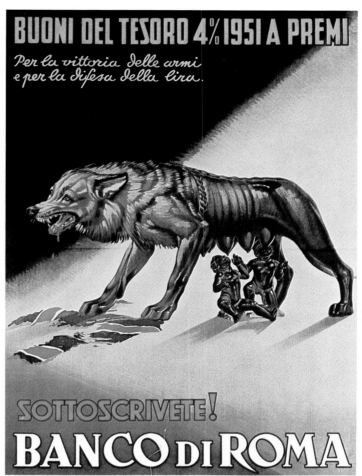

"Buy Treasury Bonds from the Bank of Rome,"
1942/Italy/A. Capitani.

"No march on Moscow without the March on
Rome," 1942/Italy/Alberto Amorico.

"All and everyone for victory," 1941/Italy/
Artist unknown.

"Enlist in the Italian SS Legion," c. 1943/
Italy/Gino Boccasile.

Anti-British postcards, c. 1941/
Italy/A. Bertiglia.

NOTIZIE DA ROMA
VE LE MANDA LA FEDERAZIONE FASCISTA DELL'URBE

Non è soltanto con l'oro che si vincono le guerre. Oltre all'oro è più importante la volontà e ancora più importante il coraggio.

SPAZIO VITALE

L'unità economica, l'omogeneità politica, la collaborazione spirituale e sociale europee che l'Inghilterra era sempre riuscita ad impedire, con la marcia vittoriosa dell'Asse diventano di giorno in giorno realtà splendente. Alle porte dell'Europa, verso l'Asia, si sta costituendo un immenso spazio destinato a servire come territorio di colonizzazione, di investimenti, di produzione per le eccedenze demografiche ed economiche continentali.

Per tale spazio, ricchissimo di risorse minerarie, agricole, zoologiche, forestali la nuova Europa si renderà del tutto indipendente nei confronti degli altri continenti. E l'America del Nord, che attraverso il bolscevismo e l'aiuto interessato prestato all'Inghilterra voleva appropriarsi di queste ricchezze costringendo alla fame e alla servitù tutti i popoli della Europa, sarà la prima a scontare la nuova situazione di fatto creata dalla illuminata volontà dei due Condottieri, il Duce e il Fuehrer, dall'eroismo dei popoli italiano e germanico e loro alleati.

Qual'è quel Paese..?

Qual'è quel Paese dove la base della Nazione non è la famiglia, ma... il divorzio?

Gli Stati Uniti d'America.

Dove è in uso la rapina e l'uccisione dei bambini a scopo di ricatto?

Gli Stati Uniti d'America.

Dove l'alcoolismo è una... istituzione? Dove lo Stato non è nelle mani del Capo, ma della di lui moglie?

Dove la Presidentessa fa la sguattera dell'ebraismo imperante e il Presidente il ragazzo dell'ascensore...?

Dove la polizia fa a mezzo con i gangsters? Dove si sovvenziona il comunismo russo, la barbarie tartara, la delinquenza serba - facendo in questo concorrenza all'Inghilterra - per rendere schiavi i popoli del lavoro, del genio e dell'arte, i veri « civilizzatori », e cioè l'italiano, il germanico e il giapponese? Dove la fame di oro e di lusso è tale che non basta più il continente americano e si vuole impadronirsi dell'Europa, dell'Asia e dell'Africa? Dove si vuol dichiarare la guerra alla... Finlandia? Dove si ignorano la storia, la luce, la verità di Roma?

Gli Stati Uniti, sempre gli Stati Uniti.

E questa gente vorrebbe dettar legge proprio a noi.

Ma la storia non è fatta dai gangsters, nè da Giuda, nè dalla coppia Roosevelt, nè da Churchill, da Stalin ecc.: è fatta dai popoli che credono nella giustizia di Dio e nel Suo nome combattono.

I convogli di Roosevelt verso la tragica meta

Certe benedizioni

Durante un banchetto di 37 portate - che razza di comunismo! - Stalin ha invocato la benedizione di Dio sul capo di Roosevelt.

Dio pronunciato dalla bocca di Stalin?

Questi sono scherzi del diavolo.

No, non lo faranno

Stalin è furibondo: lo fanno o no gli inglesi lo sbarco sul Continente europeo?

E' proprio rimbambito questo svaligiatore di diligenze: non sa ancora che gli inglesi sono specialisti in "reimbarchi„.

Roma - Anno VIII - 22 Novembre XX - N. 56 - Settimanale edito dalla Federazione dell'Urbe   SISTO FAVRE   Spedizione in abbonamento postale - Manifesto del Partito Nazionale Fascista - Esente da bollo
STABILIMENTO TIPOGRAFICO DELLA U.E.S.I.S.A.   Direttore responsabile   EDITRICE DE «IL LAVORO FASCISTA» - ROMA

*Wall newspaper of the Fascist Party, no date/
Italy/Artist unknown.*

Anti-American poster with the theme of 'cultural barbarism,' c. 1942/Italy/Gino Boccasile.

Anti-Semitic poster portraying the stereotyped
Jewish Bolshevik, c. 1942/Italy/Gino Boccasile.

"Workers, rebuild the country," 1943/Italy/
Artist unknown.

"Good blood doesn't lie," 1944/Italy/
Artist unknown.

"The spirit of Goffredo Mameli will defend
the Republic," 1944/Italy/Artist unknown.

"Italian workers, enlist for Germany," 1943/
German poster for Italy/Artist unknown.

"Bread and welfare. See the Todt Organization,"
1944/German poster for Italy/Artist unknown.

"The fate of the saboteur," 1944/Italy/
Artist unknown.

*"Kick out the Germans," 1943/OWI poster for
Italy/Artist unknown.*

The work of the "liberators," 1944/Italy/
Artist unknown.

Lavoratori d'Italia!
I "Liberatori" già da oggi pensano per l'avvenire dei vostri figli...

"Italian workers! Here's how the 'liberators' will treat your children," c. 1944/Italy/Artist unknown.

CHAPTER THREE

BRITAIN IMPROVISES
1936-1945

When the Axis powers set such store
by organization, the British applied
improvisation to good effect.

HAROLD LASWELL

Great Britain emerged from World War I with the doubtful distinction of having employed propaganda better than any other nation. This was largely due to one man, Alfred Harmsworth, later Lord Northcliffe, father of the yellow press. When the war was going badly in 1917, he persuaded Prime Minister Lloyd George and the cabinet that skillful denigration of the Germans could stimulate the flagging energies of the British people. Lloyd George let him establish a propaganda department in Crewe House. Within a year, thanks to his powerful newspaper conglomerate, Northcliffe had convinced most of his countrymen that the Germans were ruthless savages, violators of women, and inventors of the "*kadaver* factory," a chemical process by which soldiers' corpses could be converted into fats for the manufacture of explosives.

This was all primarily for home consumption. For the enemy, Northcliffe put into practice advice he had often vouchsafed, unheeded, to the General Staff—"The bombardment of the enemy mind is almost as important as his bombardment by guns." In the last year of the war, millions of leaflets composed by Crewe House—four million in August 1918 alone—were delivered across the German lines by balloon or shot over in shells. They informed the Germans of their hopeless plight, of the grand coalition now against them, with legions of completely fresh American troops, and of the hunger and starvation which awaited them as a result of the Allied blockade if they did not give in. On another level, the leaflets appealed to the large Social Democratic element still vocal in Germany, which had long admired British democratic institutions. The leaflet propaganda suggested that if the Germans would only expel their autocratic rulers, a new "liberal" Germany which the Allies would foster could be developed on Westminster lines.

But promises have to be kept. As soon as the war was over, Lord Northcliffe's department was closed, and his little group of propagandists went back to their respectable peacetime pursuits—zoology, law, teaching, and the like. No more was heard of them in Germany. The German Social Democrats complained that they had been duped by this Allied propaganda. They had done exactly what they were told—booted out the Kaiser and replaced him with a former saddler, Friedrich Ebert, as head of state. But the Allies, ran the Germans' reasoning, instead of supporting the new Weimar Republic, had done all they could to discountenance it—exorbitant reparations demands, the Versailles "war guilt" clause, and the occupation of the Rhineland by French and African troops.

Northcliffe's propaganda had a boomerang effect in another way. He was unwise enough after the war to boast publicly of what his discreditable methods had achieved. When the "German atrocities" were found to be grossly exaggerated, if not fictitious, the word propaganda became anathema for those in England who had believed them.

This disillusionment was largely responsible for the abandonment of propaganda as a government activity in England when the war ended. In any case the British, who had for cen-

(Top) Sir Oswald Mosley was the demagogic leader of the British Union of Fascists, though his public-school background added a polished tone to his conviction. After 1938, Mosley's party was torn by dissension and declined rapidly. (Bottom) Trade Unionists and Laborites came out early against the Nazis, as this 1934 poster indicates. The Peace Movement was strong in England before Germany declared war.

NATIONAL JOINT COUNCIL
Representing
The Trades Union Congress
The Labour Party   and
The Parliamentary Labour Party

DEUTSCHLAND

MADE IN GERMANY

NO MORE WAR !
REFUSE GERMAN GOODS !!!
NO MORE WAR PROFITEERING !!
NATIONAL JOINT COUNCIL
Transport House, Smith Square, London

(Top) A sign of public support for Chamberlain during the "phony war" period. That the British leader completely misjudged Hitler's intentions was made clear when Chamberlain returned from the Munich Conference with his declaration of "peace in our time." (Bottom, left) A caricature of Chamberlain made up of his famous black umbrellas. (Bottom, right) The British joked about Hitler even when under attack.

THE ENEMY ABUSED AND SATIRISED

This ugly mug, yet to be made
Commemorates the end
Of one more mug who sunk his land
And couldn't name a friend
But meanwhile (till the mug is made)
We'll drink in glasses clear
Our firm resolve to win the day
In Bulmers golden cheer

Bulmers Cider

2¼ lbs. of apples to every flagon
H. P. BULMER & CO., LTD., HEREFORD.

turies dominated half the globe, did not believe it was necessary in peacetime to advertise themselves or decry their adversaries. Northcliffe's activities were "not cricket." Nevertheless by the 1930s, British diplomatic missions in such sensitive areas as the Middle East and Latin America were becoming increasingly alarmed at the damage being done to British interests by well-directed propaganda from Italy, Germany, and the Soviet Union through government-controled press agencies, radio stations, and cultural organizations. In 1934, the British government responded to their missions' demands for something to counter this propaganda—though on a modest scale. The government established the British Council, whose charter defined its aim as "the promotion of a wider knowledge of Britain and the English language abroad, and the development of closer cultural relations between Britain and other countries." But so meager was the council's allowance that it could do little more than distribute brochures and photographs about cherished British institutions —the Horse Guards and Trooping the Color, Oxford and Cambridge, Ascot, the green sward of the Cathedral closes, and so on.

Meanwhile, the declamatory propaganda used at home in the late 1930s by the British branch of the Fascist Party under Sir Oswald Mosley did not attract the British public, which despised Mosley's demagogic methods and noisy blackshirt followers.

Yet even before Hitler came to power, there were a few men, who, having seen what propaganda had done in World War I, had been warning the government that an organized information service would be as necessary as any other line of defense in a future war. At the time of Munich in 1938 and the appeasement policy of Neville Chamberlain—which had a considerable popular following—these men, like Winston Churchill and Duff Cooper, saw the danger ahead. It was not until 1938 that government funds were made available for a foreign service of the BBC, which broadcast news, cultural talks, and English language instruction to Europe, South America, and the Middle East.

At the outbreak of war in 1939, two more propaganda bodies were founded: the Ministry of Information (MOI), principally for domestic consumption, and the Department of Propaganda to Enemy Countries, which later included enemy-occupied countries as well. The titular head of the latter organization was the politician Dr. Hugh Dalton. Its operational head was the ex-diplomat Sir Robert Bruce-Lockhart, who maintained that British propoaganda could be effective in Europe only if it were regarded as more accurate than that of the Nazis. Bruce-Lockhart also believed that, for the home front, exaggerated accounts of German weaknesses when the Wehrmacht was everywhere triumphant, had the reverse effect of that intended. Sir Robert had noted this mistake in connection with the Libyan campaign of 1941. Then, the first official army communiqués from Cairo had been almost lyrical in their optimism. The British propagandists, new to the job, had picked this up and made much of it in leaflets and broadcasts. But the offensive foundered and came to nothing, and the Germans made good capital out of the premature rejoicings.

Lockhart's department, whose official title was soon changed to Political Warfare Executive (PWE), was situated at Woburn in Bedfordshire. It was supposed to work in harmony with the BBC and the Ministry of Information in London, but its location 30 miles away from the capital did not facilitate liaison with these organizations. Hastily convened, its members were a motley crew—civil servants, barristers, university dons, journalists, army officers, advertising men, schoolmasters, and even a landscape gardener. The only thing these men had in common was that each was something of an expert on one or another of the European countries.

The first two years of PWE's existence could hardly be called encouraging. Bruce-Lockhart himself was always grumbling that they were achieving nothing. The cartoonist David Low, who did some work for PWE, was extremely caustic about it. One of his first wartime cartoons depicted the very efficient-looking Goebbels in a broadcasting studio, pouring out words into a microphone; next to him was Col. Blimp playing with a balloon. The caption ran:

"The worst cause in the world, and the best Propaganda;
The best cause in the world, and the worst Propaganda"

In his memoirs, Low relates that PWE officials showed him the type of leaflet they were dropping on Germany in the early days of the war, and asked him to do something like it. The leaflet he saw showed a Bavarian peasant in *Lederhosen* being told that Hitler had betrayed him to the Russians, and that as a result of Hitler, the Bolsheviks would soon come and take him away with all his crops. Low's acid comment was: "At that time with Hitler rampaging victorious, and the Russians practically hiding under the bed, I said it was one of the most foolish documents I had ever seen. And that if young men were risking their necks to drop this tripe over Germany, someone should be arrested."

On another occasion Low was commissioned by the Ministry of Information to design an image of Winston Churchill for the front of a Toby jug, which was to be sold in vast quantities in the United States. There was much official correspondence, congratulations, and admiration for this attempt to edulcerate Anglo-American friendship. A twin "Roosevelt jug" was even contemplated, but neither of the jugs ever got off the drawing board.

This inefficiency was also partly due to the multiplicity of commands. Lockhart's PWE team at Woburn was supposed to supervise the BBC broadcasts from London to foreign countries; but physical separation made control difficult, and the BBC was able to assert a virtual independence, broadcasting its own selection of material. Then there was the Ministry of Information, whose business was to look after home morale. In the first year of its existence it was under Duff Cooper, and was supposed to work in close collaboration with PWE. But Cooper could not abide Dr. Dalton; MOI and PWE were constantly at loggerheads. Duff Cooper says in his memoirs, "The main defect was

(Top) The cartoons of David Low were the graphic expression of Britain's wartime conscience. In this 1937 cartoon he shows Anthony Eden courting Hitler and Mussolini, oblivious to the marching troops behind them. (Middle) Low envisioned Chamberlain ringing the death knell of democary. (Bottom) The American cartoonist George Patzer was skeptical of Chamberlain's agreements with the Axis leaders.

THE AUTOGRAPH COLLECTOR

WOULD YOU OBLIGE ME WITH A MATCH PLEASE?

"GOOSE-STEPPING, NEVILLE?"

(Below) The "Hitler jig" sequence, used in British and Commonwealth newsreels, was the repetition of a little triumphal hop Hitler made at Compiègne in 1940, when the French surrendered on the very spot where Germany had been humiliated at the end of World War I. The brief hop sequence was "looped" two or three times to make Hitler look as if he were dancing a comic jig.

that there were too few ordinary civil servants in MOI, and too many brilliant amateurs. The presence of so many able, undisciplined men in one Ministry was bound to lead to a great deal of internal friction."

Later, when Cooper was replaced by Brendan Bracken, things were hardly better. In the words of the unfortunate Bruce-Lockhart, who had to take their orders: "The weekly meetings frequently ended in a wrangle between Dr. Dalton and Mr. Bracken—which would have been quite amusing, had it not deferred all progress." In his book of memoirs, *Comes the Reckoning*, Bruce-Lockhart writes, "Indeed, during this period there was more political warfare on the home front than against the enemy."

It might appear from this that Lockhart had a thankless, even a hopeless, task—particularly as Churchill himself took only a spasmodic interest in propaganda. "This is a war of deeds, not words!" the great man was said to growl if the subject came up. Nor was Air Marshal Harris, the head of Bomber Command, which had to drop the leaflets on Germany, particularly keen on exposing his air crews to danger in order, as he put it, "to drop bits of bumph." Nevertheless as the war continued, and particularly after the first German reverses, PWE began to play a more effective role. Its propaganda methods improved so much that the American propaganda expert Harold Lasswell wrote, "Part of the superiority of British propaganda was due to its amazing suppleness. They were better psychologists than the Germans and Japanese. Where these Axis powers set such store by organization—sometimes damaging their cause by over-organization—the British applied improvisation and adaptation to good effect." This was of course largely due to the change of military fortunes. As Bruce-Lockhart said himself, "Propaganda is, or should be, easy for the winning side, and difficult for the losing side."

Lockhart's two principal instruments were the leaflet, dropped over enemy territory by Bomber Command, and the radio. The leaflets ranged from single sheets to miniature illustrated newspapers. A special feature of the leaflet operation was the miniature magazine. Reviews such as *La France Libre (Free France)* and a book of Churchill's speeches were reduced to the size of a folded handkerchief. Leaflets containing portions of the text of the Atlantic Charter also played an important part. Its signatories, Winston Churchill and Franklin Roosevelt, stated, "We seek no aggrandizement, territorial or otherwise. Our countries respect the principle of national self-determination, and look forward to a peace which will afford to every nation the means of dwelling in safety within its own boundaries." Millions of Europeans in German bondage heard or read these inspiring words.

Use of the radio was widespread, with broadcasts in 23 languages. Though broadcasting to the occupied countries was relatively easy, because their inhabitants were a ready audience for anything anti-German, devising broadcasts for Germany itself was more difficult. Here Churchill and Roosevelt did not help matters, by their unconditional surrender demand established at the Casablanca conference. This was a severe setback to PWE propaganda, which had aimed at separating the German people from their Nazi leaders. Indeed, the only propagandist who benefitted from the unconditional surrender declaration was Goebbels, who plastered the walls of the German cities with extracts from it, together with passages from Lord Vansittart's *Black Record*, a philippic against the German people as a whole. Goebbels told the Germans that even if some of them did not approve of the Nazis, the peace which the victorious Allies would now impose on them would make Versailles look like utopia.

In late 1942, when the Germans were suffering their first setbacks, PWE began to make use of a new psychological weapon —"black" propaganda, as distinguished from the conventional "white" propaganda. Briefly, "white" propaganda is addressed openly to the world, making much of the victories of one's own side and the defeats of the other. It aspires to uplift home morale with eyewitness accounts of military successes, regaling the audience with jokes and cartoons about the enemy and offering examples of the gallantry of one's own forces. It is based on truth, even if the truth is twisted a little. On the other hand, "black" propaganda is sheer invention or, as its detractors would say, "all lies." By disseminating false information in the enemy camp, military and civilian, it aimed at undermining morale and generally sowing doubt, disquiet, and depression.

A good example of white propaganda was the London broadcasts of the American radio commentator Edward R. Murrow during the 1940–41 blitz. The British had learned that America could not be cajoled into the war with the old 1916–17 propaganda methods. They realized that Murrow's broadcasts were exactly what they required in the circumstances and therefore gave him free rein and every facility, even access to Churchill should he desire it. Murrow's principle, he had announced himself, was "Just provide the honest news, and when there isn't any news, why—just say so. I believe people will like it like that."

Night after night as the bombs rained down on London, he broadcast "This is London" to his countrymen in America. He described the bombing simply and factually, always calm, never polemical, never urging an opinion. He knew, as did his English hosts, that he must show no bias; that the Americans still wanted to have no part in the war. But they had heard that England was weak and decadent, had seen how she was ignominiously expelled at Dunkirk—and yet, here was their own man describing how this people was standing up alone to the steady pummeling of the German Luftwaffe. Second only to Roosevelt, Murrow did as much as anyone to make the American people realize that they must not let England be defeated by the Nazis; otherwise, the implication was clear, they would soon have the bombs on their own heads. This was white propaganda at its best.

Another example of white propaganda in action was heard all over the world when Mussolini declared war on the United States in December 1941. He announced that "Italian soldiers will be proud to fight the Americans alongside the brave soldiers of the

(Top) The bulldog with Churchill's face was used more than once to signify British determination. (Bottom) Edward R. Murrow's radio broadcasts from London during the 1940–41 blitz told Americans of Britain's courage. On August 18, 1940, his broadcast concluded with the phrase, "the defense of Britain will be something of which men will speak with awe and admiration so long as the English language survives."

(Top) A German "black" parody of a British stamp on which the head of Stalin replaces that of King George. The word "Jewish" is intentionally misspelled. (Bottom) This German propaganda postcard picturing a British Tommy with four Arabs hanging from his bayonet was thought to have been dropped over Egypt. (Opposite page) British sardonic humor was aimed at the Nazis.

Rising Sun." Unfortunately, he forgot that he had used an identical phrase in 1917 when America came into the war on the side of the Allies. As editor of *Avanti*, he had written, "Italian soldiers will be proud to fight alongside the brave soldiers of the United States—the only nation in history which has never gone to war except in a just cause." The Italian experts of PWE used these contradictory statements to good effect, broadcasting both versions to Italy.

Hitler made a similar blunder which was pounced on by PWE when he confidently announced on October 10, 1941, that the war in Russia was over. The headlines of the Nazi Party newspaper *Völkischer Beobachter* read, "The Führer announces that the hour has struck! The war in the East has been won!" Thereafter on every anniversary of that date for the next three years, PWE dropped on Germany millions of fascimiles of the front page of the 1941 *Völkischer Beobachter*, with a red strip across it, "What Hitler said in 1941."

Black propaganda is quite different. It may seem a part of "British hypocrisy" that this people, who pride themselves on gentlemanly conduct, can, when under pressure, become so adept in double-dealing, misrepresentation, and every form of shady trickery that even Goebbels in his diaries had to admit a certain grudging admiration for them. Black propaganda is addressed entirely to the enemy, confusing him by exploiting if necessary his most sacred beliefs and feelings, such as a mother's concern for her son reported missing in active service. Its principal instrument, as used by Britain in World War II, was the so-called "secret" radio transmitter, actually in England, but purporting to come from dissatisfied elements of the Wehrmacht inside Germany.

The man who was put in charge of this black propaganda was Sefton Delmer, the *Daily Express* foreign correspondent. He knew Germany intimately and spoke the language like a native. From 1933 until the outbreak of the war he had been living there, and had covered the Nazis' activities for his paper. He knew Hitler and Goebbels personally and had been invited to accompany them on their political junketings. His department of the PWE employed various German speakers pretending to be spokesmen of the Wehrmacht, hard-boiled officers representing the opposition of the military caste to the party. They interspersed wild diatribes against the Allies, Britain and America, with tales of embezzlement and sexual deviation among the Nazi leaders. Some of these were probably the most pornographic ever put on the air. Sefton Delmer appealed, he said, to "the inner pig-dog in every German."

The black emissions were faithfully modeled on official German radio lines. They opened with patriotic music and the Wehrmacht daily communiqué. Then came a list of the latest Knight's Cross awards, followed by reports from the front in which the jargon of Goebbels' men was employed (e.g. "Terror raids by the RAF"). Then came the news, of which at least 90 percent was genuine, about the German advances in Russia, the destruction of Allied shipping, isolated air raids off the English coast,

LAST WILL AND TESTAMENT
OF
ADOLF HITLER

This is the Last Will and Testament of me
Mis-Leader of Germany—Better known as the
MAD DOG OF EUROPE.

———

Fearing that my end is near—that the Die is cast, that I have shot my bolt—
that I have now gone too far.

I GIVE AND BEQUEATH all my German People that believe in me to the *Dumb Peoples
League.*

I LEAVE my Swastika to Comrade Stalin, and he can do with it what he told ME to do
with it.

I BEQUEATH all my Medals to Goering, the weight of which, together with his own,
will bring him to his knees.

I LEAVE to Goebbels my stock of two Tons of Castor Oil, so he can carry on the tradition
of Purges.

I BEQUEATH "Mein Kampf" to Colney Hatch for further investigation.

I RETURN my Moustache to Charles Chaplin from whom I annexed it.

I BEQUEATH to Herr Ribbendrops my German Chamber which he may use by merely
raising his right hand in the customary manner.

I LEAVE to Goering the Roll of Linoleum which was given to me to put up my Corridor
together with numerous hot pokers and other sharp instruments.

AS I AM GOING to the place recommended to me by many of my dear public, I leave
my Torso to the Old Maids' Hostel.

ON MY DEATH I proclaim the annexation of HELL which I have tried to give to my
German people and rightfully belongs to the Fatherland.

I APPOINT Ribbendrops and Goering to be Executors of this, my Will, as they are well
experienced in Executions.

KNOWING my ultimate destination I wish to be buried in an Asbestos Suit.

Signed and Sealed with the upraised arm
in the form of the Naazti Salute.

Adolf.

ADOLF THE PAINTER.

(Top) Posters were used to gain acceptance for a myriad of rules and regulations. (Bottom) Abram Games in his studio. Games fused contemporary artistic trends into powerful images. He believed that his war posters should make viewers think for themselves. His dramatic use of symbolism made his posters the most sophisticated of any produced during the war.

etc. But interspersed with this would be the invented item, stated simply without a word of comment.

For example, a typical black item concerned Goebbels' announcement that all bombed-out factory workers in a certain city would be given additional rations of food and, for their children, sweets. This was factual and reported as such; but the secret radio transmitter, calling itself *Soldatensender*, added that these extra rations contained special drugs to give the workers more energy. The aim of the black broadcasts was to keep the soldier at the front, the sailor at sea, the airman on the distant airfield in an occupied country, in a state of constant apprehension about the welfare of his family. Another device for the servicemen's benefit was to broadcast the names of the streets destroyed in a bombing raid the previous evening. The radio added that if the house of a sailor, airman, or soldier had been hit he could apply for compassionate leave. The soldier became extremely annoyed when he applied for leave, and it was refused because the authorities knew nothing about this dispensation.

To enhance the impression that *Soldatensender* was a German transmitter, Winston Churchill was occasionally referred to as "that flat-footed bastard of a drunken old Jew." Few Germans listening to this could conceive that British propagandists would dare to describe their country's leader in such terms.

Soldatensender sometimes announced that "the party bosses" were having a wonderful time feathering their own nests in soft billets far from the front while "our brave soldiers are freezing to death in Russia." Because of these officials' corruption, it said, the supply of winter clothing to the troops had been deliberately delayed.

Of these broadcasts Goebbels wrote in his diary, "The so-called *Soldatensender* which evidently originates in England and sometimes uses the same wavelength as our *Deutschlandsender* is certainly giving us something to think about. It does a clever job of propaganda, and from what is put on the air, one gathers that the English know exactly what they have destroyed in our cities."

Probably the most heartless of the deceptions, which Delmer himself says he felt ashamed of, was to obtain the name of a German soldier officially announced as dead, and write a letter to his mother from a "comrade" who had seen him alive and well in a neutral country, say Sweden or Switzerland, to which he had deserted. He naturally could not write himself. He was being extremely well treated and looked after, but she must on no account mention this to her friends. The delighted parents naturally gossiped, and many other soldiers imitated "the deserter" who was having such a good time. For the dead soldier's family, the reckoning came at the end of the war.

Among other black devices were letters to servicemen's families aimed at fostering distrust and dislike of high Nazi officials. Here the propaganda was based on true feelings, for everyone in Germany knew that these officials enjoyed—as high officials do everywhere—considerable perquisites denied to the man in the street. When a German soldier died in a hospital, the doctor sent a telegram by radio to the local party officer asking him to break the news to the dead man's family. This was intercepted by the PWE monitoring system, and a letter was written to the mother purporting to come from a "comrade" who had been with her son in his last hours. He described how right up to the end, her son expressed his faith in the Führer and Germany's ultimate victory. He then added that the dead man had mentioned a small possession, a ring, a watch, or a gold crucifix which he wanted his mother to have as a memento. He had sent it to the local party official, who would hand it over to her. Of course it never came, and it was clear to the family and their friends that the Nazi officials were "corpse robbers." As a variation on this theme, the writer sometimes added that the son had not died of his wounds as reported, but of a lethal injection administered by the medical officer who was a party member. The latter had decided that the patient could not recover, and his bed was wanted for another wounded soldier.

A black deception which had a direct military consequence explained why the Russians were fighting so well. It was all due to a new phosphorous shell with which the Americans had supplied them, and which could penetrate steel several feet thick; when it burst it burned up everything in sight. At the end of the war when the Cherbourg defenses were holding out desperately, it appeared that the American army would have the same problem defeating the Germans there as the Allies were having in the other French channel ports, where German units were obeying Hitler's order to fight to the last. The American commander at Cherbourg signaled to the leader of the German forces, General von Schieben, that it would be better for all concerned to surrender. To his surprise, the general replied that if they would fire one of "the new phosphorous shells" at the German fortress, he would be able to surrender honorably, as it was well known that there was no defense against them. Although no such shell of course existed, a pretense was made by firing a few incendiaries, whereupon the general surrendered with his garrison.

Occasionally the black methods had unwelcome repercussions. In mid-1942, when the Russians were under great pressure, a scheme was devised to relieve them by broadcasting to the French living on the Atlantic seaboard to evacuate and go inland, the object being to move German troops west against an invasion. Although this may have helped the Russians, when no invasion took place it had a bad effect on the morale of the French Resistance and on the French people in general. It also perplexed the Russians, who had supposed that some serious incursion was intended.

All these activities addressed to enemy countries came under PWE. Propaganda to the home front and Britain's allies abroad was the responsibility of the Ministry of Information, which had been instituted to inform the public about the war, and how they could help to win it. They had to be persuaded to volunteer for many onerous, boring, or dangerous jobs—to serve in war fac-

(Top) G. Lacoste did several humorous posters on the "careless talk" theme. Hitler was the butt of many British humorists. (Bottom) The London hoardings were thick with posters asking Londoners to lend a hand, save coal, and clean their plates. These exhortations worked for a while, but the public eventually found them excessive.

Posters for The Way Ahead *(Top) and* San Demetrio London *(Bottom). These films, which combined documentary and fiction techniques, brought a new honesty and integrity into British wartime feature production. (Opposite page) John Mills in Noël Coward's* In Which We Serve, *an emotional film about the crew of a destroyer which was sunk in the Battle of Crete.*

tories, the Home Guard and the firefighting services, to "Dig for Victory," to economize in the use of transport and gasoline, to save waste paper, to observe food rationing and avoid the black market; above all, the ministry told Britons about the progress of the war without endangering national security. For these tasks it employed every publicity technique available—films, photographs, broadcasting, booklets, posters, press advertisements, exhibitions, public lectures. It recruited many distinguished publicists, artists, and writers. Among them was J. B. Priestley, the novelist and playwright, who delivered a series of stirring broadcasts on the BBC shortly after the fall of France.

For overseas, the ministry distributed British news, to ensure that material favorable to the British cause was given the widest publicity, and that enemy propaganda was immediately and convincingly denied. It also had a Press Censorship Department, to prevent the release of information likely to be of miltary value to the enemy. For the home press throughout the war this censorship was on a voluntary basis, in the sense that editors were not bound to submit their material, and the censors had no power to prohibit publication; but by obtaining the department's permission to publish, the newspaper concerned was protected from prosecution under the Defense Regulations should it inadvertently publish information of value to the enemy. For foreign and Commonwealth correspondents, submission to the censorship of outgoing cables was compulsory.

The Ministry of Information was also responsible for producing publicity material. For this it included a Campaigns Division, handling advertising and poster campaigns, and an Exhibitions Division designing and mounting anything from major exhibitions to small window displays, both at home and abroad. Such an exhibition in 1942 was "The Unconquerable Soul," displayed at the Charing Cross underground station. Its theme of resistance in occupied countries attracted record crowds. A Publications Division prepared and distributed a wide range of official illustrated books about the war, and promoted the circulation of British newspapers and periodicals abroad.

Word of mouth propaganda was recognized as most important, and the spreading of rumors carefully planned. The aim was to get people saying "I got it from a friend of mine," or "My boyfriend heard it in The Plumbers Arms . . ." This flattered the vanity of the hearer, who was encouraged to repeat what he believed to be a piece of red-hot news. In the words of Professor Lasswell describing how the British applied their pressure on a person-to-person basis to persuade America to enter the war: "The use of persons as channels of influence was most effective . . . information spread in the United States from businessman to businessman, journalist to journalist, professor to professor . . . It was all more subtle than in the 1914–1918 war . . ."

In Britain, as in all warring countries in World War II, the cinema played an important propaganda role. Great Britain entered the war with a well-trained group of documentary film makers. The film division of MOI made a series of weekly films

(Top) Desert Victory *was a documentary record of the North African campaign, which ended in Britain's first major triumph against Hitler.* (Middle) In Which We Serve *appeared in 1942. The solidarity of a sunken ship's crew gave the British a feeling of unity when it was most needed.* (Below) The Life and Death of Colonel Blimp *was based loosely on the cartoon characters created by David Low.*

lasting five minutes each, to be shown all over the country, interpolated into the normal program. The titles are self-explanatory—"Salvage with a Smile," "Hospital Nurse," "Speed the Plough." More important documentary films were made by the Crown Film Unit. A few, such as *Men of the Lightship*, aimed patently at stirring up feelings against the Germans. Lightships have always been regarded as exempt from attack in time of war, but the Nazis—according to this film—disregarded the chivalrous code. The lightship men, who have been machine-gunned, are shown swimming vainly for shore. Only one survives. Other documentaries featured British courage or military prowess. *Desert Victory*, about the battle of El Alamein; Humphrey Jennings' *London Can Take It*, about the blitz; and Harry Watt's *Target for Tonight*, about an RAF bombing raid on Germany. The latter film was produced in 1941 at a time when the British were tired of the "passive stoicism" theme and wanted to see more aggressive action. At least three compilation films were made from the footage of Leni Riefenstahl's Nuremberg rally film, *Triumph of the Will*. Charles Ridley's *Germany Calling* mocked the rally by showing SS and Wehrmacht troops parading to the rhythm of a popular English song, "Doing the Lambeth Walk."

Some films had a purely utilitarian purpose: how to get more eggs from your hens, how to breed rabbits for extra meat, how to enjoy a Woolton pie (Lord Woolton was the hapless Minister for Food), how to dig and hoe. This last film was supplemented by a MOI mobile exhibition which toured the country explaining how to grow more vegetables on one's patch, and how to store them. *Spring Offensive*, in spite of its martial title, was also about increasing the food supply by ploughing up pasture land—the whole seen through the naive eyes of a small boy evacuated from London.

Many feature films focused on the personal experience of war. The heroine of *They Also Serve* was a suburban housewife who quietly assumed all the burdens of daily life to free her men for the front and the factory. *San Demetrio London* was about the experience of a group of merchant seamen. Noel Coward's *In Which We Serve* was also about the fighting man—in this case the sailor. In a lighter vein was *The Life and Death of Colonel Blimp*, whose hero typified the stuffy British clubman's tendency to simply "muddle through."

Another pictorial field in which the British have always, since the days of Gilray and Rowlandson, been preeminent is the political cartoon; in the Australian-born David Low, Britain possessed one of the world's finest political cartoonists. His left-wing sympathies turned him violently against the Fascist dictators. In his autobiography he says that, although he was unaware of it at the time, his cartoon campaign against Hitler began as early as 1923. One of his general themes then was that if the Versailles powers continued to treat the new German Republic like Imperial Prussia, if they thwarted rather than fostered its growth, the German militarists would soon return to power. Here he was confirmed, he says, by the Ludendorf-Hitler putsch of 1923. It inspired a cartoon depicting Ludendorf standing arrogantly on the body of a prostrate Germany (Hitler was then comparatively unknown).

When Hitler and Mussolini achieved power, Low quickly realized that to satirize them as tyrants with blood dripping from their fingers, far from embarassing them, only gratified their vanity. What piqued them, he says, was to be depicted as clowns, or as what they were, upstart plebeians. This had been done by Cavalcanti in his film about Mussolini, *Yellow Caesar*. Mussolini appears not as an awesome despot, but as a ludicrous buffoon. Low, in his political cartoons, revealed the essential commonness of these "Johnny-come-latelys" to political grandeur.

When Lord Halifax visited Germany officially in 1937, he was told that the Führer was deeply offended by Low's cartoons of him, and that the paper in which they appeared, the *Evening Standard*, was banned in Germany. The subject of the cartoon responsible for this ban was Hitler's policy of undermining the authority of the League of Nations. Low showed Hitler attempting to set fire to it, above the caption, "It worked at the Reichstag. Why not here?" On Halifax's return to London, he summoned Low and told him that his cartoons were impairing the prime minister's policy of appeasement. Low obligingly desisted—but only for a few months. Soon afterward Hitler marched into Austria and Low, realizing that Chamberlain and Halifax had been fooled, took up his brush again with renewed vigor.

Other notable artists and draftsmen employed by MOI for propaganda included Cyril Kenneth Bird (Fougasse), the cartoonist whose humorous "Careless Talk" posters were among the best-known of the war. One showed two garrulous housewives sitting in a bus, with Hitler and Goering seated primly behind them, listening. Similar warnings were given by Abram Games, who designed posters for the War Office to be hung in barrack rooms, company offices, and other locations—"Careless Talk Kills," "Keep Your Big Mouth Shut," etc. The paintings of R. H. Talmedge commemorated the RAF's battles, while Bernard Partridge, the *Punch* cartoonist resurrected from World War I, returned to the pictorial attack on Germany in his traditional style.

In conclusion, what lessons did Britain learn about propaganda in World War II, to add to her experiences between 1914 and 1918? Broadly, that propaganda, apart from its black variety—which is not strictly propaganda but deception—should always be based on the truth, even though it may distort the truth. Secondly, that it should be under a unified control. In this respect Goebbels had the advantage throughout the war. Finally, it must never be obvious. The leaflets dropped on Germany at the beginning of the war made Hitler laugh. "What do the British take us for," he said, "as stupid as themselves?" In the words of the British propaganda expert Sydney Rogerson, "Propaganda that looks like propaganda is third-rate propaganda."

(Top) David Low drew Himmler and his followers as angels of death while the Nazi juggernaut rolled across Western Europe. (Bottom) Bernard Partridge had a more old-fashioned style. Hitler, pointing to the huge hollow dove, says to Goering, "This is my secret weapon, Herman, against the Allies. I got the idea from a nightmare."

THE ANGELS OF PEACE DESCEND ON BELGIUM

Sir Bernard Partridge, Punch, London

(Below) The tongue-in-cheek humor of Noël Coward's song, "Don't Let's Be Beastly to the Germans," lightened British spirits during the darker days of the war, when morale was low.

*The bulldog symbol was revived to assert
British tenacity, c. 1942/U.S./Henri Guignon.*

Heavy "Stirling" bombers raid the Nazi Baltic port of Lübeck and leave the docks ablaze

BACK THEM UP!

From a series of posters showing the British
forces in action, 1942/England/Roy Nockolds.

ARMS FOR RUSSIA . . . A great convoy of British
ships escorted by Soviet fighter planes sails into Murmansk
harbour with vital supplies for the Red Army.

An early expression of Anglo-Soviet solidarity,
c. 1942/England/Blake.

your BRITAIN · fight for it now

ISSUED BY A·B·C·A

This scene of the South Downs aroused feelings for an
idealized pastoral Britain, 1942/England/Frank Newbould.

TITTLE TATTLE LOST THE BATTLE

Humor appealed more to Britons than heavy-handed exhortations. One of the many humorous treatments of the careless talk theme, no date/England/G. Lacoste.

Soldiers were shown the results of loose talk,
c. 1942/England/Abram Games.

A famous wartime poster, 1942/England/
Abram Games.

Another humorous treatment of the careless talk
theme, no date/England/G. Lacoste.

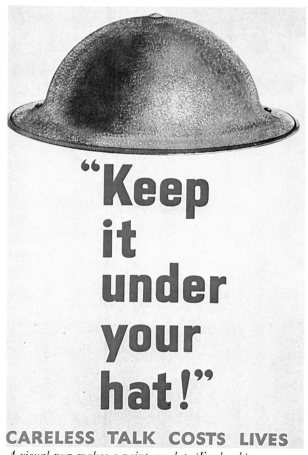

A visual pun makes a point, no date/England/
Artist unknown.

*Four variations on an important theme, no date/
England/Fougasse (Cyril Kenneth Bird).*

Games' sophisticated designs expressed simple themes,
c. 1942/England/Abraham Games.

Many posters such as this urged care with
weapons, c. 1942/England/Abram Games.

A warning to British soldiers of the danger of faulty weapons, c. 1942/England/Abram Games.

An urgent appeal for blood donors, c. 1942/ England/Abram Games.

He wanted to see inside

Accidents occur daily through wilful tampering. Taking ammunition to pieces is illegal, wasteful and dangerous. Ask the expert.

Surrealism and photomontage are used to warn soldiers against accidents, c. 1942/England/Abram Games.

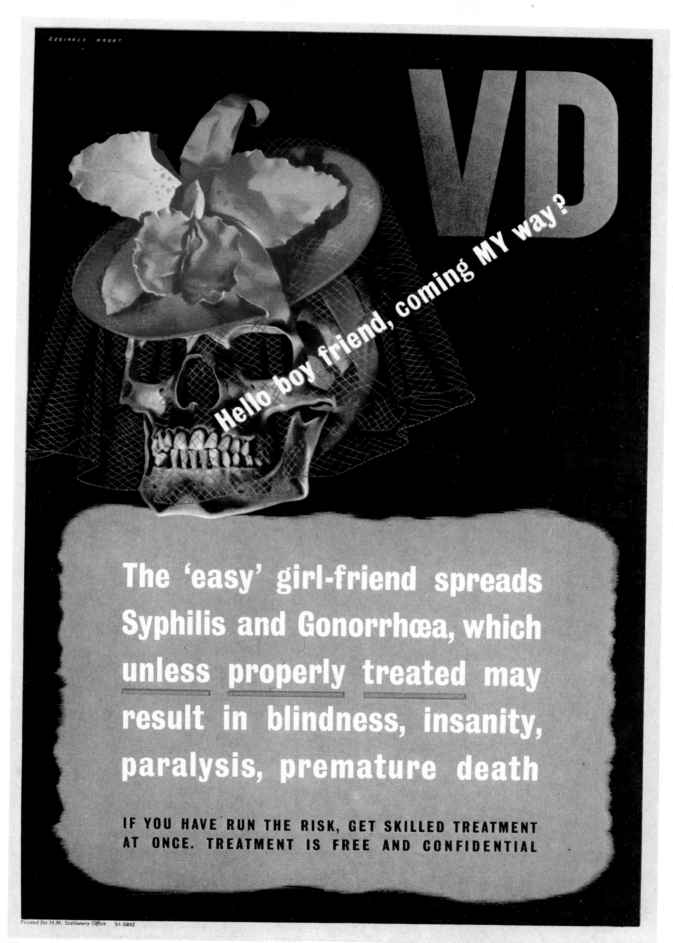

The skull and hat focused on the "easy" girl friend
as a VD source, c. 1943/England/Reginald Mount.

MAKE-DO AND MEND

says Mrs. Sew-and-Sew

ISSUED BY THE BOARD OF TRADE

Housewives were asked to make do with what they had, no date/England/Artist unknown.

BATTLE FOR FUEL

Turn it down when you are warm

USE LESS GAS

A request for fuel economy from the Ministry of Fuel and Power, no date/England/Artist unknown.

A clear plate means A clear conscience

Don't take more than you can eat

Britons eventually had their fill of such homilies, no date/England/Fitton.

IS YOUR JOURNEY REALLY NECESSARY?

TICKETS

RAILWAY EXECUTIVE COMMITTEE

An appeal to avoid unnecessary travel, 1942/ England/Bert Thomas.

I believe . . .

A symbol of Christianity's power to conquer the Nazis, no date/England/Artist unknown.

FOR THE   CONQUERED—

STEEL!

NOT BREAD

A rare anti-Nazi image, though mild compared to
American efforts, no date/England/E. McKnight Kauffer.

*Stalin replaces Queen Elizabeth on this German anti-British
"black" parody, c. 1944/Germany/Artist unknown.*

*German "black" parody of a British stamp, c. 1944/
Germany/Artist unknown.*

Poster for West Africa by a local artist, no date/
J. Olu Wright.

TRUFFLE EATER

by

OISTROS

2/6 NET

PRETTY STORIES

and

FUNNY PICTURES

Dust jacket for an illustrated "black" parody,
1940/England/Oistros

Anti-Axis propaganda for the Middle East, no date/England or Allies/Artist unknown.

An expression of British might after the tide had turned, c. 1945/England/Sevek.

THE UNITED STATES ISOLATION AND INTERVENTION 1932-1945

"The greatest propaganda force
the world has ever witnessed is the
American Film Industry."

SIDNEY ROGERSON,
PROPAGANDA IN THE NEXT WAR

Although commercial advertising is developed and respected in the United States probably more than anywhere else in the world, its political counterpart, propaganda, has generally been neglected, even ignored. The American people, who have no objection to being prevailed upon to buy anything from toothpaste to a helicopter, balk at any attempt to influence them politically, particularly in foreign affairs. They regard propaganda as an alien, un-American, method of persuading people to subscribe to doctrines in which they have no interest. To most Americans in the 1920s and 1930s this suspicion was amply confirmed by the debased uses to which they saw propaganda being put in Europe, by the Fascists, Nazis, and Communists. Before mid-1940, no government-sponored attempt to influence Americans about foreign affairs existed—for the very good reason that it would almost certainly have had the reverse of the effect intended.

There was also a perfectly good precedent. In World War I the American government had done nothing about propaganda until a week after the declaration of war in 1917. President Wilson then set up a Committee of Public Information under his friend, the well-known journalist George Creel, being careful however not to call it "propaganda." The committee played an important part in explaining to the American people why they were at war, and it even handled propaganda to the enemy, chiefly in the form of pamphlets distributed behind the lines. Nevertheless, as soon as the war was over, the committee was disbanded and its funds withdrawn. During its short and not inglorious existence it had been regarded with distaste by a section of Congress, by most American diplomats, and even by the secretary of state himself.

In the isolationist period between the wars, there was even less place for such a body. The Americans were disillusioned with the results of "the war to end wars," "the war to make the world safe for democracy." The treaty of Versailles seemed to have done little more than give birth to bellicose dictator states. Americans turned their backs on Europe. Many believed that there had been guilt on both sides, and that in 1917 they had been inveigled in by crafty British propaganda, by such slogans as "the fate of Western civilization is at stake," "the Hunnish barbarians," and stories about German troop atrocities in Belgium. When Great Britain and France went to war again with Germany in 1939, majority sentiment in America was to keep out, and propaganda from either side was considered suspect. In the words of the journalist Jay Allan, "In the Midwest you have the feeling that men are waiting with shotguns to shoot down the first propagandist who mentions Belgian babies." The greatest obstacle to Allied propaganda in World War II was the propaganda that preceded American entry into World War I.

This was the position when Franklin D. Roosevelt assumed the presidency in 1933. He was the first eminent American politician to be fully aware of the danger to America from the totalitarian states emerging in Europe. But he knew equally well that to persuade his countrymen of this would require time, tact,

While the Nazis overran Eastern and Western Europe, strong isolationist feelings kept America uninvolved until the Japanese bombed Pearl Harbor. (Top and middle) Impatience with the isolationists was expressed by cartoonists such as Clifford Berryman and Lute Pease. (Bottom) Kate Smith swelled American pride when she sang "God Bless America."

ALMOST THE LAST NEUTRAL.

PATIENCE WITH GERMANY

VICTOR

26198-A

GOD BLESS AMERICA
(Irving Berlin)
Kate Smith
with mixed chorus and orchestra

WONDER HOW LONG THE HONEYMOON WILL LAST?

and patience. In his broadcast to the American people in September 1939 he said what they wanted to hear—"This nation will remain neutral." But after describing the crisis which had led to war he added, "I cannot, all the same, ask every American to remain neutral in thought as well. Even a neutral cannot be asked to close his mind to conscience." He knew that, isolationist as most of them were, their sympathies lay with the democratic nations whose form of government they shared. An Institute of Public Opinion poll taken when World War II began revealed that 84 percent of the American public were in favor of an Allied, and only 2 percent in favor of an Axis, victory. But this was still a long way from wanting to fight on the Allied side.

The isolationists were a powerful force, consisting of many assorted elements—from the Protestant War Veterans of America, to the Catholic Irish-Americans; from midwesterners with a natural aversion to European commitments, to the large Italian community impressed by Mussolini's achievements; from Father Coughlin to Charles Lindbergh. The latter told a radio audience in September 1941, "The greatest advocates of bringing us into the war are the British, the Jews, and President Roosevelt." Other well-organized isolationist groups were the American Crusaders, the Silver Shirts, the Christian Front and, most powerful of all, the "America First" Committee which engaged one of the first New York advertising agencies, Batton, Barton, Durstine and Osborn, to mount a propaganda campaign against intervention and aid to Britain. Added to these were many socialists, opposed to British imperialism and her exploitation of India, and the Communist Party, just recovering from the sommersault they had been forced to turn following the Nazi-Soviet pact of August 1939. All these zealots emitted a stream of anti-British abuse and propaganda, which found a ready audience in a people who have always preferred peace to war.

The most voluble of the isolationists was Father Coughlin. Every week he broadcast to 3½ million Americans, warning them against the guile of the British and Jews. He said that President Roosevelt was a warmonger, and that his real name should be "Rosenfeld." He edited a well-written magazine, *Social Justice*, full of thinly veiled apologies for Nazi Germany. It had a circulation of half a million; and the St. Louis journalist, Marquis Childs, said that one of its articles was a word-for-word translation of a radio speech by Goebbels. Father Coughlin coined the phrase "the blood business" for those Americans who wanted to enter the war, he alleged, for financial gain. On February 19, 1940, his magazine published a manifesto entitled "Beware of the British Serpent," divided into sections each addressed to an ethnic group who had, allegedly, suffered at British hands; Polish-Americans, Irish-Americans, Italian-Americans. As a priest, Father Coughlin enjoyed a certain immunity from criticism, and he had a large following throughout the country.

As for the Nazis themselves, their propaganda problem in the United States was relatively simple (compared with that of the Allies). The Nazis knew they could expect no help of any kind

(Opposite page, top and bottom) Clifford Berryman and other cartoonists were skeptical of the 1939 Nazi nonaggression pact with the Soviets. (Top) Russia was portrayed as an aggressor nation before U.S. foreign policy did a volte-face when America entered the war and Russia became an ally. (Bottom) Father Coughlin and other pro-Nazi demagogues carried on an extensive propaganda campaign to keep America neutral.

(Top) A 1934 cartoon by Herblock, who foresaw Hitler's ambitions of conquest before most Americans took the Nazis seriously. (Middle) Many cartoonists treated Hitler as a joke. (Bottom) Fritz Kuhn, leader of the German-American Bund. The Bund attracted many German sympathizers in the late 1930s, but collapsed in 1939. (Opposite page, top and bottom) Registration forms for Bund members and sympathizers.

DER FUEHRER

from America. They could, however, by encouraging groups like Father Coughlin's, neutralize America, so that she would give help inadequately, or not at all, to Britain and France. But they started from a number of dubious premises. They believed that of all the democracies America was potentially the most anti-Jewish; they thought they could count on the support of a number of native anti-Semitic groups, such as the Klu Klux Klan, the Crusaders for America, the Paul Reveres, the American Patriots, Inc. They also believed that the large colony of German descent, some 20 million, would be firmly on their side. For this purpose Goebbels had created and encouraged the German-American Bund, which was headed by Fritz Kuhn, a fanatic German who had migrated to the United States in the late 1920s. But the Nazis were never renowned for their subtlety (indeed they openly scorned it), and here they overplayed their hand. The Jewish pogroms in Germany and the Nazis' vicious anti-Semitic propaganda only alienated Americans, whatever their personal feelings about Jews. Also, the Nazis do not seem to have fully understood that the United States is not Sweden. They had mesmerized the smaller nations of Europe into terrified inaction with their threatening propaganda—such fearful films as *Baptism of Fire* about the Polish campaign—and their belief that the "big lie" if repeated often enough will finally be believed. But the Americans proved singularly unimpressed by the big talk, which only served to strengthen anti-Nazi feeling. It soon became impossible for a Nazi propagandist to appear on an American platform; and even first generation German-Americans were quick to dissociate themselves from the German-American Bund (whose demise came in 1939 when Fritz Kuhn was indicted and imprisoned for stealing the organization's funds). The "blood calls to blood" propaganda which had been so successful in certain European countries made little impression in the United States.

In spite of this, the problems which confronted President Roosevelt after the fall of France in 1940 were prodigious. For Americans to be negative about Germany did not necessarily mean that they were positive about Germany's enemies. To convince his countrymen that Britain must at all costs be saved for America's own safety proved to be extremely difficult. Moreover, it is far harder to persuade people in a democracy than in a dictatorship. The latter possesses the great advantage that decisions can be taken swiftly and acted on at once. These in turn require that the people are ready to accept them without hesitation; this they do thanks to having been properly indoctrinated before. But in the democracies there is, far from unhesitating acceptance of the leaders' decisions, frequently criticism of them. Although in wartime internal conflicts are most damaging, in the democracies they cannot be suppressed. All democratic propagandists can hope for is to persuade people that for the duration of the war it is best not to exercise their inalienable rights—the right to grumble, to reject conscription, to be pacifists or conscientious objectors, the right to hate blacks, Catholics, Jews, the right to grow flowers instead of potatoes in the

German American Bund

ADDRESS: GERMAN AMERICAN BUND, P. O BOX 1, STATION "K", NEW YORK, N. Y.

DISTRICT ....
SECTION ....
UNIT ....
ADDRESS ....

Application for Membership

*) Payable when applying

Initiation Fee $1.00
Monthly Dues $0.75
Voluntary Donation $0.50 up

I hereby apply for admission to membership in the „German American Bund". The purposes and aims of the Bund are known to me, and I obligate myself to support them to the best of my ability. I recognise the leadership principle, in accordance to which the Bund is being directed. I am of Aryan descent, free from Jewish or colored blood.
Please write distinctly.

Full Name .... Occupation: ....

Exact Address .... Telephone: ....

Born .... Place of Birth: .... Single/Married/Widowed: ....
        Day   Month   Year

First Papers No .... What Court and when obtained: ....

....

Final Papers No.: .... What Court and when obtained: ....

....

When and where immigrated: .... Passport No.: ....

Two References: (1) ....
                (2) ....

To what Organisations do you belong? ....

Only U. S. Citizens are eligible for office. First Papers suffice for Membership in "Prospective Citizens' League"

Paid Dues	
Initiation Fee .... $:.........	
Monthly Dues .... $:.........	
Vol. Donation .... $:.........	

Date: ....

....
Applicant's Personal Signature
....
Unit Leader

Please do not use this space

No. ....

German American Bund

ADDRESS: GERMAN AMERICAN BUND, P. O BOX 1, STATION "K", NEW YORK, N. Y.

DISTRICT: ....
SECTION: ....
UNIT: ....
ADDRESS: ....
....

Sympathizer's Registration

*) Payable when registering

Registration Fee $1.00
Monthly Contribution $0.75
Voluntary Donation $0.50 up

I hereby register as a Sympathizer of the "German American Bund". The Aims and Purposes of the Bund are known to me and I obligate myself to support them to the best of my ability. I am of Aryan descent, free from Jewish or Colored Blood.

Name: ....

Address: ....

(The address need not be given. A Pseudonym may be used.)

Paid	
Initiation Fee .... $:.........	
Monthly Contribution . $:.........	
Vol. Donation .... $:.........	

Date: ....

....
Applicant's Personal Signature
....
Unit Leader

Please do not use this space

No. ....

(Top, bottom, and opposite page)
Three cartoons by Daniel Fitzpatrick
of the St. Louis Post-Dispatch.
Fitzpatrick's powerful images of the
German juggernaut brought home the
dangers of Nazi expansion.

ORIENTAL END OF THE AXIS.

THURSDAY, JULY 10, 1941.

TO WHOM IT MAY CONCERN:

SATURDAY, SEPTEMBER 28, 1940.

back garden.

Propaganda is also more difficult to organize in democratic countries, because lies can be more easily exposed than in dictatorships. The big lie cannot be continually repeated or it will become ludicrous and have the reverse effect. Therefore the attitude adopted by the propaganda department which President Roosevelt set up in 1940 (naturally not under that name) was that it must always retain the essence of truth in what it said. It could embroider the truth, but there must be some truth to embroider.

In November 1940, he had sent Colonel Donovan on a reconaissance tour of the principal warfronts. On a visit to Britain he was introduced to the newly formed British Psychological Warfare Department. He reported so favorably on this to the president that in July 1941 Roosevelt appointed him Coordinator of Defense Information; he immediately set up a political warfare department. By the time of Pearl Harbor, this was already in action, and thereafter it functioned with growing effectiveness. The organization was at first known as the Office of Facts and Figures, and its chief function was to explain the need for helping the Western democracies with as much aid as possible short of war. Its main theme was that a Germany victorious in Europe would be strong enough to flout the Monroe doctrine and—with the British fleet eliminated—would launch an attack on South America. Here, the propagandists knew, American public opinion was particularly sensitive. Robert Sherwood, the playwright and a staunch interventionist, was enrolled as a propagandist; he announced, "If Great Britain is defeated, then the next war will follow quickly, and it will be fought in this hemisphere." Another eloquent Anglophile was the journalist Dorothy Thompson; she was an interventionist not, she said, for Britain's sake, but for America's.

In Germany, Goebbels controlled the entire propaganda apparatus in every media, which responded instantly to the touch of his hand on the tiller. In the United States, as in Britain, propaganda was bedevilled by a multiplicity of squabbling departments, often fighting one another more than the enemy. The Americans repeated and aggravated British mistakes by setting up two psychological warfare departments, the Office of War Information (OWI) and the Office of Strategic Services (OSS), the first with responsibility for overt or "white" propaganda, the second for covert or "black" propaganda. Both groups wanted to gain the ear of the president, who did not improve matters by granting them charters which were vague in defining their respective spheres of authority.

At the head of OWI was Elmer Davis, a well-known radio commentator. His task was not made easier by Washington because a sizable element in Congress still regarded propaganda as a kind of wasteful mumbo jumbo. He was even accused of using his organization to advance the cause of the Democratic party—presumably because Roosevelt had set it up. In fact, Davis was always complaining that he could hardly ever have access to the president to obtain rulings. His staff, which had

WINGS OVER EUROPE.

WEDNESDAY, MAY 15, 1940.

The "Safe Conduct Pass" was one of
the most successful leaflets devised
by the Office of War Information. The
leaflets were snapped up by German
and Italian soldiers in North Africa
because they were assured of being well
looked after and removed from the
danger zone.

been hastily cobbled together in 1942, contained, inevitably, a
large foreign element, some of whom were prima donnas more
concerned with propagating themselves than America. This gave
fuel to the well-known American suspicion of "foreign intellectuals." He also had friction with the services' high command,
whose generals and admirals regarded propaganda much as they
did psychiatry, unnecessary and unmanly. In November 1942,
at the time of the invasion of North Africa, General Eisenhower
said, "I don't know much about psychological warfare, but I
want to give it a chance." After the war, the Army General
Board, in its final report, concluded that "propaganda has been
a neglected and ineptly used political and diplomatic weapon."

The American propaganda bodies clearly could not compare,
at least at the outset, with Goebbels' mammoth and monolithic
structure. But the Americans, slow to anger, when finally roused
are unstoppable, particularly in spheres which they regard as
their own. In two of these during World War II, they surpassed
all other nations in propaganda achievment. One was the use of
the leaflet for offensive propaganda, and the other, films for
domestic consumption.

In wartime when frontiers are closed, the leaflet dropped from
the air is the surest way of getting at enemy civilian morale.
(Radio of course is another, but many people are frightened
of listening to forbidden foreign radio stations.) But when things
are going badly in the war, and wherever you turn in the street
or the countryside you find leaflets telling you day after day,
week after week, in the simplest terms what is happening in the
war, it soon has a cumulative effect. The Americans used the
leaflet to announce facts without commentary, telling the Europeans in the tersest terms what their leaders were concealing
from them—the territory gained by the Allies, the progress of
the war in the various theaters. Here the vast American airfleets
that dominated the skies literally swamped the enemy cities with
paper.

A special squadron of Flying Fortresses was set aside to do
nothing but carry out leaflet raids. During the last years of the
war, the OWI was showering occupied Europe with 7 million
leaflets a week (compared to the total of 3 million American
leaflets distributed throughout all of World War I). A young
American air force captain, James Monroe, made this possible
by inventing a leaflet bomb—a cylinder of laminated paper,
five feet long and one and a half feet in diameter, which could
hold 80,000 leaflets. When the bomb had fallen to a height
of 1,000 feet, an automatic fuse opened it, the leaflets were
released and fell concentrated on the target. Before his invention, the leaflets were simply tossed out of the bomb hold from a
great height and dispersed far and wide.

On July 10, 1943, 7 million of these leaflets were scattered
on German and Italian positions in preparation for the Sicilian
invasion. A few days later on July 16, millions more were
dropped in every part of Italy, informing the Italians that they
could either die for Mussolini and Hitler, or live for Italy. On
August 15, 1944, they were dropped in similar numbers on

German troops in southern France. Some leaflets were in the form of "safe conduct" passes for enemy soldiers, luring them to desert with promises of good treatment and illustrations of this treatment in comfortable surroundings away from the front. The "safe conduct" passes always contained a box written in English instructing the American soldiers whom they approached with the leaflets: "The man who carries this leaflet is no longer an enemy. Under International Law, you will ensure that he is guaranteed personal safety, clothing, food, living quarters and if necessary medical attention." Other leaflets contained instructions on how to malinger or feign illness. Others came in the form of counterfeit ration cards, coupons, stamps, and currency. All these operations on so vast a scale were made possible, it should be noted, by one main factor, the vast airplane production of the American factories.

Aerial supremacy was used again for dropping on France a tabloid newspaper produced by OWI called *L'Amérique en Guerre* (*America at War*). It described factually the American war production figures, the weapons and ships being turned out daily, hourly, by the greatest industrial power in the world. It listed Allied advances with names of places in North Africa, Sicily, and Italy now in Allied hands. By D-Day 1944, 7 million copies of this journal were being dropped weekly in France. Similar newspapers were delivered to Norway, Spain, and Ireland.

In mid-1944 the leaflet hailstorm was diverted to Germany itself. One side of one leaflet bore the American flag, the other the ominous words, "Adolf Hitler declared war on the United States on December 11, 1941." Later, a news tabloid *Sternebanner* (*The Star-Spangled Banner*) was dropped weekly on the German cities. On the lines of *L'Amérique en Guerre* it too was strictly factual—so factual that it occasionally carried news unfavorable to the Allies. This raised objections in high Allied military circles; but it made *Sternebanner* credible to its German readers because, as OWI had reasoned, credibility could not be achieved without objectivity. Another German-language paper, *Frontpost*, was also distributed weekly on the Italian front by shellfire as well as by air. That so much artillery and air power could be diverted from their usual deadly business was in itself, to the enemy soldier, a depressing sign of the vast armaments mounted against him.

Ronald Seth, in his book *The Truth Benders*, says that each leaflet was read by at least six people, and that there could have been very few men, women, and children in the occupied countries who did not see them. One important reason why they were read eagerly was because they were often essential to the safety of the civilian. They often gave a warning of coming bombing attacks, thus allowing time to leave the area and harm's way. They were used in this way at Monte Cassino, when all civilians who were sheltered in the monastery were warned twenty-four hours before the attack began.

The second propaganda medium which was particularly effective in wartime America was the radio. It has always been

The Japanese attack on Pearl Harbor, December 7, 1941, was the decisive blow that brought the United States into World War II. (Top) A recording of President Roosevelt's address to the Congress on December 8, 1941. (Middle) Roosevelt kept the public informed of the war's progress through his quiet, intimate "Fireside Chats." (Bottom) Sammy Kaye's rendition of "Remember Pearl Harbor" fostered patriotic feelings.

*(Below and opposite page)
After the United States entered World
War II, songwriters began to turn
out music to keep spirits up on the
home front. Styles ranged from popular
ditties to semireligious spirituals.
People danced to "Goodbye Mama—
I'm Off to Yokahama" and other tunes
played by the swing orchestras of the
day.*

more important in America than in smaller countries because her vast size precludes any newspaper's having a national circulation. Radio alone could create a truly national public opinion. Also, the special radio announcers and commentators in America were given much freer license than their European counterparts. They have developed to a high pitch the art of playing on the emotions of the public.

It is appropriate that the American who did more than anyone else to bring his country into the war on the side of the Allies should also have been its finest radio speaker—President Roosevelt. His mastery of the medium dates back to the early 1930s, when he persuaded a recalcitrant public that the New Deal was their only salvation. On March 12, 1933, he inaugurated his famous series of radio "fireside chats" from his room in the White House. Unlike Hitler and Mussolini, who also took every advantage of the new medium to expound their views, and whose bombastic radio speeches were made against a background of mass hysteria, Roosevelt preferred a more intimate approach. He spoke calmly, sharing his thoughts and ideas with, as it were, all the families of America. Many felt he was talking to them personally, and that he understood their problems. By his measured tones they felt assured that he was at once their leader and their friend. During the Depression these chats helped the New Deal, "this socialist measure" as a hostile Congress often called it, to become law.

Evidence of the success of the fireside chats came by mail after each broadcast. Before them, the presidential mail had been handled by one secretary. After March 1933, half a million unanswered letters piled up in the White House, and the secretarial staff had to be greatly enlarged. Radio was the medium, too, with which after September 1939 President Roosevelt again addressed a recalcitrant audience, telling them that if Britain were defeated they would soon have to face the greatest danger in their history—the European continent united at last under the most bellicose power in the world.

Apart from Roosevelt's fireside chats, American radio in the period September 1939–December 1941 had remained as far as possible neutral, avoiding great controversial European issues. After Pearl Harbor this quickly changed. So frightened were many people living on the West Coast that they demanded the immediate incarceration or removal to the interior of the considerable Japanese-American colony living peaceably there. The fear of a Japanese invasion may not have been entirely justified, but it at least woke up the West and Midwest, the traditionally isolationist areas of the country.

In February 1942 "This is War," a 13-week series produced by Norman Corwin, began. It aimed at inspiring, informing, and ultimately frightening people into action. The titles of the series were self-explanatory—"The Enemy," "America at War," "Your Navy," "Your Army," "The United Nations," "Mr. Smith against the Axis." The series was broadcast on all the nationwide networks every Saturday night, and was heard by some 20 million Americans. It was also short-waved to the

VICTOR

P 20-1   26516-A

BALLAD FOR AMERICANS—Part 1
(John Latouche—Earl Robinson)
Paul Robeson, *Basso*
American People's Chorus
directed by Earl Robinson
Victor Symphony Orchestra
conducted by Nathaniel Shilkret

COLUMBIA

36445
(CO 31617)

(There'll Be Bluebirds Over)
THE WHITE CLIFFS OF DOVER
Fox Trot - Vocal Chorus by
Harry Babbitt and Glee Club
-Burton-Kent-
KAY KYSER and
his ORCHESTRA

COLUMBIA

For perfect tone
use Columbia Needles

36640
(11CO 901)

PRAISE THE LORD AND PASS THE
AMMUNITION!
Fox Trot - Vocal Chorus by Glee Club
-Loesser-
KAY KYSER and
his ORCHESTRA

BLUEBIRD

For best results
use Victor Needles   B-10881-A

THERE'LL ALWAYS BE AN ENGLAND
(Parker-Charles)
The Happy Gang
Vocal by Bert Pearl with chorus by Bob Farnon,
Eddie Allen, Blain Mathe and
Kathleen Stokes at the organ

VICTOR

For best results
use Victor Needles   27407-B

BLESS 'EM ALL—Vocadance
(Hughes-Lake-Stillman)
Barry Wood and The Four King Sisters
with Orchestra

VICTOR

For best results
use Victor Needles   20-1661-A

BELL BOTTOM TROUSERS—Fox Trot
(Moe Jaffe)
Tony Pastor and his Orchestra
Vocal refrain by Ruth McCullough
and Tony Pastor

Every popular art form was a propaganda medium during the war. (Top) Al Capp promoted the national campaign to save fat and scrap metal. (Bottom) A recruiting poster in comic-strip style.

rest of the world. By 1943, of the twenty N.B.C. serials which went out weekly, only five were unconnected with the war. Some, such as the one featuring Ma Perkins who lost a son in the fighting, were aimed at the home front; she was constantly telling housewives to save fat and collect tinfoil. The results were encouraging. By August 1942, fat and grease salvage had increased by 3 million pounds, and by March 1943 by 7½ million pounds. Victory gardens for home-grown food-stuffs were dug by an extra 2 million families. Information about war bonds, victory loan, Red Cross, victory food, student nurses, and shoe rationing was heard by millions of listeners. After a two-week appeal, 30,000 Grade-A glider pilots volunteered for the air force. The OWI, which organized this radio campaign, claimed that each adult in the United States heard four war messages a week. The radio was also used offensively in the theaters of war. The Italian navy in 1943, after being urged by American radio broadcasts every quarter of an hour to deliver itself to the Allies, did so. Of this, a British admiral commented that the American radio propagandists had "accomplished in one day" what he had not been able to do for three years.

Though the poster could make no claim to competition with radio in its influence on the American public, nevertheless a barrage of posters was issued by assorted government agencies and private corporations during the war years. They exhorted factory workers to boost their production, warned civilians against careless talk, and encouraged everyone to help defeat the enemy. Posters were commissioned from such prominent artists and designers as Ben Shahn, Normal Rockwell, and David Stone Martin, but well-designed as these were, they could hardly influence the public as much as the day-to-day events to which it was exposed through radio, newsreels, and newspapers.

Among newspaper cartoonists, Daniel Fitzpatrick of the *St. Louis Post-Dispatch,* Herblock, and others had continued throughout the 1930s to remind Americans of events in Europe. Fitzpatrick gave the swastika a menacing interpretation by drawing it as a huge steamroller and as a greedy octopus stretching its tentacles across the English Channel. Cartoons by Lute Pease and Clifford Berryman showed the continuing pressure on Uncle Sam to absolve his neutrality. After Pearl Harbor, the key events in Europe and the Pacific were interpreted for the public by many cartoonists in newspapers throughout the country. Bill Mauldin's grubby, mud-soaked G.I.s, Willy and Joe, served as a reminder that war was anything but heroic. Mauldin's cartoons implicitly asked the people to support the men in uniform, who were enduring untold hardships to preserve the democratic way of life.

Another domain in which American propaganda distinguished itself during the war was film. Goebbels had realized its immense importance years before, making it his special province. But when the war began he could not compete with Hollywood. Film is the American art—or craft—par excellence. Each week 85 million Americans sat in the blackened halls for hours. In the magniloquent but only too justified boast of a Hollywood tycoon, "Influence is exerted by Hollywood over the thought processes and emotions of 120 million Americans. The clothes that are worn by Hollywood today are worn by the nation tomorrow. The games that are played in the parlors of the Hollywood great become the pastimes of America. That which is done by Hollywood today will be emulated by American cities big and small, and by the citizens who live in them." It was clear that this formidable weapon must be enlisted in the service of its country—but how? The Hollywood moguls were particularly independent-minded men.

For decades Hollywood had been turning out between six and seven hundred films a year, principally domestic comedies, westerns, police thrillers, romances, and musicals. They were addressed to the more primitive emotions—which was of great value in making the change from peace to war production easier than had been expected. Hollywood, with its strong Jewish and British elements, was overwhelmingly on the side of the Allies, and it wanted to do what it could to help them—but of course in such a capitalist organization, without sacrificing profits. For this reason, any war propaganda contained in a Hollywood film had to be incidental to the entertainment. Americans went to the cinema to be thrilled, harrowed, amused; they were unreceptive to political propaganda. It was soon found that the stereotyped mystery thriller lent itself admirably to Nazi fifth-column stratagems, as did mobland shootings to Nazi cruelty. The "bad guy" gangster became the "bad guy" Nazi; while the hero, the clean-cut, upstanding American could become the clean-cut, upstanding British fighter pilot (or a young American who had volunteered for the RAF). Single-handed they outwitted scores of Nazis and purloined the secret plans for the Nazis' new deadly ray gun or secret new explosive. The Nazis, on the other hand, were not capable of much more than taking pot shots at defenseless pilots as they floated down to earth on their parachutes.

Simple-minded plots were nowhere more prevalent than in the serials, which theaters showed in installments over a period of weeks to accompany the features. In *Secret Service in Darkest Africa*, the hero, Rex Bennett, has a life-and-death duel with a Nazi. After disposing of him he throws his sword into a portrait of Adolf Hitler. Other stock characters in the serials were Spiderman, Batman, Spy Smasher, the Masked Marvel, Secret Agent X-9, and the Jungle Queen, who stymied Nazi plans for taking over Africa. Once the United States became involved in the fighting, even Tom Mix was enlisted to have a go at the Japanese. One of his films depicted a giant King Kong who terrorized the countryside; he turned out to be a huge balloon manipulated by Japanese agents.

More serious films, such as Chaplin's satirical *The Great Dictator* (1940), *Mrs. Miniver*, showing the stoicism of Britain under the blitz, and *The Moon is Down*, about the ruthless Nazi occupation of Norway, became immensely popular—although they were very powerful, if veiled, political propaganda. In 1940 the America First Committee had attacked Hollywood for incorporating anti-Fascist propaganda in films such as *Confes-*

(Top) A biting caricature of the Axis leaders by Arthur Szyk. (Middle) An unsuccessful poster by Jean Carlu to increase factory production. Workers thought the top figure was a gangster because of his cap. (Bottom) Bill Mauldin's Willy and Joe were reminders to the folks at home that war was a tough grubby business.

"Just gimme a coupla aspirin. I already got a Purple Heart."

German emigré actors found work in Hollywood as Nazi officers. (Top, left) Conrad Veidt as General Kurt von Kalb in Escape. *(Top, right) Peter Lorre in* Cross of Lorraine. *(Bottom) Erich von Stroheim in* North Star. *(Opposite page) Helmut Dantine in* Edge of Darkness, *a melodrama about the Norwegian resistance.*

sions of a Nazi Spy (1939), which exposed the danger of a fifth column in the United States. The movie men countered that they had always catered to popular taste commercially and this is what they were still doing.

By 1943 three out of ten films made in Hollywood were connected with the war. After the Nazi invasion of the Soviet Union, the United States did an about-face and Hollywood began producing films which glorified the Soviets, or at least treated them sympathetically. *North Star* (1943) was probably the first serious attempt to portray Soviet Russia on the American screen.

Hitler, Mussolini, Tojo, and their followers were also the butts of much film humor. They even appeared in cartoons, where they were outwitted by the likes of Bugs Bunny and ridiculed by Donald Duck in Walt Disney's *Der Führer's Face.*

Until the war, the documentary or information film had hardly been able to compete commercially with the Hollywood entertainment film. Among the small number of the former was the series *March of Time,* which began in 1935 and appeared monthly. Produced by the publishers of *Time* magazine, it was in theory impartial, but the antitotalitarian atmosphere was clear in the accompanying commentary. For this reason it ran into much criticism in isolationist circles.

When the Japanese bombed the U.S. Navy gunboat *Panay* on the Yangtze River in 1937, Universal and Fox Movietone cameramen were on the spot. Their film was rushed back to the United States and attracted large crowds when it was shown in theaters across the country, accompanied by a soundtrack opposing Japanese militarism. About the same time, a film about the bombing of Shanghai made by Fox Movietone was openly partisan. At one point it showed a helpless crying baby whose parents had been killed in the attack. That baby's pathetic face was seen by 136 million Americans. But these films were exceptions. Before the war, foreign politics were seldom seen on American screens. In fact, the intense desire to avoid controversy led Pennsylvania film distributors to enter into an agreement in 1936 that no newsreel bearing on political issues would be seen in their theaters.

But as the war in Europe continued, the people turned gradually away from the isolationist view, and more and more documentaries and newsreels were shown. By the time the United States entered the war the motion picture industry, as well as the public, was taking documentaries seriously for the first time. Within a matter of months of the American entry, Hollywood directors including Frank Capra—who was summoned to Washington to see the president—were producing documentary films explaining the war and why the totalitarian states had to be defeated. Capra gathered a talented team of directors around him: Anatole Litvak, John Huston, and Eric Knight. His famous series "Why We Fight" was made to explain to the American fighting man the background of the war up to America's entry. *Prelude to War* (1942) described the rise of Fascism, Nazism, and Japanese militarism between 1931 and 1938. *The Nazis Strike* (1943) dealt with events in Central Europe from the Aus-

Hollywood producers manufactured their own version of World War II. (Left, top to bottom) Robert Young (left) and Dan Dailey, Jr. in The Mortal Storm; *Otto Kruger (seated) and Tim Holt in* Hitler's Children. *(Right, top to bottom) Erich von Stroheim (left) in* Five Graves to Cairo; *Skippy Homeier (right) in* Tomorrow, the World; *George Sanders in* Confessions of a Nazi Spy; *Raymond Massey (seated) and Henry Daniell in* Hotel Berlin; *Otto Preminger in* The Pied Piper. *(Opposite page, top row, left to right) Humphrey Bogart in* Sahara; *John Garfield (left) and Alan Hale in* Destination Tokyo; *Richard Conte in* Guadalcanal Diary. *(Middle row, left to right) Burgess Meredith in* The Story of G.I. Joe; *Irene Dunne and Alan Marshall in* The White Cliffs of Dover; *Tallulah Bankhead in* Lifeboat. *(Bottom row, left to right) Rains, Henreid, Bogart, and Bergman in* Casablanca; *The Andrews Sisters in* Buck Privates.

*A full array of heroes and villains
appeared in American war films.
(Left, top to bottom) Dana Andrews in
The Purple Heart; Cary Grant in
Destination Tokyo; This is the Army.
(Right, top to bottom) Song of Russia;
Walter Huston in Mission to Moscow;
Robert Watson as Hitler in The Hitler
Gang. (Bottom and opposite page)
Charlie Chaplin as Adenoid Heynkel in
The Great Dictator.*

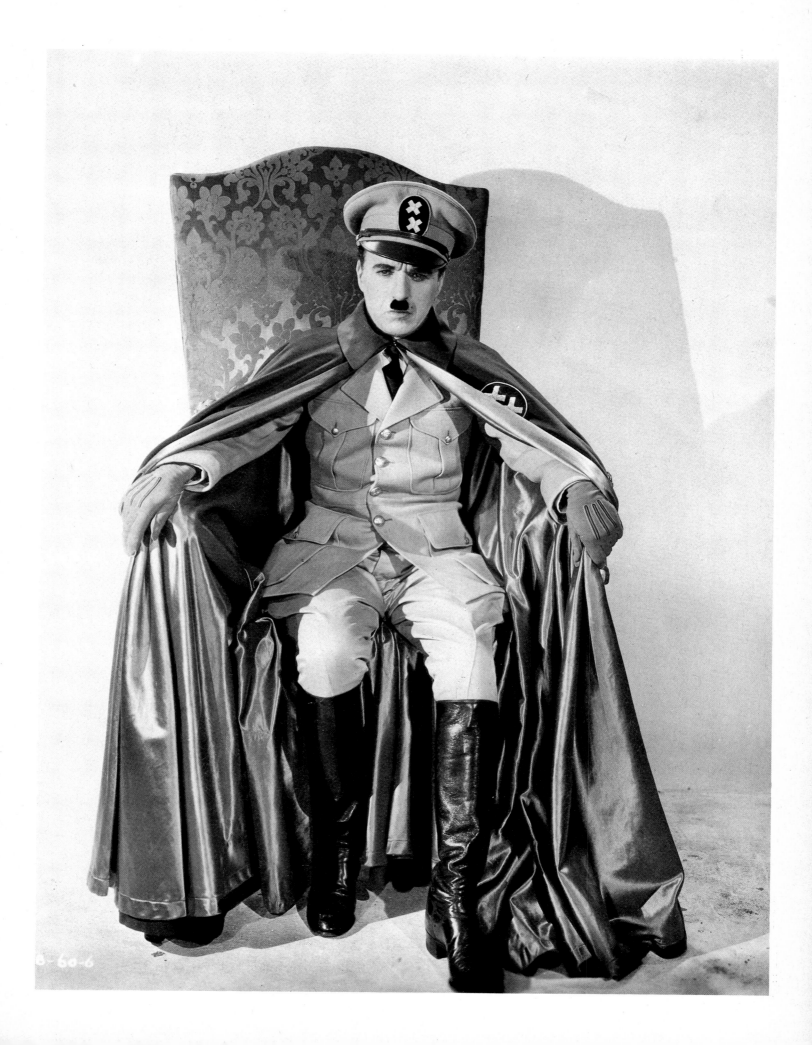

(Top) The song "Der Führer's Face"
was a high-spirited poke at Hitler.
(Middle and bottom) Victory through
Air Power, Walt Disney's cartoon for
the Air Force. (Opposite page, top and
bottom) Donald Duck in Disney's
Der Führer's Face. (Following page,
top) Frank Capra discussing his
Why We Fight series at the War
College, 1941. (Bottom) A scene from
Battle of Russia, one of the films in the
Why We Fight series.

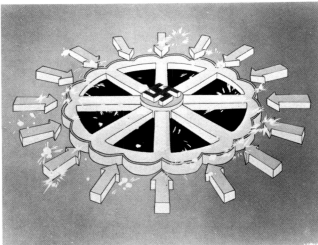

trian Anschluss to the invasion of Poland. This was followed by
Divide and Conquer (1943) about the German invasion of Scandinavia, the Low Countries, and France. *The Battle of Britain* (1943) showed the gallant defense of England by the Royal Air Force. With the remaining films, *The Battle of Russia* (1943), *The Battle of China* (1944) and *War Comes to America* (1944), the American soldier was given a complete picture of the origins of the war and its progress. In Britain the entire series was shown to the public by order of Churchill himself.

Because of the opposition from Congress and Hollywood, few official propaganda films were made for domestic consumption. For audiences abroad the United States government financed its own newsreel series, "United Newsreels," which was released in sixteen languages for viewing in friendly and neutral countries. The government also produced the bimonthly *Army-Navy Screen Magazine*. This newsreel kept the armed forces informed about current events at home and abroad. It also reminded them of the factory workers who produced the weapons they fought with. In the later stages of the war these films gave details of the concentration camps in occupied Europe and Nazi cruelty to their defeated enemies. The films were accompanied by a lively use of the vernacular, to appeal directly to the G.I. in his own language.

More than a year before the capitulation of Japan, the War Department commissioned the film *Two Down, One to Go* to explain to American troops in Europe that even when Germany and Italy were beaten, Japan still remained. This was to counter the men's natural longing to return home in June of 1945. The film told them instead that they would soon be transferred to the Pacific theater of war.

The main conclusion to be drawn from the use of propaganda in and by the United States during World War II is that propaganda cannot do much against an enemy who is fresh and confident. It is only when defeat sets in, that propaganda begins to work. This situation started to develop in Europe within a year of America's entering the war. At the root of it all lay the American industrial system. Mass production was, and is, its specialty. A single example suffices. In the autumn of 1942, the United States had only three aircaft carriers. A year later there were fifty in the American fleet; by the end of the war, over 100. This extraordinary achievement was matched by an increase in aircraft production which was no less remarkable. It was merely a question of letting the enemy know this, and of the fearful retribution which would increase in geometrical progression with every extra day he resisted. This the Americans did primarily by leaflets, using their immense air fleets. Italian morale was broken, German confidence weakened, French resistance stimulated, and finally Japanese surrender obtained. Political propaganda, a device fundamentally distasteful to the American character, was most effectively employed by the neglected and often despised ad hoc organizations set up by President Roosevelt to help save the American people from themselves.

Isolationist sheet music cover, 1940/
USA/Artist unknown.

Bubble gum "War Cards" carried the following legends "To know the HORRORS OF WAR is to want PEACE," 1938/USA/Artist unknown.

DECEMBER 7, 1941

*This caricature, appearing several days after Pearl Harbor, probably
did little to arouse American ire, 1941/USA/Arthur Szyk.*

As the war progressed, America felt more confident
about defeating Japan, 1944/USA/Artist unknown.

Poster produced for factory workers by Texaco,
c. 1943/USA/Artist unknown.

Patriotic songs, both serious and comic, boosted
American morale, no date/USA.

Even popular song themes promised Japan's defeat,
no date/USA/Artist unknown.

Even early in the war, Americans could laugh at Hitler, 1942/USA/Walt Disney Studio.

Adolf Hitler—Napoleon Jr., an early magazine caricature, 1933/USA/W. Cotton.

Hitler as an aspiring world conqueror, 1942/ USA/Boris Artzybasheff.

Cover for a book of anti-Axis drawings, 1941/ USA/Arthur Szyk.

Szyk's mordant caricatures sometimes appeared on Collier's covers, 1942/USA/Arthur Szyk.

Even Captain Freedom joined the fight against the Axis, c. 1943/USA/Schomberg.

Songs mocking the Nazis were popular with the public, no date/USA/Artist unknown.

Caricature showing Mussolini subservient to Germany and Japan, 1942/USA/Arthur Szyk.

KOEHLER
ANCONA

This is the Enemy

WINNER R. HOE & CO., INC. AWARD — NATIONAL WAR POSTER COMPETITION
HELD UNDER AUSPICES OF ARTISTS FOR VICTORY, INC. — COUNCIL FOR DEMOCRACY — MUSEUM OF MODERN ART

*This aristocratic officer seems a far cry from the crudeness of most
Nazi leaders, 1942/USA/Karl Koehler and Victor Ancona.*

The emotional appeal of the threatened mother and child
made this poster a success, 1942/Canada/G. K. Odell.

*A grim picture of Axis occupation to spur the
American fighting spirit, 1942/USA/Ben Shahn.*

*Again, c. 1943/USA/
Thomas Hart Benton.*

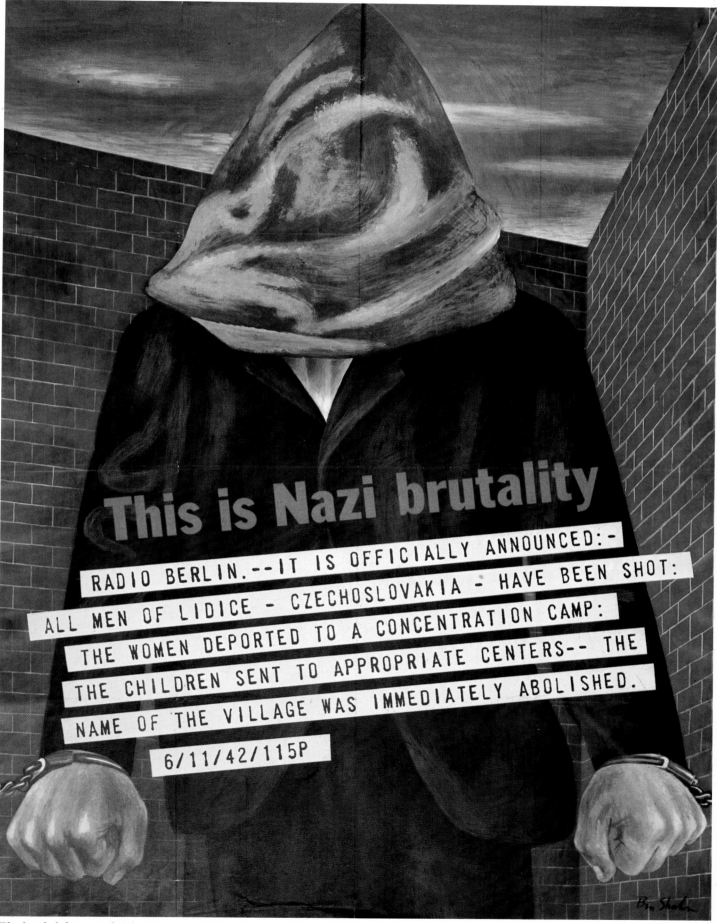

The hooded figure and ticker-tape text made
this poster effective, 1942/USA/Ben Shahn.

Connecting loose talk with a sunken ship,
1942/USA/Henry Koerner.

Someone Talked!

U.S. SHIP SUNK BY

A more abstract statement of the careless talk
theme, 1943/USA/Steven Dohanos.

AWARD

FOR CARELESS TALK

DON'T DISCUSS TROOP MOVEMENTS · SHIP SAILINGS · WAR EQUIPMENT

This poster was well designed but too sophisticated
to have much influence, c. 1943/USA/Steven Dohanos.

a careless word

...another cross

A simple image shows the results of careless
talk, c. 1943/USA/John Atherton.

We'll Finish the Job!

Flagg's avuncular Uncle Sam got tough as victories mounted, 1944/USA/James Montgomery Flagg.

-UNLESS WE KEEP 'EM FIRING!

This poster played on the theme that danger was also close to home, 1942/USA/Artist unknown.

A realistic rendering of the American soldier in combat, 1942/USA/Norman Rockwell.

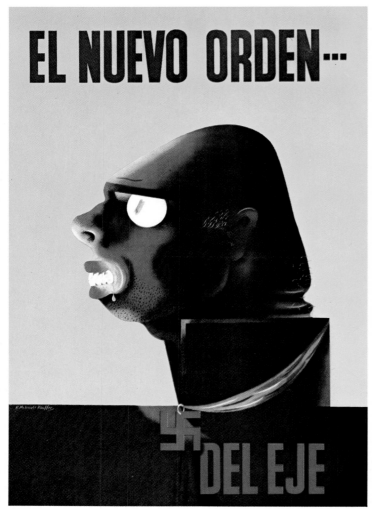

The New Order of the Axis (Office of Inter-American Affairs),
c. 1944/USA/E. McKnight Kauffer.

Hands Off the Americas (Office of Inter-American Affairs),
1942/USA/John Gaydos.

As One Man (Office of Inter-American Affairs),
c. 1942/USA/Arias Bernal.

Though strong graphically, this poster's message
and intent were unclear to factory workers,
1942/USA/Glenn Grohe.

When you ride ALONE you ride with Hitler!

Join a Car-Sharing Club TODAY!

Civilians were strongly exhorted to share
resources, 1942/USA/Weimer Pursell.

STOP HIM

AND THE JOB'S DONE

U.S. ARMY OFFICIAL POSTER

The oversized Japanese soldier is intended
to threaten the viewer, 1942/USA/Artist unknown.

STOP

**STOP STEALING TOOLS!
THAT CREW WILL NEED THEM IN COMBAT**

A frank admittance that factory thefts occurred,
even in wartime, 1944/USA/Artist unknown.

**Stop this monster that stops at
nothing... PRODUCE to the limit!**

This is YOUR war!

A plea for more production to fend off the
Axis brute, 1943/USA/Bert Yates.

(Top) Win the War issue, 1942/USA/Artist unknown. (Bottom) Issued to commemorate the battle of Iwo Jima, 1945/USA/Artist unknown.

RULE AND RESISTANCE IN 'THE NEW ORDER' 1936-1945

> "France has lost a battle;
> she has not lost the War."
>
> CHARLES DE GAULLE
>
> *Broadcast from London to Occupied France,*
> *June 18, 1940.*

When in 1936 Hitler repudiated the treaties of Versailles and Locarno and marched his troops into the Rhineland, he took a calculated risk. He knew that if the French marched too, he was lost. But he did not think the French would attack him; and he was right. The French and their British allies wanted peace at any price. This was confirmed when the Spanish Civil War began three months later. The Western powers postulated the farce of nonintervention, which Hitler and Mussolini, now openly contemptuous of them, brazenly flouted. They found the Civil War a most convenient testing ground for their new weapons, which Goebbels justified by making great play of the atrocities allegedly committed by the Reds in Spain—the torture of nuns and hostages, the killing of children, the destruction of churches, convents, and religious shrines. He warned the world that Spain was being used by the Bolsheviks as a base for an attack on Western Europe. The liberals in England and France, as usual, did not see the danger. Goebbels presented the Fascist powers as upholding European civilization in Spain against the forces of "Jewish Bolshevism"; Germany had eradicated this cancer at home in 1933, and would now be proud to lead a crusade to help other countries do so. In every way Spain proved to be an excellent dress rehearsal for the much bigger "crusade" Germany was to lead in 1941 against the cradle of Bolshevism.

In the three years 1936–1939, Nazi foreign propaganda was to foster with every means in its power the defeatism which was revealed in France at the time of the Popular Front, so that France would at the moment of Hitler's choosing fall into German hands without a struggle. Hitler wanted to avoid wasting force on the Western powers if he could neutralize them by other means. He would reserve his military strength for the inevitable struggle in the East with the tough Soviet army. As he said to Rauschnigg, "Why should I bother to use military means, if I can do it better and more cheaply in other ways? . . . if I can break down the enemy psychologically before the armies begin to function at all? . . . By provocation of unrest in French public opinion, France can easily be brought to the point where she will be able to use her army too late, or not at all." In due course, all this came to pass. Hitler overcame France in six weeks, with military losses smaller than those Germany had sustained in a single battle of World War I. In this success, the machinations of Goebbels played a cardinal role.

One of his propagandists was Otto Abetz, a personable German who professed a great affection for France. In the years immediately before 1938 he lived in Paris, posing as an advocate of Franco-German understanding. Moving easily in Parisian society, he found a ready audience for his proposal that differences between the two countries should be settled amicably. Germany, he said, had absolutely no quarrel with France, nor designs on Alsace-Lorraine; all that was over, the 1914 war forgotten. Playing on anti-Semitism and anticommunism, he convinced many influential and patriotic Frenchmen that German and French interests could be identified.

(Top) "England, this is your work." A 1938 German poster in Poland shortly after the occupation. (Middle) "Monster, you made us suffer." This German poster for Belgium blamed the war on Churchill. (Bottom) The "falling leaf" which the Germans dropped on Parisians during the phony war. "The leaves fall because of God but you will fall because of the English."

In the early months of the war, German propagandists discovered how to create anti-Semitic propaganda by reversing the title of the London newspaper, The Times. (Top) An anti-British postcard. (Bottom) The "puzzle" leaflet was a later version of the same idea. The fragments were dropped on French soldiers in the Maginot Line.

War -„Times"

The next propaganda move was to divide France from her ally, Great Britain. Here Abetz and his French friends had the support of eminent French writers like Marcel Déat, whose theme was, "Why should we die for Danzig—because Britain has guaranteed Poland?" The French government was "the tool of British diplomacy," and the British would always "fight to the last Frenchman." All this became much more virulent during the Phony War in 1939–40. From the radio studios in Stuttgart, Goebbels' man Ferdonnet poured out a flood of propaganda asking why the British had only a few thousand troops in France, while France had mobilized her whole manpower in millions? He told the French that the British troops were much better paid than the French soldiers, which gave them the advantage for the favors of French women. In the weeks before the attack of May 1940, millions of German leaflets dropped on France showed the tired and dirty French poilu at the front, while the British soldier lay in the arms of French prostitutes well behind the lines. The most famous of these leaflets was "The Falling Leaf," actually shaped like a leaf, which littered the streets of northern French cities. Its legend above the death's head of a French poilu was "The leaves fall because God wills it—but we shall fall because the English will it. Next spring no one will remember either the leaves fallen this year, nor the French soldier fallen this year. Life will pass over our tombs . . ."

Against all this during the Phony War, the Western Allies were badly prepared. The British Ministry of Information was not yet in working operation; and no Ministry of Information existed in France until the May–June crisis of 1940. The French case was hardly presented at all, and when it was, its advocates seemed always on the defensive, trying to refute some piece of German propaganda, using such phrases as, "It's not true that . . ." or "It is inexact that . . . ," which only drew more attention to the German allegations. Until the 1940 crisis, the French director of information was the playwright Jean Giraudoux, of whom de Rochemont, the Paris correspondent of *Life*, wrote, "His feeling about Germany is comparable to that of a brother whose sister has gone on the streets and developed homicidal tendencies. He is full of pity, terror, to some extent shame—but mostly of sorrow."

In March 1940 Giraudoux's *Ondine* was the most popular play in Paris. It told of an immortal maiden beneath the sea, wooed by a mortal prince to the chagrin of her father and other submarine folk. The legend was really another verison of the *Rheingold* story. *Ondine* seemed to attract the Parisians in the same rather surprising way that Wagner did. Was such a man as Giraudoux a worthy opponent of Goebbels?

Goebbels' propaganda to France leading up to May 10, 1940, had been carefully planned. As Hitler had said earlier to Rauschnigg, "The place of artillery preparation will be taken by propaganda, before the armies arrive . . . mental confusion, indecision, panic, these are the first weapons. When the enemy is thoroughly demoralized from within, when social unrest is rife, that is the right moment. A single blow will then suffice." It did.

The problem for the Nazis after June 1940 was to govern the huge territories they had annexed so rapidly—France, the Low Countries, Denmark and Norway, as well as half of Poland—while preparing the final blow against Britain. Here propaganda, they knew, would be less effective in undermining the will to resist. Against an island people they would have to employ more material means; this was why they now tried to enlist France as an ally in the projected invasion.

Although the German press and radio had often discussed plans for the reorganization of Europe after the final victory, no serious attempt had been made to describe how the "New Order" was to operate—until July 1940, when the Nazi minister of economics, Walter Funk, went into the matter in some detail. From his speech it was immediately clear that the Nazis were primarily interested in the commercial exploitation of the occupied territories, and that all the grand talk about the New Order was mystification. The Germans wanted a continent at peace, self-sufficient economically and completely self-contained politically, in which the Greater German Reich would exercise hegemony.

The immediate problem was to present this *Grossdeutsche Reich* as offering France a prominent role in a noble enterprise on behalf of all Europe. Before the war and during the Phony War, the Goebbels propagandists had done all they could to divide the French among themselves, to put class against class. But after the fall of France and during the Occupation, they exhorted the French to pull together and forget their mutual antagonisms and class hatreds, in short to emulate Germany and the German virtues of hard work and sobriety; to work for collaboration, not revenge. Had not Germany, they asked, been exceptionally magnanimous to France in defeat, leaving her in possession of her navy and her colonies? While the British had, as usual, abandoned France in her hour of need. At Dunkirk, the British forces had been evacuated first, and the French were left to sit on the beaches waiting for death or captivity. A contemporary German cartoon shown in France had twin pictures, one of which shows a British Tommy and a French poilu standing together at the edge of a blood-filled swimming pool, poised to dive in. The British soldier is counting, "Ready? One . . . two . . . " The second picture shows the poilu, having dived in, floundering about and gulping, while the British Tommy is still standing on the edge, grinning and shouting, "Three!"

Posters on the walls of Paris and the provincial cities recalled the treatment meted out to France throughout the centuries by the hereditary enemy, "perfidious Albion." One of them, entitled *"L'appetit du dogue Britanique"* ("The appetite of the British bulldog"), showed a voracious looking bulldog, his jaws clamped on the world's Western hemisphere, which was marked with the names of the various territories taken from the French since early times. "England!" ran the caption, "YESTERDAY —in the 14th century she devastated Gascony . . . she burned Joan of Arc at Rouen . . . she stole French possessions in Canada, India, the West Indies, Malta. . . . she left Napoleon to rot on Saint Helena. . . . she humiliated France at Fashoda and

(Top left) During the phony war, cartoonists warned the French public against Hitler's tyranny. (Top, right) "Silence, the enemy is listening," a 1938 poster by Paul Colin. (Middle) A poster by Jean Carlu promoting Anglo-French solidarity, 1939. German propaganda at that time tried to drive a wedge between the two countries. (Bottom) French propaganda before the German invasion could still mock Hitler.

(Top, left) The Germans pasted this poster on Belgian walls. It condemned the British and Canadian troops for the attack on Dieppe in August 1942. (Top, right) "Don't forget Oran," a German poster seen in Paris after the British sank the French fleet at Oran. (Bottom) Anti-Semitic films like The Eternal Jew *were shown in Holland and other occupied countries.*

CIMETIÈRE DES ALLIÉS

N'oubliez pas Oran!

DE EEUWIGE JOOD

OOK U MOET DEZE FILM ZIEN!

EEN DOCUMENTAIRE FILM OVER HET WERELD-JODENDOM.
NAAR EEN IDEE VAN Dr. E. TAUBERT. SAMENSTELLING: FRITZ HIPPLER
MUZIEK: FRANZ R. FRIEDL

expelled her from Egypt . . . TODAY—she causes French blood to flow at Mers-el-Kebir, at Dakar, at Gabon, in Syria, Madagascar . . . TOMORROW—what new robbery and French bloodletting is she planning . . . ?"

Here, the British destruction of the French fleet at Mers-el-Kebir in July 1940 was an unexpected windfall for Goebbels. Posters were immediately placarded all over France showing a despairing French sailor drowning in the harbor of Oran, still clutching the tricolor. Another showed Churchill as an octopus, his tentacles stretching out to glean any possible prey.

This Nazi propaganda had some effect in Vichy, where the ministers around Pétain tended to be Anglophobe, and on that considerable portion of the French public for whom Pétain was regarded with almost religious veneration as the savior of France. In the later months of 1940, it was therefore possible to obtain some results from the "perfidious Albion" propaganda. But to present the Germans, if not the Nazis, as friends and confederates of the French proved somewhat harder. One of the most ubiquitous posters of this time in occupied France showed a tall, clean-cut, chivalrous looking Wehrmacht soldier comforting a young French widow with her children, taking them fondly in his strong arms; below was the caption, "Abandoned French populations! Have confidence in the German soldier!" Another poster celebrated the advantages of volunteering for work in Germany. It showed a poor French woman saying to her ragged children as she opened a letter from her husband in Germany, "Look! Now at last we have some money from him!" An attempt was even made to present Hitler as a simple soul, humble in his triumphs, tearful over his wounded soldiers, also a child lover. But this never really caught on.

The cinema was of course used freely by Goebbels as a propaganda medium. He founded a special French production company, the Continental, to make films for French consumption, on which he spent vast sums of money. His department supervised all branches of the French film industry—studios, printing works, production, distribution, publicity, even movie houses. This last led to the acquisition of many cinemas belonging to Jews; by 1944 one-third of the French film industry was in German hands. All film scripts had to pass two censorship bodies, the German and the Vichy. A typical example was *Les inconnus dans la maison (The Unknowns in the House)*, a film adaptation of a prewar Simenon novel, about a young Jewish maiden who perverts a good provincial bourgeoise and leads her from the straight and narrow path. But this sort of propaganda was too obvious for the French, as was *Jew Süss* and *Ohm Kruger*, and they tended to boycott such programs.

Pétain and his regime endeavored to convey to the French people the notion that France had sinned in the lotus years of the 1920s and '30s, that the defeat of 1940 was a condign, even divine, retribution. To account for French depravity in these years, Vichy adduced a host of curious reasons—contraception and the low birth rate, gambling, the immoral writing of Marcel Proust and André Gide, Pernod, permanent waves, bathing suits

. . . In the atmosphere of almost permanent self-castigation after June 1940, the aged marshal's cry of *"Travail! Famille! Patrie!"* ("Work, Family, Fatherland")—which replaced the traditional *"Liberté! Egalité! Fraternité!"*—seemed to sound a new and healthier note. To show how the country had changed for the better, a film was made to contrast the new "clean" life under Vichy with that in the decadent Anglo-Saxon countries. The French cineasts obtained a number of American newsreels and documentaries about life in New York; they selected certain episodes about speakeasies, nightclubs, call girls and the like, strung them together and released the film in France under the sardonic title *La Libre Amérique* (*America the Free*). The trouble was, however, that the French public, far from being shocked, was delighted with *La Libre Amérique*; they flocked to see it not for edification, but for vicarious pleasure.

Pétain's savior image was encouraged by the German propaganda machine. The poet Valéry-Larbaud compared Pétain resurrecting France with Christ resurrecting Lazarus; and a religious postcard showed two adjacent medallions, one bearing the effigy of Christ, the other of Pétain. When Paul Claudel's play *L'Annonce faite à Marie* (*The Annunciation to Mary*) was performed in Vichy, the dramatist wrote a laudatory ode to the marshal.

When after a year of Nazi-Pétain collaboration the war in Russia began, the Nazis thought they had a trump card in the large anti-Bolshevik element in occupied countries. Their propaganda now took the dual form of "Utopia round the corner," in a Europe under German "protection," and "Europe as a slave camp" if the Soviets won. When representatives of the Axis powers, their satellites, and sympathizers from Vichy France and other occupied countries gathered in Berlin in November 1941, it was to celebrate the "New Order in Europe" as a European crusade against Bolshevism. The Légion Volontaire Française was formed for those Frenchmen who believed in it, and were prepared to fight alongside the Germans in Russia. In commemoration of the occasion, the German radio stations broadcast a new "Song of Europe," and the Nazis issued a special stamp inscribed "European United Front against Bolshevism," against a background of a Europe decorated with a sword and a swastika. It was at this time in 1942 that Goebbels coined the term "Iron Curtain" (popularly and erroneously ascribed to Winston Churchill in his Fulton speech after the war). Goebbels told the occupied countries of Western Europe that if Germany did not destroy the Soviet Union, an "Iron Curtain" would descend over all Europe, separating its ancient and glorious civilization from the rest of the world. When in 1941 England espoused the cause of Soviet Russia, Goebbels deplored the ignorance of the British who had not learned the lesson of Kerenski.

For about six months all this crusade propaganda had some effect in Western Europe, but it never took real root and, after the first German reverses in the snows of the East, it began to lose its attraction. The Scandinavian countries, near neighbors

(Top, left) A poster announcing a rally of the Nasjonal Samling, the Norwegian Nazi movement led by Vidkun Quisling. (Top, right) A Nasjonal Samling recruiting poster, "Fight with Heroes." (Middle) An anti-German leaflet from Belgium. (Bottom) Poster columns such as this one in Holland were plastered with German propaganda during the occupation.

(Top) During the Nazi occupation of Holland, a strong resistance movement and underground press affirmed the Dutch loyalty to Queen Wilhelmina. Underground papers ranged from simple stenciled sheets to handsomely printed journals. This cartoon was published in a clandestine magazine, De Groene Amsterdammer. (Bottom) A symbol of occupied Holland drawn by an Australian cartoonist.

of the Soviet Union, might still lend an ear to it; but the French people were too cynical to be taken in by it.

After the Wehrmacht's initial "correctness" in France, which had a limited success, the SS and the Gestapo spoiled it all with their Draconian measures. They began the fatal policy of executing hostages in retribution for German soldiers killed by the French Résistance. Their crude anti-Semitism had no appeal to a people which had once been divided by the Dreyfus affair. Particularly appalling was the Vélodrome d'Hiver episode, when Laval rounded up tens of thousands of French Jews for dispatch to the extermination camps in the East.

In other parts of Europe overrun by the Nazis, strenuous attempts were made, as in France, to woo the people to the cause of the New Order. In both Norway and Belgium, the Germans established pro-Nazi movements under Quisling and Degrelle respectively, which had some initial success. In Holland, where the Dutch Nazi party was headed by Anton Mussert, the Germans took over the Hilversum radio, using as a broadcaster Max Blokzijl, a conservative journalist who eloquently preached the Nazi gospel. Although known as "Lying Max" by the patriots, his programs nevertheless had a wide following. Another popular Nazi radio program in Holland for a while was a political cabaret which ridiculed the Allies and their Dutch supporters. In the first year of the occupation these efforts made some headway, and a number of volunteers from the occupied countries enlisted in the Waffen SS for service in Russia.

Broadly, one may say that the German propaganda to the occupied countries failed. It had worked well enough for years before the war, most effectively in preparing the military offensives in the West, acting as "softening-up" artillery on the enemy—that is to say acting negatively. But when the Nazis were confronted with the more prosaic business of administering the conquered territories, of winning the hearts and minds of the populations, they had nothing positive to offer. The fault lay not in Goebbels' propaganda, but in the very nature of National Socialism itself. After the military victories had been won, it was found to be barren. There was nothing to propagate, except stale racial theories which had no place in the modern world, where communications had brought people closer together than ever before. The New Order was a vision not of a brave new world, but of something resurrected from the mists and fogs of the Niebelungen.

"Propaganda," according to Maurio Megret, "takes as its objective the mind of the enemy, and makes use of the intellect *to compensate for the inadequacy of material resources.* It is therefore the weapon par excellence of the weak." This might well apply to the occupied countries in the early days. Organized resistance was not so much weak as nonexistent. Everything had happened too quickly. Isolated, unknown to one another, the potential resisters' only weapon was psychological. For over a year, France had no unified or disciplined resistance group. The first acts of resistance were therefore individual, by men and women acting on their own initiative. Their only value in 1940 and 1941 was that these small acts, if repeated, irritated the Germans—irritated rather than harrassed them—making them feel uncomfortable, aware that they were living in a hostile environment. When the first men of the Résistance daubed the letters RAF, or the V sign, or the Cross of Lorraine on the walls and pavements of Paris, they were obeying one of the basic rules of psychological warfare—to inform the enemy that, although he may have the upper hand militarily, he is surrounded by hostile, elusive, and immeasurable forces. Springing up ubiquitously and irregularly, these symbols were also an affirmation to other resistance groups that they were not alone.

In the early days after the western blitzkrieg, these spontaneous acts were puny and unplanned. At Bar-le-Duc, the secretary general of the department flew the French flag at half-mast and refused to take it down. A mayor in Seine-et-Oise stopped the town-hall clock to show that he did not recognize "the new time." In Chartres, the prefect instructed all mayors not to hang German notices on the walls of their offices. In Alsace, where German was understood and where German official notices for the civil population were appearing everywhere, they were defaced. The last six letters of the instruction *Achtung! Verdunkelung!* (Attention! Blackout!) were obliterated, so that the notice read, *Achtung! Verdun!* The word *offen* (open) on the compartment windows of trains was amplified into *Hoffen* (hope). *Raucher* (smoking compartment) on the trains became *Rache* (revenge). One journalist always made the same typing error in republishing material fed to him by the Gestapo; he continually referred to Hitler's masterwork as *Mein Krampf* (my cramp). Assemblies being forbidden in occupied France on the traditional public holidays (July 14, May 1, etc.), people foregathered spontaneously at the last moment, as if by chance, before the municipal war memorials. In all offices and factories, work would suddenly cease for a minute.

It was the same in the other occupied countries. In Holland, the Nazis had forbidden all official and semiofficial references to the exiled royal family, the House of Orange. Opposition to this was expressed in the pins and pendants made from the proscribed coinage bearing Queen Wilhelmina's head. The Dutch also often displayed or carried orange flowers. A favorite piece of wall propaganda used by the Dutch resistance was the number six and a quarter with a slash through it (6¼). This was a play on the Dutch *seis en kwart* (six and a quarter) and Seyss-Inquart, the chief Nazi occupation official in the Netherlands.

In Poland, a senior SS officer in the Government General named Moder was always referred to by the Poles as *Mörder* (murderer). On the walls of Warsaw the Nazi slogan *Deutschland siegt an allen Fronten* (Germany is victorious on all fronts) became *Deutschland liegt an allen Fronten* (Germany is prostrate on all fronts). In Brussels the annual parade at the tomb of the unknown soldier of the 1914 war was banned, so that day the Belgians marched past the Column of Congress, the monument to national independence. When this too was forbidden, students

(Top) A Belgian resistance sticker opposing Leon Degrelle's pro-Nazi Rexist movement. The demands of indigenous Nazi groups were ignored by the Germans, who relied on physical force rather than ideology to maintain the New Order. (Bottom) Posters such as this one for a German film were daubed with anti-Nazi drawings and slogans by resistance propagandists.

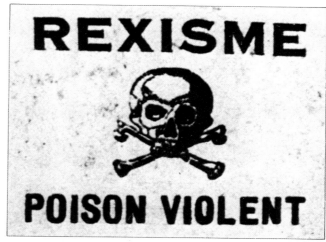

Variations on the Allied use of the
"V for Victory" theme. (Top) A rebus
with Churchill's cigar, Roosevelt's
cigarette, and Stalin's pipe. (Second
row, left) Churchill made the V
sign famous. (Third row, left) A
British cartoon reinforcing the V for
Victory idea. (Opposite page) Paul
Henried as the Czech underground
leader, Victor Laslo, in Michael
Curtiz's Casablanca (1942).

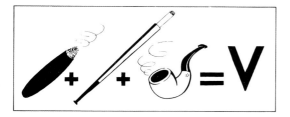

boarded trams which passed the column, made them slow down while they passed and threw out flowers at the foot of the column.

The most effective form of passive resistance was the V sign. Two Belgians working for the BBC Foreign Service knew that their countrymen at home, listening night after night to the British bombers overhead on their way to the Ruhr, often scrawled on factory walls the cheering letters RAF. But to write these clearly could take time, during which they might be arrested. The Belgians in London therefore invented for their own bilingual people (Walloon and Flemish) a simpler sign, the letter V, which stood for *victoire* for the French speaking Walloons, and *vrijheid* for the Flemish. It could be daubed on walls and pavements in a second. They suggested it to the deputy editor of the BBC, "Colonel Britton," who agreed that it should be tried out in Belgium. It was so successful that it was recommended to other occupied countries. Soon the V sign was appearing all over occupied Europe—even in countries where the word for victory does not begin with a V. Thus, in Czechoslovakia, V recalled the words of the great Czech patriot Jan Huss, *"Pravda vitezi"* (Truth shall prevail), which became the motto of the first president of the new Czechoslovakia, Thomas Masaryk. It also had a musical connotation, because the Morse code for the letter V is . . . —, three dots and one dash. These were the opening bar of Beethoven's Fifth Symphony, which he had explained as "Fate knocking at the door." It was easy to tap on door and window, and was henceforth to symbolize fate knocking at the door of the Third Reich.

Although at first scorned and ignored by the Germans, the V campaign was soon infuriating, and finally haunting, them. They ordered shopkeepers and householders whose walls and windows were marked to obliterate the V sign, or be held responsible for it. It was displayed not only on these surfaces, but in other more unusual ways. In the Paris metro, people alighting tore their tickets into the shape of Vs and threw them down, so that the metro floors everywhere became *Champs de Victoire*. After failing to outlaw the practice, the Germans decided in desperation to adopt it themselves, to appropriate the V as a symbol of German victory. They announced that *Viktoria* was an old, perfectly good, Teutonic-Latin word for victory, which had only been replaced by *Sieg* in relatively modern times. In June 1941, therefore, they began to use posters in the occupied zone of France bearing a huge white V beneath which was a pendant swastika. Below this was written, *"Viktoria*—the victory of Germany which is fighting for the New Europe." They even painted the V on their own vehicles. The most prominent of these plagiarized signs was on the Eiffel Tower, and on the pediment of the Chambre des Députés, on the front facing the Pont de la Concorde. Here, two gigantic Vs forty feet high were erected, with the motto beneath, *"Deutschland siegt an allen Fronten."* This German use of the V continued throughout the occupation, until in the summer of 1944 they began to use the letter for another purpose—the V-1 and V-2 (*Vergeltung*—vengeance) rockets which fell on London.

C.617

*The Nazis tried to turn the "V"
campaign to their own use. (Top)
A German poster, "V—Germany
victorious on all fronts." (Second row,
left and right) The V in occupied
Holland. (Third row) The Germans
equated the V with the Latin word
victoria. (Bottom row) An anti-Semitic
leaflet. (Opposite page, top left) A
German poster issued in connection
with the 1941 Allied collapse in Greece.
(Top, right) The German long-range
rockets were called V-1 and V-2.
(Bottom, left) A Dutch postcard
published by the Germans. (Bottom,
right) A Nazi propaganda postcard.*

Unlike the Germans, the various resistance movements could not use the poster as a form of propaganda; it was too dangerous to put up. But they could deface German posters. Never before, it was said, had Paris known such a plague of posters. Tearing them down was a punishable offense. A man who tore down a caricature of Winston Churchill as an octopus was given a three-month sentence and a heavy fine. Much quicker, and less dangerous, was to scrawl the V sign on the German poster.

The propaganda material employed by the resistances came largely from British and American sources. Not long after the evacuation of Dunkirk, the RAF was already dropping leaflets on the French, informing them that the British would come back.

The Allies took some time to realize that the propaganda they provided had to be adapted to the psychology of the occupied country in question. Before attempting to influence public opinion, care had to be taken not to offend it. In unoccupied France, for instance, in 1940 and 1941, it would have been impolitic to defame Marshal Pétain, whose popularity was then at its height. It proved more rewarding to attack his subordinates, in particular Pierre Laval, or at the most to refer sympathetically to the baneful effects of old age on human judgment.

Nazi propaganda in the experienced hands of Dr. Goebbels was by 1941 presenting the war as a grand crusade to save Europe and the world from Bolshevism. The Allies had to counter this logically, explaining why they were now joined with the Soviet Union in the struggle. This they did by quoting Winston Churchill, who had said he would make a pact with the devil to destroy such an evil thing as Hitlerism.

As the war progessed, the Allies also learned that the military situation must be reported accurately to the occupied countries, without concealing Allied reverses. In any case, these reverses would be given full publicity by the Nazis. To anticipate their announcement was a sure sign of confidence and self-assurance. Unlike the Nazis, whose propaganda was broadly addressed to the lowest human denominator—as Goebbels himself boasted— the Allies appealed to reason and the critical sense of their European audience. In the early stages they made many mistakes. During the fighting in Norway in April 1940, the BBC made extravagant claims for Allied successes, which only made the Norwegians disillusioned with the West when the Germans occupied the entire country. Here the British prime minister, Neville Chamberlain, did not help matters with his confident "Hitler has missed the bus" speech. As late as August 1944, the BBC made a premature announcement about the fall of Paris, which might have been costly and bloody for the jubilant Parisians. On the whole however the influence of Allied propaganda, principally the BBC and the American leaflet campaigns, in the occupied territories was to uplift morale and to inspire the inhabitants to greater feats themselves. This was confirmed in thousands of letters from listeners which came through Spain and Portugal, or from those who had escaped. From Bergen to the Basque country, from Amsterdam to Athens, every evening in thousands of homes and shops, the shutters would be closed

"V 1..."

"Ja, Johnny - en dat is nog maar het begin!!"

VICTORIA

Pierre Laval as seen by the American cartoonist, Daniel Fitzpatrick, (Top) and the Russian artists, the Kukriniksi (Bottom). Though Marshal Pétain became chief of the French State after the Germans occupied France in 1940, Laval, by 1942, emerged as the virtual dictator of the Vichy regime. Following the liberation, he was sentenced to death and executed.

early, the lights extinguished and the inhabitants would gather in silence round the radio, straining to catch the muffled tones of London.

Charles de Gaulle, leader of the "Free French" in exile, frequently broadcast to his countrymen, urging them to resist until the Allies arrived; and the daily broadcasts of Queen Wilhelmina from London were a ray of hope to the Dutch, who accepted her as the symbol of national independence and survival.

When America was still neutral, her short-wave broadcasts to occupied Europe were often more effective than the BBC emissions. Many Europeans felt that a neutral country was more likely to tell the truth than was a belligerent. Moreover, the American broadcasts revealed where American sympathies lay, although she was neutral; and this in turn persuaded the people in 1940 and 1941 that, in spite of all appearances to the contrary, Britain's chances of winning must be good. Penalties for listening to these foreign broadcasts increased as the war continued. In 1943 the Nazis began confiscating radio sets in Holland. But people handed in only their old, broken-down sets and kept the good ones. At the end of the war, 20 percent of the sets, it was estimated, were still concealed and listened to at night.

Early in the occupation, a clandestine press appeared, the fruit of spontaneous efforts by the occupied peoples themselves. Editing was relatively easy—with material obtained chiefly from American and BBC broadcasts and leaflets—but printing and distribution, the shortage of paper and equipment, and the stringent security measures which had to be applied, presented exceptional problems. A rotary press was difficult to acquire, and the essential collaboration of professional printers could not be relied upon. In Poland, small hand presses were set up in the cellars of townhouses or, if they were too noisy, in shacks in the woods. News from all over the world was collected by radio monitors concealed in soundproof cellars, forest huts, and barns with false roofs. Farmers' carts brought paper to the printers, concealed under loads of hay or vegetables. Distribution was on the "threesome system," each distributor knowing only the person who handed him the paper and the one he passed it on to. The news sheets were also distributed through shops, concealed in goods, or sometimes sold openly from street kiosks, hidden inside the pages of German newspapers.

In Belgium, two clandestine papers appeared as early as June 15, 1940: *Chut* (*Buffoon*) in Brussels and *Le Monde du Travail* (*Working World*) in Liège. A month later, history repeated itself when *La Libre Belgique* (*Free Belgium*) appeared, to carry on the clandestine tradition of its famous namesake under the 1914–18 occupation. Its articles were remarkably outspoken. On August 15, 1941, an unusual anniversary, it wrote:

> After overrunning Belgium and France, the Führer said that by August 15, 1940 he would be reviewing a parade of his troops in London. His astrologers and pythonesses had told him! But he lost the air battle over London, and now. . . . the Boche marches furiously up and down the channel coast looking out impotently on the twenty-three miles of water

which separates him from what Hitler thought would be an easy prey. . . . Because of a shortage of metal, Hitler then attacked Russia. . . . now the RAF is nightly giving him more metal than he wants. . . .

When the Nazis took over the principal Brussels newspaper *Le Soir*, the Belgians immediately rechristened it *Le Soir Volé* (*Le Soir*, stolen). On November 9, 1943, thousands of copies of a fake *Le Soir* were delivered by bicyclists to all the Brussels kiosks, an exact imitation of the paper under German control, containing nothing but anti-German propaganda. Just before the liberation in 1944, 275 clandestine newspapers, many in Flemish as well as French, were being published in Belgium.

In Holland on May 15, 1940—two days after the capitulation —a Haarlem tapestry maker launched the first clandestine news sheet, *Action de la Gueux (Beggar's Action)*. By 1941, 120 clandestine news sheets were circulating in the country. Much the same could be said for Denmark and Poland. In France, the Résistance newspapers bore significant names—*Combat, Libération, Franc-Tireur, Valmy*, etc. In Paris Emilien Amanauny founded "Le groupe de la rue de Lille," an organization which provided Résistance papers with news and other press facilities. It was never discovered by the Gestapo. By 1944, over a million copies of the clandestine press were circulating in France.

All these newspapers and sheets specialized in detailed accounts of what the people could not otherwise know, particularly the German military setbacks. Among other regular themes was "how the Germans are plundering our food supplies"—most apposite and widely read in a period of acute food shortage. There were, in fact, a number of other reasons for the food shortage, including the Allied blockade, but only "the German occupation" was given. Some clandestine news sheets were even addressed directly to the soldiers of the Wehrmacht, to awaken their *Heimweh*, or longing to return home to a normal existence with their families, and to remind them constantly of the dangers their families were now exposed to by the Allied bombing. Foreign units incorporated in the Wehrmacht were also canvassed; ethnic Germans from Poland, Slovakia, Transylvania, and the Ukraine. What were they doing here, so far from home, waiting to be killed by the Anglo-Saxons on behalf of Hitler? Another regular press feature was the action of the resistance, details of trains derailed, bridges blown up, factory stoppages, all aimed at encouraging emulation. The news sheets also informed people how to hoard those metals necessary for the German war effort, such as copper and nickel, how to sabotage machinery and how, for the younger and more active, to kill with the hands.

The use of the cinema for resistance purposes was severely limited. Most French directors, prevented by the censorship of scripts from supporting it openly, could only indulge in elaborate fantasy, or historical films in which an intelligent audience might see a parallel with the present. Such a film was *Pontcarvel*, about the 1815 Restoration of the Bourbons. It was full of double entendres about the Vichy regime, which escaped the censor and delighted the French audiences. The hero, Colonel

In all occupied countries, the underground press served as a lifeline for resistance groups. Two Belgian clandestine newssheets were L'alouette (Top) and La Meuse (Bottom). These papers were crudely reproduced. They contained news gleaned from short-wave broadcasts, editorials, and poetry. In France, several clandestine journals had circulations of more than 10,000.

(Top) A poster for a Franco-American festival in Paris after the liberation. (Middle and bottom, right) Two scenes from Rene Clement's Bataille du Rail (Battle of the Rails, 1945). The film described the sabotage of the French railroads by the resistance during the German occupation. (Bottom) A French poster by Raymond Gid commemorating those missing during the war.

THÉÂTRE NATIONAL DE L'OPÉRA · 24 JUILLET 1945

PACIFIQUE 45

APRES BERLIN...TOKYO!
FESTIVAL FRANCO-AMÉRICAIN

SEMAINE DE L'ABSENT
24 DÉCEMBRE-1·JANVIER

Pontcarvel of the Empire, barricades himself in his house and fights off the reactionary troops. He became a symbol of the Résistance, one of whose military leaders took the name Pontcarvel. In *Les Visiteurs du Soir*, the film makers returned to the Middle Ages, the time of the devil and his sorcerers. On the one hand are the good beings, those sanctified by love; on the other, the evil ones led by the devil. Originally the script writers intended the devil to be a portrait of Adolf Hitler, but this allusion could not be fully realized without too great risks. However the point was clear. In the last scene, the devil turns the young lovers into stone but—so runs the fantasy—they are only united in love in the stone statue, and their hearts beat there in unison . . . an image of petrified France itself. Evil is powerless to conquer love and goodness.

In Denmark a similar effect was obtained in a documentary made by the Danish Agricultural Pests Commission. This was about an insect plague, the *sitophilus granariae*, which destroys the crops. Passed by the German censor on nutritional grounds, it was shown throughout the war to Danish audiences who fully appreciated the satire. Everyone knew what the last line meant: "Remember that Danish crops are at stake."

Ironically, the success of the resistance propaganda was due principally to its use of the very weapons which Goebbels had perfected in the 1930s. The radio with which he had indoctrinated the Germans and terrified half of Europe with Hitler's threatening speeches, boomeranged against him during the war from the stations of the BBC. Without their constant broadcasts, high morale could not have been maintained in the occupied territories, nor could instructions for sabotage have been so easily conveyed. Without the airplane, with which Germany had rocked the continent in 1940 and 1941, no leaflets could have been dropped. Without modern printing, hundreds of clandestine newspapers could not have been read. When Winston Churchill wrote that the Nazis had conquered half of Europe, benefitting "from the lights of perverted science," he was referring to the destructive uses to which they had put these new propaganda weapons. However, as Goebbels was to learn, they proved also to be very two-edged weapons.

LE VRAI VISAGE DE REX

Comité de Vigilance des Intellectuels Antifacistes

"The true face of Rexism," 1939/Belgium/
René Magritte.

"Unification," c. 1937/
Republican Spain/Artist unknown.

"To defeat Fascism, join the Air Force," c. 1937/
Republican Spain/Artist unknown.

Anti-Italian poster, c. 1937/
Republican Spain/Artist unknown.

(Top, right) Commemorative for the 2nd anniversary of
the Defense of Madrid, November 7, 1938/Republican
Spain/Artist unknown. (Bottom) Commemoration of the
150th anniversary of the U.S. Constitution, June 1, 1938/
Republican Spain/Artist unknown.

Marshal Petain issue, 1941/
France, Vichy government/J. Piel.

COMPAGNONS DE FRANCE

"Men of France," no date/France, Vichy
government/Artist unknown.

"The women and children of Europe accuse the RAF,"
1940/German poster for France/Theo Matejko.

"Thanks to the British, our cross we bear," 1940/
German poster for France/signed SPK.

CONFIANCE...

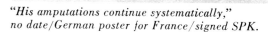

AMPUTATIONS SE SUIVENT MÉTHODIQUEMENT

"*His amputations continue systematically,*"
no date/German poster for France/signed SPK.

ILS DONNENT LEUR SANG

DONNEZ VOTRE TRAVAIL
pour sauver l'Europe du Bolchevisme

"*They give their blood, give your work.*" *Give your work
to save Europe from Bolshevism, c. 1942/German poster
for France/Artist unknown.*

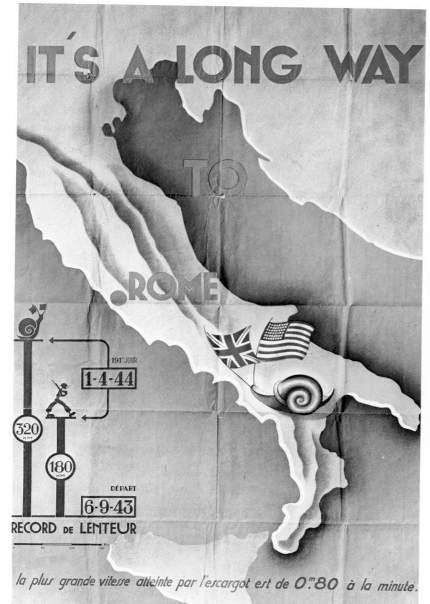

"*The Allies are advancing at a snail's pace,*"
1944/German poster for France/Artist unknown.

"*Europe united against Bolshevism,*" *c. 1943/*
German poster for France/Artist unknown.

"Black market, crime against the community," 1943/
France, occupation government/Ph. H. Noyer.

"And you? Become a W.A. Man," no date/
Holland, occupation government/Lou Manche.

"Dutchmen, fight Bolshevism in the Waffen SS,"
c. 1943/German poster for Holland/Artist unknown.

"Bolshevism is murder," no date/
German poster for Holland/Artist unknown.

"Moscow commands," no date/German poster
for Holland/Artist unknown.

"Prove you're a true Dutchman, join the Waffen SS,"
c. 1943/German poster for Holland/Artist unknown.

"The 'liberators' will save European culture from its downfall,"
1944/German poster for Holland/Leest Storm.

"All is well, Madame la Marquise . . . ," no date/
Belgium, occupation government/Artist unknown.

"Join the National Socialist Transport Corps,"
no date/German poster for Belgium/Wieland.

"Europe is prepared. Join the Flanders Legion,"
c. 1943/German poster for Belgium/Claudius.

"Waffen SS Recruitment Command," c. 1943/
German poster for Belgium/Bertau.

"Danger threatens from the sky. Take air raid precautions," 1938/Finland/T. Kivihariu.

Published by the Free French Movement in
America, no date/USA/Jean Carlu.

Published by the Free French Movement in
America, no date/USA/Henri Laussucq.

Published by the Belgian Information Center,
c. 1944/USA/V. Rotter.

Published by the Belgian Information Center,
no date/USA/R. Sturbelle.

The Danish church as a symbol of resistance,
no date/USA/Artist unknown.

Published by the Czechoslovak Information
Service, no date/USA/Adolf Hoffmeister.

Published by the Greek War Relief Association,
no date/USA/Artist unknown.

A vision of the Yugoslav spirit, no date/USA/
Vladimir Ivanovic.

*Anti-German postcards, 1945/Holland/Nico
Broekman and Smits.*

Anti-German postcard, 1944/Belgium/
Artist unknown.

CHAPTER SIX

THE SOVIET UNION PROPAGANDA FOR PEACE 1917–1945

We think it will not be much longer
before Alexander Nevsky will be
shown in public theatres again.

SERGEI EISENSTEIN
to Margaret Bourke White,
shortly before the
German invasion in June 1941.

One feature which the Soviet and Nazi regimes had in common before the Second World War was their regard for the technical inventions of the 20th century—the radio, the cinema, the popular press (as well as automobiles, airplanes, and wireless telegraphy). These were seen by the two regimes as a means of dominating their fellow men. Whereas in the Western democracies in those years, the communications media were mostly in private hands, for entertainment and commercial gain, in the Soviet Union and Germany they were state monopolies, used primarily for disseminating propaganda.

Other similarities in the propaganda systems of the two countries are well enough known: the indoctrination of youth at an early age; the constant repetition of slogans and catchwords; the diatribes against the bourgeois "plutocracies;" the censorship of all news from abroad; the sudden switches of government policy. In one aspect of propaganda, however, there was an important difference.

Whereas the Nazis, as well as Mussolini's Fascists, presented themselves essentially as warriors, and attempted by a continuous show of force—military parades, rallies, and bellicose speeches—to terrify the rest of Europe into submission (e.g. the effect of the Nazi film *Baptism of Fire* on Norway and the Low Countries in 1940), the Soviets always posed as men of peace. Hitler and Mussolini were forever strutting about in uniform; but the Russian leaders, on the few occasions when they showed themselves outside the Kremlin, appeared dressed in their neat dark suits and Trilby hats, the personification of civilian propriety. Indeed, the Soviets' appropriation of the word "peace" is one of the most remarkable propaganda achievements of our time. They took possession of it completely, arrogated it as it were to their exclusive use.

A glance at the names of some of their front organizations in the United States alone reveals this: The American Committee for the Struggle against War, The American League against War and Fascism, and The World Congress against War, to mention only a few. For the average Western citizen not much interested in politics, but aware of the horrors of modern warfare, this all sounded much more attractive than the martial rodomontades of Hitler and Mussolini.

Where the propaganda machinery is state controlled, it is easy to account for contradictions in meaning by the use of a special vocabulary. To most people, for example, the Soviet invasion of Finland in 1940 was "war." But to the Soviet propagandists it was "A rectification of frontiers to protect the pacific Soviet state against an attack by the Western Imperialist warmongers."

Long before Goebbels appeared on the scene, the Communists were fully alive to the importance of propaganda. Already in 1902 Lenin, in his book *What Is to Be Done?*, had expatiated on its revolutionary value. By 1910 his lieutenant in Baku, Joseph Stalin, was running a full-scale propaganda bureau, financed from the proceeds of bank raids. With the triumph of the October Revolution in 1917, they set up the Department of Agitation

(Below) Until the end of 1933, the Soviets maintained friendly relations with Nazi Germany. Though Hitler had annihilated the Communists in Germany, the Soviets felt less threatened. They saw Nazism as a desperate attempt to stave off the inevitable proletarian revolution in Germany and expected it to fail. After the signing of the German-Polish Nonaggression Pact in January 1934, the Soviets shifted their stand, suspecting that Germany would help Poland to seize parts of the Ukraine. From 1934 until the signing of the Nazi-Soviet Nonaggression Pact in August 1938, Soviet propaganda, such as this 1936 cartoon by Boris Efimov, attacked Hitler and the Nazi Party.

ON A SHAKEY THRONE.

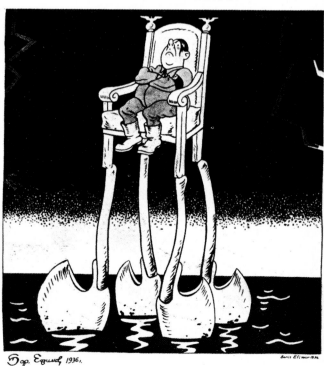

(Below) Sergei Eisenstein directing the Battle on the Ice sequence for Alexander Nevsky *(1938). The tension in this sequence was heightened by the closely coordinated score of Sergei Prokofiev. The film, which dramatized the Russian victory over the Teutonic Knights near Novgorod in the 13th century, was a thinly veiled challenge to Hitler's* Drang nach Osten. *(Opposite page, top) Nicolai Cherkasov as Nevsky. Cherkasov closed the film with a patriotic declaration spoken directly to the audience. "Whosoever comes against us by the sword shall perish by the sword. Such is the law of the Russian land and such it will always be." (Opposite page, below) The soldiers of Novgorod massing for the battle against the Teutons on ice-covered Lake Peipus. Following the Stalin-Hitler Pact,* Alexander Nevsky *was removed from circulation until the Germans invaded the Soviet Union in 1941.*

and Propaganda in Moscow, which took complete control of all information media. In *What Is to Be Done?* Lenin had made an interesting distinction between the two concepts, agitation and propaganda. "Agitation," he wrote, "is for the ignorant masses, presenting them with a single, simple idea which by constant repetition will be rammed home. The propagandist, on the other hand, deals with more complex issues and ideas—so many that they can be understood only by a few people." The agitator therefore, according to Lenin, was inclined to the spoken word, the propagandist to the written. In another book, *The Rape of the Masses,* the writer Serge Chakotin made much the same distinction about the Russians; he divided them into two categories, the 10 percent who were the active minority, and the 90 percent who formed the dull, brute mass. For the masses, propaganda had to be simple, categoric, direct.

Within a short time all forms of printing—books, newspapers, pamphlets, and posters—were in the hands of the State Publicity Corporation, which controlled not only the publishing operations but the printing machinery and paper supply. It was endowed with a censorship department which examined all book manuscripts, film scripts, drawings, music, and even maps. On November 12, 1920, the Main Political Education Committee of the Republic was set up, branches of which were attached to the political division of every region, district, town, and village.

Widespread illiteracy was the immediate problem, and it was here that the recently invented radio and cinema came to the rescue. In rural districts, radio receivers were placed in communal "reading huts," clubs, dormitories, houses of culture, museums, parks, and other public institutions where the peasants were encouraged to congregate and listen. In the reading huts they were exposed to posters as well as radio broadcasts. The huts were rudely built and generally had earthen floors. The peasant would have to come to them for information about the food situation and rationing, local notices, etc.; while there, he would also receive a broadside from the radio about the iniquities of the old Czarist system, and the benefits of the new Bolshevik one.

For the illiterate in those early days, the wall poster also proved invaluable. While the Civil War was still in progress, the windows of the press agency, Rost, in every town and village were plastered with brilliantly colored posters by such well known artists as Mayakovsky, depicting the triumphs of the Red Army. Illustrated wall newspapers were also used to give a simplified account of the Five Year Plan.

The Communists were equally quick to make use of the cinema for the illiterate. They were innovators in the documentary field and their films had a strong element of persuasion. *Turksib,* for example, discarded the narrative and human aspect, in favor of a plea for the building of the Turkestan-Siberian railway. Other topical themes were taken from the Five Year Plan, to persuade workers and peasants that no sacrifice could be too great to achieve its goals.

When it became clear in the 1930s that Germany would be

(Below) Sergei Mezhinsky as a Jewish surgeon persecuted by the Nazis in Professor Mamlock *(1938), directed by Adolf Minkin and Herbert Rappoport. One of the strongest anti-Nazi films made before the war,* Professor Mamlock *was also used as propaganda in the United States and England shortly after its completion. Mamlock is humiliated solely because he is Jewish and finally shot for offering open resistance to the Nazis. (Opposite page, top) A scene from Grigori Roshal's* The Oppenheim Family *(1939), another strong anti-Nazi film released at the height of the tension just before the Nonaggression Pact. The film was adapted from a 1933 novel by the Jewish writer Lionel Feuchtwanger; its theme, the persecution of a Jewish family. (Opposite page, below) Another scene from* Professor Mamlock. *The Jewish surgeon is paraded through the streets and scorned by Nazi sympatherizers.*

the enemy in any future war, a number of films were made to prepare the public. The great director Sergei Eisenstein was commissioned to do a film about Alexander Nevsky, the 13th-century Russian hero and conqueror of the Teutonic Knights who had invaded Russia in 1242. The implication was that what the Russians had done under Nevsky, they could do again under Stalin. *Alexander Nevsky* (1938) was immensely popular and was shown all over the Soviet Union. Eisenstein received Russia's highest award, the Order of Lenin. He was congratulated by Stalin, who had taken a personal interest in the filming. When the Soviets signed the nonaggression pact with Germany in 1939, the film was withdrawn from circulation—until the Nazi invasion of the Soviet Union in 1941. By a happy coincidence, Nevsky's defeat of the Teutons in 1242 took place at Lake Peipus near Leningrad, where the same humiliation was inflicted on their Nazi heirs in 1944. Other anti-Nazi films were *The Oppenheim Family* (1939), about Jewish pogroms and concentration camps in Germany, and *Professor Mamlock* (1938), about an eminent Jewish surgeon who opposed the Nazis. These too were withdrawn from circulation in 1939 and later rereleased after the German invasion.

In the early days after the revolution, when propaganda was in its infancy, the Bolsheviks, its first modern protagonists, made many mistakes. They were perceptive enough to see that religion, Lenin's "opium of the people," would be a powerful psychological enemy. In their determination to control people's minds, they decided that religion must be obliterated overnight. Here they overplayed their hand. Their "Union of the Militant Godless" organized a procession through the streets of Moscow of all the gods and prophets. It included Buddha on horseback in a state of priapic lubricity, the Virgin Mary lying on her back, also in a voluptuous posture, and a repulsive-looking Catholic priest making overtures to a beautiful maiden. In December 1922 in Leningrad, the Union of the Militant Godless erected a scaffold in the middle of the Nevsky Prospect, on which effigies of the gods, saints, popes, and prophets were ceremoniously beheaded and burned. In the Soviet press, the clergy of every faith were ceaselessly attacked for the alleged gluttony and drunkenness which accompanied their religious festivals. At Easter, a shop window in Moscow was decorated with a waxwork of six priests in a small boat swilling vodka, with quantities of empty bottles littered around them. This early period was also one of confiscation, and often willful destruction, of church property. The churches with everything they contained, such as sacred vessels, liturgical vestments, church bells, etc., were proclaimed national property and turned into warehouses, cinemas, and stables.

This sort of thing may have had some effect, but most of the workers and peasants—the new regime's main concern—were deeply shocked by this sacrilege. A leading Communist, Zarianov, complained about the indifferent results obtained from this anti-God propaganda. He said that when soldiers who had been subjected to it during their army service returned home,

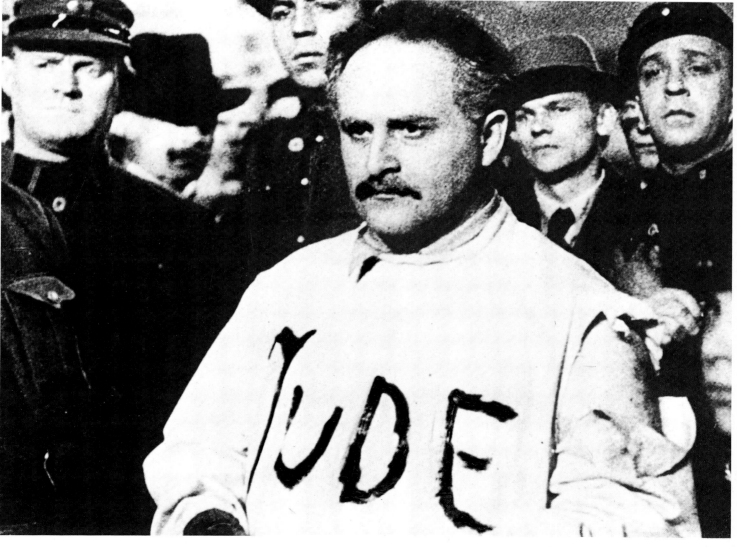

(Top) Daniel Fitzpatrick's cartoon from the St. Louis Post-Dispatch *showed Stalingrad as a death trap for the German army. (Bottom) Boris Efimov's comment on the subservient German press, c. 1936. After Hitler and Stalin signed the Nonaggression Pact, German papers were directed not to refer to ideological differences between the two countries and to use only "favorable comments from friendly and neutral countries."*

GATEWAY TO STALINGRAD
NOVEMBER 25, 1942

COUNTENANCE OF THE UNIFIED PRESS.

they were consulting the priests again within a couple of weeks, and paying them to say masses. He said that the "Anti-God Campaign" had been grossly mishandled. The 2,000-year reign of the church could not be effaced by crude stump oratory.

The Communists still intended to eradicate religion, which they described as "an evil no less pernicious than alcoholism or prostitution." But they now refrained from persecuting it directly, and adopted subtler methods. Ribald parodies of sacred themes and dignitaries were replaced by serious lectures, discussions, and seminars with scientific arguments. The process of fostering antagonism between religious sects and creeds was unobtrusively encouraged, and the priests were allowed to go about their daily business without being insulted.

Communist propaganda to foreign countries was always more subtle, based on the peace theme, and it took account of national character and temperament. The United States, in terms of communist ideology, was the most important country of all. Of it, Stalin said, "When a revolutionary crisis develops in America, that will be the beginning of the end of world capitalism as a whole."

When the American League for Peace and Democracy proclaimed, "Let us work towards the stopping of the manufacture and transport of munitions and other materials essential to the conduct of a Fascist war," many Americans could only applaud such a desirable aim. Nor was there much objection to the proclamation by the Communist Party of California, "Remember that the Soviet Union with 185,000,000 people is antiwar. Join in the defense of the peace policy of the only socialist country in the world, the Soviet Union."

In the 1920s, before Nazi Germany became the principal enemy, Soviet propaganda was directed largely against the powerful Western "plutocracies," and the horrors which their capitalist system had unleashed on the world between 1914 and 1918. The world was told that the capitalists would do it again, this time against the Soviet Union, because she was "the motherland of the international proletariat, and the only factor for its emancipation." The Communists even presented the coming war as desirable, because it would weaken capitalism more than communism. In the words of the 1928 Comintern Congress, it would "broaden the base of the proletarian movement everywhere, and bring nearer the world victory of Communism." This propaganda was broadcast on short-wave from the Soviet Union all over the world, in seventeen languages. The transmitter at Noginsk near Moscow was one of the most powerful in the world. In 1942, when Tito's partisans became active in Yugoslavia, the USSR set up a transmitter at Tiflis known as "Free Yugoslavia," purporting to be from within Yugoslavia. Later, it did the same for Bulgaria and Slovakia.

In the Soviet Union, as in Germany, Italy, and other countries where all communications media were centralized, an entire propaganda campaign could be changed overnight. On August 23, 1939, the Soviet Union and Germany, who had been insulting and threatening one another for years, signed a pact of friendship and nonaggression. It contained their agreement to the partition of Poland. A few days after its signature, on September 1, 1939, Germany invaded Poland and World War II began. Three weeks later, when Polish resistance was completely broken by the Germans, the Soviets also invaded. Yet the pact was explained in Moscow at the time as a "peace" measure, in these terms:

"The signing of the nonaggression pact between the USSR and Germany is not a war alliance between the two powers. It is not an agreement for the partition of Poland. . . . In this sense, the pact is the only real contribution to the security of Poland that has been made to date. In doing this, the Soviet Union had made a real contribution to an understanding of the present crisis in Europe. It has made a real contribution to the peace and security of Europe, the United States, and the world. . . ."

The war of 1939 brought immediate propaganda changes within the Soviet Union. Although still presenting itself as a "champion of peace," the Soviet Union now began to prepare its people for war. The armed forces were greatly expanded. A small but significant indication of this change was the issue of postage stamps depicting Soviet military power. Stamps now showed Red Army soldiers hurling grenades, and Soviet airplanes diving on enemy tanks. When in June 1941 the Germans attacked and the Soviet Union found itself allied with the Western democracies, postage stamps depicting the Big Three leaders in fraternal discussion, with the national flags of their countries intertwined above their heads, were issued. At the same time, the emphasis on the international nature of communism was reduced. The will to resist was encouraged in the Russian people by appeals to their patriotism rather than their communism; the war was described officially as "The Great Patriotic War." Films were made with such significant titles as *No Greater Love* and *In the Name of the Fatherland.* History was also rewritten to a certain extent; those czars who had distinguished themselves on the battlefield in the past were honored and held up as shining examples for the present. Stalin's frequent references in his speeches to Alexander Nevsky and Suvorov made everyone conscious of the link between the Russian past and present. An early wartime propaganda poster showing a Russian worker in combat with an aristocrat—probably inherited from Civil War times— was quickly withdrawn. The struggle now was national, not social.

The broad directives for propaganda came from the fountainhead itself, Stalin's orders of the day and his speeches on National Days. In his "Holy Russia" speech of November 6, 1941, the 24th anniversary of the revolution, he kindled national pride by recalling not only the great Russian generals of the past, but by associating them with great cultural figures like Pushkin, Tolstoy, Chekhov, and Tchaikovsky. The general line of propaganda was then determined by the Council of Peoples' Commisars and the Political Bureau of the All Union Communist Party. It was issued by the Propaganda Ministry to the country's many social and technical organizations—the Trade Unions

(Top) Soviet poster artists pulled no punches in depicting the Nazis as beasts and vermin. The text of this 1941 poster declares, "We'll destroy your teeth, hangman. We'll also cut your head with the red sword of retaliation." (Bottom) A 1941 Ukranian poster which proclaims "Destroy the Serpent." After initial setbacks, the Red Army fought valiantly to defend the Ukraine against Hitler's forces.

(Top) Goebbels was singled out for special attack by Soviet cartoonists, particularly Boris Efimov and the Kukriniksi. They found myriad ways to call him a liar. Efimov drew him as an aircraft gunner behind a battery of spouting fountain pens. (Bottom) The Kukriniksi drew Goebbels as a machine gun used by Hitler to spew forth propaganda instead of bullets.

GOEBBELS ANTI-AIRCRAFT BATTERY

The Fascist Lie-Gun

Cooperatives, the Communist Youth Movement, the Union of Intellectuals, the Cinema Workers' Union, the Writers' Union, the Union of Workers in Art, to name only a fraction. All had special directives adapted to their particular needs.

The most effective means of conveying propaganda to the less literate—as the Soviet leaders had discovered twenty years before, during the Civil War—was the poster. The first of these, with the caption "We Shall Crush and Exterminate the Fascist Viper," appeared on the streets of Moscow the day after the German invasion. Within a few days, the editorial board of the "Tass Windows" had been formed and the Tass posters began to appear shortly thereafter. When Lord Beaverbrook visited the Soviet Union in 1941, he was so impressed by the Soviet posters that he asked Stalin for a collection to take home to England (where they were later exhibited). The tradition of Mayakovsky and the Civil War was revived by some of the best-known artists in wartime Russia—Sokolov-Skaya, Denisovsky, Lebedev, the Kukriniksi (a pseudonym derived from the names of three artists who worked as a team for twenty years—Mikhail Kuprianov, Porfiri Krylov, and Nikolai Sokolov). Many of the posters recalled the exploits of Russia's old national heros. In one, Alexander Nevsky, the victor over the Teutonic Knights in 1242, stood beside Suvorov, who defeated the Turks in the war of 1787; beside them, to bring it up to date, was Vasily Chapayev, who led a Bolshevik division against Kolchak's White forces in the Civil War. A parallel with the great Soviet counteroffensive of 1941–42 west of Moscow was suggested by a poster depicting General Kutuzov who, one hundred and thirty years before, had repelled another invader, Napoleon's army, before the gates of the capital.

In the gloomy days of 1941, the aim of these propagandists was to persuade the people that Mother Russia must finally prevail. Posters of huge Russian hands and steel pincers tightening on a German throat expressed the confidence which came with the first successful counterattacks. The posters often took the form of caricatures of the Nazi leaders; in particular Goebbels, who was depicted by Efimov in the satirical magazine *Krokodil* as Mickey Mouse with a swastika tail, and by Lebedev as a braying donkey. Pétain was shown placing France under the Nazi jackboot; and Hitler, dangling Hess on a fishing line as a bait to England to join the anti-Bolshevik crusade. A book of drawings by Sharmidov showed German war atrocities: looting, hanging mass burials.

These designs, rapidly produced by the stencil method, also acted as wall newspapers, announcing political and military successes. They could be as large as 10 feet high and half as broad, using fifteen to twenty different stencil colors. Some 200 artists in Moscow alone worked on these posters, which again, as in the Civil War, were displayed in the windows of the Tass press agency (formerly Rost) offices throughout the country. They were also distributed to every factory, farm, institute, hospital, army unit, and naval vessel, so that no Soviet citizen went untouched by them. They often included a pungent verse commentary by well-known poets like Marshak or Bedny, the children's book author.

The widespread popularity of war posters and cartoons in the Soviet Union was due to their simplicity and the talent of the Soviet artists who drew them, using a popular, comprehensible form of art. During the war this poster art went through several phases of development. The first posters, especially those by Moor, still showed certain influences of the Civil War posters. Abstract symbolic treatment of subjects, pronounced schematism of forms and limited color range (red, black, and white) were typical of this phase. Later war posters acquired new characteristics. This was largely explained by the fact that artists who had previously worked in easel painting or book illustration now tried their hand at posters. It was they who introduced heroic figures with emotional and psychological elements. Conventional decorative composition was replaced by realistic interpretation. The defeat of the Germans at Moscow, the gigantic battle of Stalingrad, the victorious advance of the Red Army, the liberation of Soviet territory, the fighting qualities and victories of the Allies were all reflected in the "Tass window" posters. There was not a single event in the war, in international or domestic affairs, which was not depicted in one Tass poster or another.

One exclusively Soviet wartime feature was the propaganda railway train. Its compartments were converted into printing presses and portable cinemas, and it was staffed with teams of lecturers, actors, and artists. They toured the country making speeches and supplying information about the war; they even penetrated into the battle zones, where the train stood in a siding camouflaged behind the lines.

The cinema also played an important role in the Soviet war effort. Within three days of the Nazi invasion, the first newsreels from the front were released. Thereafter, newsreel cameramen covered the war on all fronts; film projectors were installed in the big Moscow subway stations so that the public did not have to pay to see the commentaries. Films such as Eisenstein's anti-German *Alexander Nevsky* were resurrected; other films in the same patriotic vein, about Russian heros such as Kutuzov, were turned out. The barbarism of the Germans was depicted in *Zoya* (1944), about a real woman, Zoya Kosmodemyanskaya, a partisan who worked behind the German lines, where she was captured, tortured, and hanged. Another film about partisan activity, *Secretary of the District Committee,* was awarded the Stalin Prize for 1942. To depict the horrors of life inside Nazi Germany, Mikhail Romm's *Girl No. 217* (1944) told of an inhuman German family who had acquired a Russian slave girl.

The documentary studios were reorganized and famous directors employed. As speed was essential, the first documentaries were short, but by the end of the war they formed a complete chronical of its history—*The Defeat of the German Armies before Moscow* (1942), *Siege of Leningrad* (1942), *Battle for the Ukraine* (1943), *Battle of Orel* (1943), *Berlin* (1945), *Vienna* (1945). These documentaries described not only how the battles were won, but how they were planned.

(Below) In this 1941 cartoon by the Kukriniksi, a team of three Soviet artists, Goebbels tries to cover the fact that the Soviet air raid on Berlin took the Germans by surprise. Goebbels' greatest triumph as a speaker was his 1943 Sportpalast speech in Berlin where he managed to cover up the harsh facts of the German army's devastating defeat at Stalingrad and turn a total disaster into a cry for "total war." Germans joked about Goebbels' facile ability to churn out lies. (Following spread, left) The Kukriniksi ridiculed Goebbels' propaganda efforts which were no match for the Soviet air force. (Following spread, right) As the Russians piled up victories against Germany, Goebbels was portrayed as a desperate man rather than a comic figure.

LIE-LOCATORS

GERMAN COMMAND'S REPORT OF MILITARY OPERATIONS

КУКРЫНИКСЫ-41.

LES MENTEURS DE BERLIN

(Top) In 1942, when the Germans were on the offensive, cartoonists could only warn that the harshness of the Russian climate and terrain would defeat the Germans. (Bottom) The turning point was the victory at Stalingrad. Throughout the rest of 1943, propagandists like the Kukriniksi capitalized on a steady string of Soviet victories. (Opposite page) A more serious view of Hitler by the Kukriniksi.

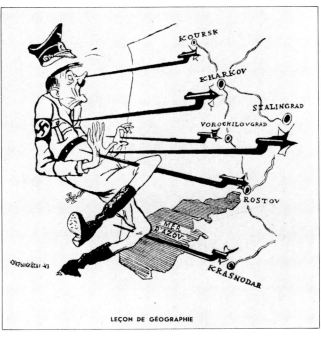

LEÇON DE GEOGRAPHIE

To improve relations with the capitalist states, now the Soviet Union's allies, the Comintern was dissolved and the revolutionary "International" removed from the Soviet song book. In July 1941 Stalin, in order to make his regime appear more respectable in the eyes of the Christian world, did a political somersault. Up to and during the 1939–40 war, when the Soviets were invading eastern Poland, the Baltic states, parts of Finland, and Rumania, he had continued the atheist policy. The Union of the Godless under Jaroslavski had extended its activities to these conquered lands; 4,000 clerics of various confessions were deported from eastern Poland alone before mid-1940, and replaced by 25,000 antireligious agitators. But all this was changed overnight. One of Stalin's first acts after the German invasion in June 1941 was to announce the death of Jaroslavski (not, it later transpired, from natural causes). Stalin even told the Polish-American priest, Stanislas Orlemanski, that he would like to "collaborate with the pope against the coercion and persecution of the Catholic Church in Germany," adding that he was "a champion of freedom of conscience and religion." A Soviet Deparment of Church Affairs was set up in Moscow, its function being "to organize friendly relations between the government and the confessions." At this fearful moment with the Germans at the gates of Moscow, the Soviets were prepared to canvas support from every conceivable quarter. They even permitted the Polish forces under General Anders to have their own army chaplains; some fifty Polish Catholic chaplains who had disappeared into Soviet concentration camps in 1939 were released for this purpose. In Moscow, the French church was reopened and placed at the disposal of the Polish Catholic community.

In its propaganda to the Germans, the Soviet Union took a different line from that adopted by the Western Allies, who had decided at Casablanca in 1942 on the policy of unconditional surrender. They made no distinction between Hitler and any alternative German government, should the Nazis be overthrown internally. The Soviets however distinguished very carefully between the German people and their Nazi leaders, the "Hitlerites" as they were contemptuously called. In their broadcasts to Germany, the Soviets said they would have no truck with the Hitlerites, but with the people of Germany, the workers whom they assumed must be on their side, they had no quarrel. Stalin's statement, "The German state passes—the German people remain," summed up the Soviet attitude.

Soviet propaganda to the German prisoners of war—of whom there were tens of thousands after the Stalingrad victory—was aimed primarily at persuading them to turn against the men who had misled them. Playing on professional pride, they even persuaded a group of German generals, by showing them that Hitler was ruining the Eastern campaign with his bungling, amateurish methods, to lead a "Free German" movement against him. They had so many prisoners that the German General Staff could not keep track of the dead and wounded, whom they posted simply as "missing." The only way that German families could find out if their men were still alive was by listening to the Soviet radio

КУКРЫНИКСЫ 43.

(Top) A poster by Dementry Shmarinov
declares "Revenge." In 1942, while the
Germans overran vast areas of Russia,
propagandists had to arouse the spirit
of vengeance in the Soviet people
with images such as this mother holding
her dead child. (Bottom) When victory
was close at hand, poster artists lost
no time in proclaiming the strength of
the Red Army.

programs beamed to Germany, in which from time to time lists
with names of German prisoners of war were read. The radio
would announce that a prisoner was to be brought to the microphone, so that his relations could hear his voice. Time was given
for the next-of-kin to be called to the radio; so that while waiting,
the German relations had to listen to political and military talks
of indeterminate length describing the German catastrophes and
Allied victories. The Russian announcer would then address
himself to the prisoner's next-of-kin: "Frau A. of Munich, your
husband is here in the studio. He was taken prisoner near Rostov.
He lost an arm but, as you will hear from his own lips, he is
receiving good medical care and he will recover. You are lucky,
Frau A. When the Hitlerites have been destroyed, you will see
your husband again. But millions of other German wives and
mothers are not so lucky. Their husbands and sons will not
return. The criminal ambition of the Hitlerites has cost them
their lives." Or the announcer would sometimes say, "Herr Z.,
here is your son. He was wounded and captured on the road to
Bobruisk. Herr Z., what was your son doing on that wintry,
snowy road to Bobruisk, so deep in Russia?"

The Russians were fortunate in one respect, thanks to the
extraordinary psychological purblindness of the Germans in
dealing with the occupied Eastern territories. In the Ukraine and
White Russia, they had the most promising opportunity, for
many people were violently anti-Soviet and welcomed them with
open arms as "liberators." Yet Goebbels' great propaganda
machine hardly went into action, nor indeed did it in all the
Russian territory conquered in 1941 and 1942. No Ukrainian or
Russian Ferdonnet broadcast to his people exploiting the weaknesses and shortcomings of the Communist party, or playing on
the differences between the Russian people and their leaders.
The reason was quite simple. The Nazis regarded the Slavs as
illiterate subhumans on whom propaganda was wasted. They
were to be beaten into submission by sheer brute force. Had the
Nazis approached the Ukrainians with more subtle methods, the
result might have been different. But the propaganda opportunity was not taken and the Nazis remained prisoners of their
racial arrogance.

The Soviet Union's wartime propaganda, both abroad and to
their own people, was remarkably successful. Abroad the Soviets
could play on the sympathies of the British and Americans as
allies sharing the same tribulations and the same hatred for a
common enemy. They posed as liberators who would, after the
victory, vacate the countries they had liberated in Eastern Europe.
In a speech on November 6, 1941, Stalin had said: "Our cry is
—No intervention of any kind in the internal affairs of other
peoples! The equality of nations! The inviolability of territory!"

At home the propagandists had the advantage of dealing with
a people accustomed after twenty years of communism to
Draconian discipline and innumerable political volte-faces. This
discipline, and the appeal to the people's deep-seated feeling
for their homeland, enabled Stalin to mount a more successful
military campaign than Hitler could ever have imagined.

"The proletarian counterattack will destroy the fascist beast, 1930/USSR/Viktor Deni.

ВСТРЕЧА НАД БЕРЛИНОМ

НАЗНАЧИЛИ НАРОДЫ-БРАТЬЯ
НАД ВРАЖЬИМ ГОРОДОМ СВИДАНИЕ.
ОТ ЭТОГО РУКОПОЖАТЬЯ
НЕ ПОЗДОРОВИТСЯ ГЕРМАНИИ!

ХУД. КУКРЫНИКСЫ   ТЕМА- И. ЛИВШИЦ   ТЕКСТ С. МАРШАК

БЕРЛИН

(TRANSLATION) MEETING OVER BERLIN
THE BROTHER-NATIONS ARRANGED
A RENDEZVOUS OVER THE ENEMY'S TOWN.
THIS HANDSHAKE WILL NOT BE HEALTHY FOR THE GERMANS

Artist: KUKRINIKSY.   Theme by I. LIVSHITZ.   Words by S. MARSHAK.

Meeting over Berlin, c. 1941/
USSR/Kukriniksi.

УБЕЙ ФАШИСТА-ИЗУВЕРА!

"Kill the fascist beast," 1942/
USSR/Viktor Deni.

"Remove your hat" says the fascist; "Off with your head"
is the partisan's response, 1941/USSR/Kukriniksi.

Pincers within pincers, c. 1942/
USSR/Kukriniksi.

WHAT IS AN "ARYAN"?
HE IS HANDSOME

AS GOEBBELS

REPRODUCED FROM SOVIET WAR POSTER 1941 · BY RUSSIAN WAR RELIEF INC.

Goebbels as Mickey Mouse, 1941/USSR/
Boris Efimov.

"The Big Three will tie the enemy in knots," 1942/
USSR/Kukriniksi.

Weapons for the front from the Soviet women,
1942/USSR/Alexei Kokorekin.

"May the example of our predecessors inspire you
in this war," 1942/USSR/Viktor Ivanov and O. Burova.

*More weapons and ammunition to defeat the
enemy, 1942/USSR/Viktor Ivanov.*

"The fascist pirate can't escape the Marine Guards," c. 1942/USSR/Vialov.

"Follow this worker's example. Produce more for the front,"
1942/USSR/Alexei Kokorekin.

ВИННИЦА

*Winniza, Jewish commisar, no date/German
poster for occupied USSR/Artist unknown.*

Poster proclaiming Russian atrocities, no date/
German poster for the Ukraine/Artist unknown.

Brat-Brata, no date/German poster for Eastern
Europe/Artist unknown.

"*Fight vigorously, sons of Suvorov and Chapayev,*
1941/USSR/Kukriniksi.

"*The strength of our weapons is hurled against*
the enemy," *1941/USSR/Mal'tsev.*

**Во имя Родины
Вперед Богатыри!**

For the Motherland's Sake, Go Forward, Heroes

"For the Motherland's sake, go forward, heroes,"
c. 1942/USSR/I. Toidze.

Mother's Farewell to a Soldier Son ("Be a Hero!"),
1941/USSR/Artist unknown.

Issued to honor Soviet war heroes and commemorate
the 25th anniversary of the Young Communist League,
1942-1944/USSR/Artist unknown.

Commemoratives of war medals. (Top) Patriotic War Order; Order of Prince Alexander Nevsky. (Bottom) Order of Field Marshall Suvorov; Order of Field Marshall Kutuzov, 1944/USSR/Artist unknown.

(Top) Issued to honor Soviet war heroes. (Bottom) Issued to commemorate the Day of the Nations United Against Germany, June 14, 1944/USSR/Artist unknown.

Donkeys and Goebbels make the same noises,
no date/USSR/Vladimir Lebedev.

*The East Front general seeks orders and Hitler
deliberates, 1944/USSR/Kukriniksi.*

"*Comrades! Your renewed efforts will help hoist
the victory flag over Berlin,*" 1944/USSR/Viktor Ivanov.

THE RISE AND FALL OF JAPAN
1931-1945

Let's refrain from all senseless
entertainments. Let's all do physical
exercises in the open air for at least
two hours a day. Let's all thank our
farmers at every meal, and see that
not a single grain is wasted.
JAPANESE WARTIME SLOGAN

At the beginning of this century Japan was regarded by the West with a kind of benevolent condescension. America's Commander Matthew Perry had brought to the Japanese in the mid-1850s the doubtful advantages of "Western civilization;" and another American naval officer, Lieutenant Pinkerton of Puccini's *Madama Butterfly*, had helped create in Western minds the image of "the land of the cherry blossom and the chrysanthemum." Of the other Western nations, Great Britain—impressed by Japan's conquering of the Russian colossus in 1904—had welcomed "the gallant little Jap" as an ally in World War I. Yet within a decade of the war's end this genial image had vanished almost without trace. "The gallant little Jap" had become in Western eyes "the Prussian of the East." How did it happen?

In 1900 when Japan was still emerging from her medieval cocoon she had, with her population of 50 million, offered a most profitable market for Western goods; one of the cheapest dumping grounds in the world for American and European manufacturers. But as soon as the last remnants of medievalism had been cast off, she became, within two decades, an industrial power in her own right. Thanks to a large and cheap labor force, she was soon usurping not only traditionally Western markets, but underselling the Western nations in their homelands.

During the depression of the early 1930s, the Americans and Europeans applied severe tariffs against Japanese products. Japan was therefore forced to look elsewhere for outlets. Her chief source of coal and iron was China; and it soon became clear that here, and in neighboring East Asia, she must secure the markets on which she could permanently rely. This was bound to bring her into conflict with the Western powers who had hitherto dominated the area politically and commercially. The favorable Western image of Japan began to change.

This process was accelerated by increased unpopularity in the West after Japan invaded China in September 1931, on the pretext that the Chinese had blown up a portion of the Japanese-owned Manchurian railway at Mukden. The destruction was, in fact, engineered by the Japanese army as an excuse to go to war. The invasion was greeted with almost universal hostility in America, which was beginning to regard Japan rather than any European power as her future potential enemy. Although Congress passed neutrality legislation and declared that the United States would remain aloof from the Sino-Japanese conflict, both American and British sympathies lay with China, whom these countries helped by building the Burma road for the supply of war material. On April 18, 1933, Japan warned that China was her preserve, and she showed her displeasure at Western criticism by leaving the League of Nations, and later the Naval Conference. It was clear that a confrontation of some kind with the West must sooner or later ensue.

China had to defend herself against a modern military power as best she could, on her own. Her propaganda in the rural areas, where illiteracy was general and where radio and press were almost unknown, relied almost entirely on the spoken, sung, or

(Top) The Kellogg-Briand Pact, signed by fifteen nations in August 1928, was an agreement to renounce war and to adhere to arbitration for settling international disputes. Japan broke the pact in 1932 when she occupied Manchuria. As this American cartoon from the early 1930s shows, the League of Nations was too weak to oppose her. (Bottom) A Chinese poster showing Japan as the greedy aggressor.

他的貪慾能滿足嗎

"YOU CAN'T APPEASE THAT APPETITE!" a copy of a Poster by Chang Ting. 8

Posters supporting the Chinese Nationalists. (Top, left) A poster for Chiang Kai-shek, one of the Big Four Allied leaders. (Top, right) A poster expressing British solidarity with the Chinese. (Bottom) A poster promoting the Chinese air force. (Opposite page) A Chinese woodcut poster. The text reads "National Unity! Defense in Depth to make China a fortress that will destroy the enemy."

acted word—for acting has always been much appreciated by the Chinese peasantry. The poster, too, was used by the Chiang Kai-shek government with great effect to mobilize the population for military service. Propaganda squads toured battle areas behind the troops, traveling in trucks with as many as fifty actors, musicians, or poster artists. In the event of a retreat, they plastered the walls with posters written in Japanese, pointing out that it was uncivilized of the Japanese to bomb fellow Asians, and that the Chinese were too civilized to undertake reprisals in kind. It was about all they could do, because the Chinese did not yet possess an air force capable of retaliation. Wherever printing and other methods of dissemination were not available, the *Pi Pao*, a hand-written wall newspaper, was employed. Consisting of brief articles, illustrations, poems, songs, and cartoons, it was pasted on the walls for the passer-by to see. It attacked the Japanese and celebrated events of national importance such as new treaties with the United States or Britain, or the suppression of the opium trade. In 1937 a "defense film organization" was created in British-occupied Hong Kong, consisting of several small companies making propaganda films cheaply and quickly in the Cantonese dialect.

The Japanese invaders, for their part, also used posters to convince the Chinese that the Europeans, in particular the Americans and the British, were their worst enemies. They dramatized all the evils of the opium trade, allegedly encouraged by these two Western powers for their own sordid commercial ends. Local actors were arrayed as caricatures of typical Westerners, with long wax noses and curly blond wigs.

Until the invasion of China, the Japanese had regarded propaganda with a certain disdain. They even refused to use the word, calling it "thought war." Tradition had taught them that they were a more "spiritual" people than the Westerners, that they lived in a divine land, and that their emperor was a direct descendant of the sun goddess. They had observed the uses to which propaganda had been put in World War I by the Europeans, and considered themselves above such deceits. As late as 1937, a Mr. S. Shiba summed it up in a letter to the *Japanese Times* in which he deplored Japan's inability to state her case to the world. "The Japanese," he wrote, "still think that thought war is incompatible with the true spirit of Japanese knighthood—that *bushido* and propaganda are poles apart."

But just as "Westernization" could not be avoided in industrial advance—otherwise the superior armaments of the West could not be matched—so Western psychological warfare had to be equaled as well. From the beginning of the Chinese campaign, the Japanese Foreign Office had been organizing unofficial propaganda in the form of tourist agencies, traveling lecturers, trade delegations and so on. A Bureau of Thought Supervision was founded by the Ministry of Education in 1932. The army and navy inaugurated their own press services. Attached to the prime minister's office was a Cabinet Information Bureau, whose function was to guide public opinion at home, and enlist sympathy for Japan abroad. The bureau had closely examined the

Japanese walls were plastered with posters to promote the war effort. (Top, left) A 1939 poster to encourage air travel. (Top, right) "People's Anti–Air Raid Exhibit." (Bottom) Tojo's face smiles from a wartime wall bulletin produced by the Matsushita Electric Company. (Opposite page) The ABC Weekly was an English-language propaganda sheet for the Co-Prosperity Sphere.

propaganda techniques of Britain and Germany in World War I, and now began imitating them. As the groupings of the "have" and "have not" nations in Europe began to form, Japan's natural allies became, inevitably, the self-proclaimed "have nots," the Fascist states. Taking a leaf from *Mein Kampf*, Japan proclaimed that she too was being starved of *Lebensraum*; that the Western imperialists were drowning her in her own home waters.

In many ways the Japanese leaders, although late starters, had an easier task in shaping public opinion than Goebbels had in Germany. The Prussian spirit of obedience, which Goebbels fostered so ardently, did not prevail throughout the Reich. But the Japanese were, in this spirit of obedience, all "Prussian." The average Japanese had been formed by centuries of strict conformity to a rigid code of values. Isolated from any non-Japanese habit of thought until the late 19th century, he had never known the democratic tradition, the liberal notions of participation in government, the rights of the individual, of free speech, and so on—of which the Germans, who had felt the Renaissance and had been through the Napoleonic wars, were at least aware. From early times, Japan had been governed by a small oligarchy imposing its will on a docile populace.

In 1924, the *Kokuhonsha* association was founded by Baron Miranuma, "to guide the people's ideologies and make known the *kokutai*"—which means roughly "the uniqueness of Japan in being governed by a ruler having spiritual origins." By the 1930s, it had become the most important association in Japan; and a text on *kokutai* was distributed by the Ministry of Education to all schools and universities. Much was also made of *Hakko Ichiu*, another patriotic catchword resurrected from the past. According to Japanese tradition, it was used by the first human emperor of Japan, Jimmu, to describe Japan's divine mission. The phrase, which means "to bring the eight corners of the earth under the same roof," gave a religious flavor to what was to be a blatantly expansionist policy. The whole world would become a happy family with Japan as paterfamilias guiding all the nations. In Japan, statecraft and practical politics had always been interwoven with religion. The intricate political game was played behind a religious screen.

By the mid-1930s the government of Japan, following this trend, had become an appendage of the armed forces. The generals had acquired both legislative and executive power, and formed an independent body answerable only to the throne. Henceforth, the Diet (Japan's parliament) played the same role as did Hitler's Reichstag, rubber-stamping government decrees. The miltary not only carried out policy, they formulated it. In 1935 General Sadao Araki became minister of education, a post later assumed, when war broke out, by the prime minister, General Tojo. In the military indoctrination of youth, the Japanese generals showed that they had little to learn from Hitler and Mussolini. Military penetration soon transformed the educational system into a reliable weapon in the new thought war. Children were taught that soldiers killed in battle waited on the gods at the Japanese Valhalla, Yasukundi, and that the war with

[The　A B C　Weekly]　大正四年二月八日着三種郵便物認可　第六十六巻第九號毎週一回月曜發行　定價二錢

THE ABC WEEKLY

Vol. 66　No. 9　Tokyo, Mon., March 4, 1940　(Edited by N. Imai)　Price 2 *sen*

ARCH 10 is the Army Day. The War Ministry has **issued** many **posters like the one** shown here.

It has also published 120,000 pamphlets to **remind** the people **of** the day.

*　　*　　*

A future **grand champion** sumo **wrestler** is in Fukuoka Prefecture.

He is K. Minematsu **by name.**

Though only 16-years old, he is already five feet, eight inches tall.

He **weighs** 150 pounds.

March 10=the 10th of March (三月十日). **the Army Day** (陸軍紀念日). **the War Ministry** [mínistri] (陸軍省).

cf. {**the War Minister** (陸軍大臣).

has issued [iʃuːd] (發行した). **póster** (ポスター、ビラ). **like the one shown here** (こゝに示したものゝ様な).

cf. {I want to have **one** like that.
(それのやうなのが欲しい).
It's not the **one** I lost.
(それは僕のなくしたのではない).

álso (亦). **has públished** (刊行した). **pamphlet** [pǽmflit] (パンフレット、小册子). **to remind the people of the day** (國民に當時を想起せしめるために).

cf. {The picture **reminds** me **of** my childhood.
(その寫眞を見ると私の子供時代を想ひ出します).
I beg to **remind** you **of** your promise.
(約束を御忘れない様に).

*　　*　　*

ɒ **fúture gránd chámpion** [tʃǽmpiən] (未来の横綱、横綱の卵子). **súmo wréstler** [réslə] (相撲、力士). **Prefecture** [piːféktʃə] (縣). **by name** (名は).

cf. {Do you know all the students **by name**?
(生徒の名を皆知つて居るか).
No, but I know every one of them **by sight**.
(否、しかし顔は皆知つて居る).

Though only...... (まだ......だけれども). **already** (子でに). **is......tall** (身長が......だけある). **weigh** [wei] (體重がある). **pound** (封度).

〈▷ 本文應用練習課題 ◁〉

❶ このポスターや小册子は戰地 (the front) へ送られます.
❷ 僕も君の持つてるやうなのを買ひ度い.
❸ 陸軍省は上記の命令 (order) を發した.
❹ 彼の顔を見たら先日の約束を想ひ出した.
❺ Answer :—
1. How tall do you stand?
2. How much do you weigh?

(Top) A leaflet proclaiming Asian solidarity against the Anglo-Americans. Japan saw her destiny as the leader of a resurgent Asia. Though "Asia for the Asians" was an omnipresent propaganda slogan, the Japanese occupation of other Asian countries was often harsh and oppressive. (Bottom) Japanese leaflet which falsely declared that the United States was prepared to negotiate peace with Japan in 1942.

ONE BILLION ASIANS AGAINST ANGLO-AMERICANS

EXTRA

The Yankees Tender The Olive Branch Singapore Neutral Zone?

Lisbon 14th.

News has been received here that America has proposed her separate peace negotiation to Nippon. The proposal was made on 14th January 1942.

President Roosevelt is of the view that Singapore ought to be declared a Neutral Zone.

The Nippon is considering this Peace Proposal.

China was just, and had the support of the gods. In every school, the morning's work began with a procession to the courtyard, where the Japanese flag was run up and the national anthem played. Every family was urged to start the day at the same hour with radio calisthenics. Army officers were attached to all higher education establishments, to give military training. Unauthorized absence by students from any training session was punishable, and three such absences could result in expulsion. The officers would walk into the lecture rooms unannounced and, if they felt so inclined, criticize the lecturer in front of the students. In the Jesuit university of Jochi, the teaching fathers were made to undergo military training alongside the students. Scholarships were granted not for intellectual achievement or hard work, but on how well the student satisfied the Japanese military ideal. History books were revised, until history teaching was transformed into a course of ethics and morals. Books on the divinity of the emperor and the duty of the citizen to place everything, including life, on the imperial altar, became compulsory reading in all high schools and colleges. Until 1939, university officials were still appointed by the respective faculties; after that date, by General Araki. When World War II broke out, special emphasis in all educational establishments was laid on "navigation, aviation, horsemanship, and mechanics."

The Japanese militarists had also learned from the Nazis that broadcasting can play an important part in the indoctrination of the young. Unlike the textbook, the radio responds immediately to daily events. In 1935, school broadcasting was established on a nationwide basis. A radio "Morning Address" to schools was given twice a month, in which contemporary events were authoritatively discussed. Typical titles of these talks were: "The Spirit of Loyalty, Filial Piety, Devotion, and Obedience"; "One Strength—the Japanese"; and "Why Our Military Forces Are Strong."

Of the written word—books and the press—control had already been taken in the early 1930s by the Board of Information. Writers were urged to join national service groups, which gave instruction on what themes to choose. The number of newspapers was reduced, allegedly because of paper shortage. The real reason was that press power was to be concentrated in the hands of the progovernment newspaper magnates. The 1,200 newspapers circulating in 1936 had, by 1940, been reduced to 900. Just before the outbreak of war in 1941, all newspapers were converted into "public utilities."

Japanese newspaper correspondents abroad were rigorously controled. They had to submit their dispatches through the local Japanese embassies, legations, and consulates, which eliminated any material considered unsuitable. On arrival in Tokyo, these dispatches underwent a further pruning by the military censor. By the time they reached the editor's desk, they were seldom more illuminating than the releases of the government press agency, Domei. This body, which was founded in 1936, had a near monopoly of foreign news; no paper could exist without its services (c.f. D.N.B. in Nazi Germany, and Stefani in Fascist Italy). Domei issued directives about what newspapers could print, what material they should emphasize, and what attenuate. Before the advent of Domei, two press agencies had existed in Japan, one Nippon Dempo in private hands, and another semi-official. Both were fused in Domei.

In wartime, all these forms of governmental control were greatly extended. In 1942, the National and Patriotic Association of Publicists was founded, with thousands of "writers, speakers, novelists, historians, and philosophers." When the war began to go badly for Japan, they were charged with a series of lectures throughout the country "to educate the people on the danger of defeatist thoughts." "Literary patriotic rallies" were organized to study a series of books dealing with "the extermination of the British and Americans." To purge the nation entirely of the debilitating influence of American jazz, the All Japanese Songsters' Association was founded, and such harmless tunes as "Dinah," and even "Auld Lang Syne," were forbidden. Huge meetings were held all over the country entitled "To crush America and Britain." After the radio and press, these monster rallies on Nazi lines proved to be one of the government's most effective propaganda weapons.

Also modeled on the Nazi example were various patriotic weeks, organized at regular intervals, to remind the Japanese people of their civic duties. "The Week for Good Commercial Morals and Shady Transactions Prevention" suggested that the black market was active; the "Week against Rudeness and Bad Manners," that war weariness had set in. There was also a regular "Anti-Espionage Week." Japan had always been extremely spy-conscious, and much domestic propaganda warned against disclosure of information to strangers. Posters were widely distributed to portray the famous monkey trio—Hear no Evil, See no Evil, Speak no Evil.

Propaganda against the Americans and British had of course started much earlier, in the late 1930s. The term "dangerous thoughts" was then coined for all notions of Western civilization which conflicted in any way with Japanese social institutions. The Anglo-Saxon nations were depicted in Nazi terms as a plutocracy run by Jews, a soulless, godless civilization whose only idols were "materialism, utilitarianism, and individualism" —in contrast to the Japanese "spiritual" values. Sometimes they were referred to as the "redheaded barbarians from the West." American civilization was shown as at once barbaric and decadent; statistics about racial oppression and the lynching of blacks in the United States were given great prominence. Hollywood's conventional portraits of gangsterism and crime were quoted as typical of everyday life in America. The British came in for much the same abuse in short-wave broadcasts to the peoples of southeast Asia. They were portrayed as tyrannizing the natives in Malaysia, Burma, India, and Hong Kong, who were urged to rise and throw off the British yoke under which they labored and suffered.

In contrast to this anti-Anglo-Saxon propaganda was the cam-

(Top) A Japanese anti-American leaflet for China. The text reads "American victory means enslavement and Chinese victory, peace and prosperity." (Bottom) A scowling Chiang Kai-shek watches smiling Chinese stream toward the fortress of the Japanese puppet government at Nanking. This leaflet promised starvation and death under Chiang's Chungking regime.

(Top) Five Scouts (1939), the first important Japanese war film, told the story of a group of Japanese soldiers caught in the middle of hostilities in northern China. (Bottom) Mud and Soldiers (1939) was another realistic wartime film. (Opposite page, top) A scene from The Flowering Port. (Opposite page, bottom) The Story of Tank Commander Nishizumi (1940) reflected prewar humanist ideals.

paign to glorify the Fascist powers, whose methods the Japanese militarists admired. After the signature of the anti-Comintern Pact with Germany, cultural exchanges on a wide scale between the two countries began. In December 1941, a German-Japanese cultural agreement was signed, and the *Reichsrundfunk* programs were broadcast to Japan by relay—and vice-versa for Japanese programs to Germany. These cultural exchanges did not always have the happiest results, particularly regarding the cinema. The Japanese realized, as did the Nazis, that for influencing the illiterate masses there was no better medium. The cinema enthusiast Goebbels persuaded the Japanese to collaborate in a joint celluloid venture to enshrine the unity of the Nazi group spirit with the racial spirit of the Japanese—to the detriment of the feeble and decadent spirit of the democracies. It was to be called *The New Earth*, and would be codirected by the German Arnold Fanck (Leni Riefenstahl's mentor) and Mansaka Itami, one of Japan's leading cineasts. Fanck wrote the script, which was about a renegade Japanese hero's conversion from democracy back to the faith of his fathers and the Japanese family creed. But Fanck did not—at least according to his colleague, Itami—understand the Japanese mentality sufficiently, and the script was so full of psychological errors that Itami insisted on reediting it. This infuriated the great Fanck, with the result that two versions of the film were produced: one for German, the other for Japanese consumption. Although *The New Earth* was a complete failure, Goebbels insisted on another joint production, *The Oath of the People*. This was an even bigger fiasco. After these two expensive attempts at collaboration, the Japanese turned to Asiatic partners for any joint film productions.

On the whole, the Japanese were good film makers; they had even in one short decade established a tradition of humanist films, such as *Five Scouts*. This was about the war in China, surprisingly free of Japanese nationalism and depicting in a completely objective manner the grim destiny of the soldier. But with the greater war approaching, their cineasts had to conform to a stringent code of instructions laid down by the Home Ministry. It prescribed "healthy entertainment value, with themes showing persons ready to serve patriotically." Subject matter included Japanese industrial and food production, and life in farming communities. After Pearl Harbor, the Japanese government encouraged warlike themes—known euphemistically as "national polity themes." The military leaders were very much impressed by the Nazi war films *Baptism of Fire* and *Victory in the West*. Japanese film makers were instructed to emphasize the spirit of complete sacrifice to the nation and the need to follow prescribed behavior regardless of difficulties. Individual success, love, or amusement were not to be emphasized. "Slice-of-life" films dealing with individual happiness, the life of the rich and idle, women smoking or drinking in cafes, and scenes of sexual frivolity were prohibited. One day of each month was set aside as free admission day to the cinemas for families with members doing their military service. On this

day in every cinema and theater, one minute of meditation was required at midday to pray for those relations.

Apart from a spate of films about war heroics, with obvious titles such as *Torpedo Squadrons Move Out*, about three young officers sinking an American battleship (a film aimed at submarine recruitment), or *Falcon Fighters*, or *Volunteers of Death* about Pearl Harbor, there were one or two which were more subtle. *A Record of Love* aimed at inducing spinsters to marry disabled soldiers; it told of a woman who falls in love with a permanently disabled war hero, whom she marries and supports all her life by her own work. But there were few of these films. Most of them had the usual wartime propaganda themes; actresses being heroines in steel foundries or, as in *Most Beautifully*, a girl working in a military optical factory; or work in an aerial-torpedo factory, depicting the "life" of the torpedo from its manufacture to its final disintegration under an American hull.

Then there were the usual themes about espionage, such as *Fifth Column Fear* and *Miracle Worker*, to make the public suspicious of foreigners because "they wander about with their true intentions unknown as tourists, technicians, businessmen, students, and missionaries." The title of *The Last Days of the British Empire* is self-explanatory. A more unusual anti-British film, *International Smuggling Game*, depicted the British Consular Service running an opium smuggling ring, with which the British consul, Mr. Perkins, weaves a Machiavellian scheme for subduing Japan as the British had subdued China. *The Opium War* was also about the British stupefying the Chinese with vast quantities of the drug. *You're Being Aimed At* was about American agents trying to spread bacteriological disease throughout Japan. No doubt all this reinforced patriotic ideals and maintained the image of the Allies as nefarious villains. In this way the Japanese cinema fulfilled its wartime role.

The superiority of the Japanese over the Anglo-Saxons seemed confirmed, at least militarily, between December 1941 and June 1942. In those six months, the Japanese chased the Europeans to the limits of Eastern Asia, and overran a tenth of the surface of the globe, an area which included all French Indo-China, Thailand, Burma, the Philippines, the East Indies, and large tracts of China. To the peoples of this huge area, the "spiritual" nature of the hard Japanese rule was stressed. "This war differs from all others," wrote the Japanese-controled *Shanghai Times*, "in that it is a war of construction, not destruction. It is a 100 percent unselfish crusade undertaken by Japan in the interests of all the East Asian nations."

The new Japanese empire was disguised under the attractive name of "The Greater East Asia Co-Prosperity Sphere," in which everyone would work for the common goal of "Asia for the Asians." This latter was an excellent slogan, most fair sounding, much more precise than Hitler's "New Order." It was nothing less than the Asian version of the Monroe doctrine—just as the Co-Prosperity Sphere was the Japanese equivalent of

(Below) This Japanese leaflet shows the Philippines being rescued from the shoals of American imperialism and racial prejudice by the solidarity of her fellow Asians under Japan's leadership. The Japanese used such phrases as "the spiritual renovation of the Philippine people" while they marched thousands of Philippine soldiers to their death at Bataan. In 1938 Prince Konoe had proclaimed Japan's intention to establish a "New Order" which would insure the permanent stability of East Asia. After 1941, this doctrine was widely broadcast in Asia with the emphasis on Japan as the liberator. Though the Japanese granted the Philippines "independence" under quisling Jorge Vargas, it was for tactical reasons only.

the Allies' "Atlantic Charter." The word *kodo* was also used as the Japanese version of "the white man's burden."

That the average Japanese at home saw only idealism in the Co-Prosperity Sphere was indicated by the prize-winning titles in a competition for slogans run in early 1942 by the *Japan Times*:

1. Japanese action spells Construction
   Enemy action spells Destruction
2. With Firmness we fight
   With Kindness we build
3. Fight on until Asia is Asia's own
4. In the Freedom of the East
   Lies the Peace of the West

In an eruption of euphoria, every public meeting in Japan concluded with the singing of the *"Kimigayo,"* the national anthem, and a recital of the imperial declaration of war.

Now that the British and American imperialists had been expelled, all varieties of Asian culture, oppressed for so long, would blossom. Such phrases as "the spiritual renovation of the Philippine people" were coined. The Philippines would henceforth be able to live "in strict observance of the traditional Oriental principles." An independent Philippine government under the quisling Jorge Vargas was installed.

During the short period of fighting in the Philippines, leaflets were dropped by air to persuade the natives that the Japanese came as friends, not enemies:

Don't Obey the Americans!
Japanese forces are friends, not enemies of the Filipinos. Don't obey America's orders, which may change your city into a battlefield. Never obey them. Keep all things as they are, don't destroy anything that belongs to the Filipinos, and we shall protect you and your city.

Another said:

Save the beautiful Philippines from war's havoc! Give up at once, lay aside your arms. Don't shed your blood for America. Return, return to your own sweet homes!

To reasure the strong Catholic element in the Philippines, a leaflet was dropped which cited the support of Pope Pius XII for the Imperial Japanese Army's campaign to foster freedom of religious worship, and it promised the army's protection of the Christian churches.

During the Japanese advance through Malaya in 1942, a variety of propaganda leaflets was disseminated. One of these addressed to enemy soldiers gave instructions on how to desert: "After fixing a white cloth to your left arm, climb down to this side under cover of darkness and meet your Japanese soldier brothers. All of them are looking toward and for you."

A crude sketch on one leaflet showed British soldiers carrying off native women by force. Another showed the British carousing while the Indonesians fought. A leaflet signed by the commander of the Japanese fleet began with the biblical quotation, "Now is the time of war. Verily, this is the day of your deliverance." It assured all educated Indonesians of religious freedom and "great power."

(Below) A leaflet exhorting solidarity between Japan and the Philippines. Japanese propagandists wrote books and magazines for schoolchildren in the Co-Prosperity Sphere. For the lower grades, they produced Frontline Diary *and* The Co-Prosperity Sphere Children's Stories: *for the upper grades,* Military Talks *and* Wartime Geography. *The Japanese language was used in official documents and taught in all the schools. To reach the illiterate, Japanese propaganda was delivered by film and radio in local dialects. People in the occupied territories had to honor the emperor and celebrate Japanese festivals. For the organized reception of propaganda, Neighborhood Associations and East Asia Youth Leagues were formed.*

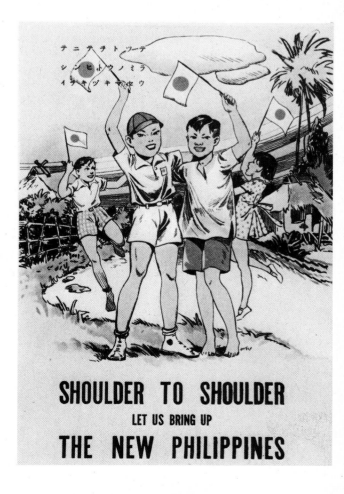

SHOULDER TO SHOULDER
LET US BRING UP
THE NEW PHILIPPINES

(Below and opposite page) Iva Ikuko Toguri, known to thousands of GIs in the Pacific as Tokyo Rose, was a Japanese-American with a degree in zoology from UCLA. She had visited Japan after graduation and war broke out before she could return home. She agreed to make daily broadcasts to American soldiers in the Pacific, combining popular music with a soothing patter intended to make them homesick. After the war she was convicted as a traitor, imprisoned and fined. Tokyo Rose was not the only American to broadcast to her country-men for the enemy. The soft voice of Axis Sally, broadcasting from Berlin, was heard on European battlefronts by American troops. Like Tokyo Rose, Axis Sally was also found guilty as a traitor when the war ended.

In all these occupied countries, the Japanese immediately founded mutual cultural societies in the capital cities to ingratiate the natives, the principal aim being to foster the use of the Japanese language throughout the East, replacing English as the lingua franca. In Indonesia they also founded a more ambiguous organization, "The Virgin's Association." Its aim was "to rally all Indonesian girls to cooperate with the Japanese Army."

The vast territories which the Japanese had annexed so rapidly presented them with a number of problems similar to, but more complicated than, those which confronted the victorious Hitler in 1941. He too had bitten off more than he could immediately digest. But, as a comparison of the European and Asian maps reveals, he at least was working on interior lines, in hundreds rather than thousands of miles, and on land. The neo-Japanese empire, thousands of miles square, embraced an area which was mostly water, studded with innumerable isles of all sizes. Controling this maritime expanse politically proved to be an engineering problem, to which short-wave radio alone provided a solution.

The Japanese had had some experience with the propaganda uses of short-wave broadcasting and, lest their own people should be tainted with it from abroad, had in 1932 banned the ownership of short-wave receivers throughout Japan. Therefore the first task of the Japanese invading forces was to install a short-wave broadcasting system embracing the entire Co-Prosperity Sphere, with powerful transmitters in Batavia (Jakarta), Singapore, and Saigon. From here, night and day for the next four years, an uninterrupted flow of propaganda about Japan's plans for Asian welfare, together with denigration of the "Anglo-Saxon tyrants," poured forth.

The next immediate goal was Australasia, which was subjected throughout 1942 to this intense radio war. In attacking the "White Australian" policy which had for over a hundred years kept Australia a preserve for Europeans, the Japanese had the right approach. There were only 7 million people, nearly all of European descent, in Australia, a continent which at a conservative estimate could nourish at least 100 million. Why should the tropical northern and desert areas be kept empty, the Japanese asked, simply because no European could live in such a climate? The more industrious and frugally living Asiatics could irrigate these areas and turn them into a cornucopia. If they were prepared to come and make the Australian deserts bloom like roses, why should they be denied? Why should the Anglo-Saxons keep this vast continent entirely to themselves, in complete disregard of other people and the well-being of their neighbors?

This all went down very well in the early days when Japanese arms were everywhere triumphant. Modeling themselves on Germany, the Japanese established communal listening to this propaganda for their new subjects. Loudspeakers were hung at street corners all over the occupied territories. Known euphemistically as "singing trees" and "singing towers," they were also introduced into elementary schools throughout the

(Below) *As the war progressed, the Americans dropped numerous leaflets such as this on the Japanese. The leaflets, produced by the Office of War Information, were the most effective means of propaganda in the Far East. At first they were dropped by plane on combat troops in the South Sea battle areas; but in late 1944 and until the end of the war, the home front was showered with a barrage of messages. As American bombers moved closer to Japan, the leaflet campaign was stepped up. The leaflets showed the falsehood of the Japanese government's domestic propaganda and prepared the people for surrender. In the spring and summer of 1945 leaflets fluttered down daily on Japanese cities, announcing warnings of impending bombing raids.*

Co-Prosperity Sphere.

Particular importance was attached to India, now on the frontier of the new empire, and through which the Japanese hoped soon to pass on their way to shake hands with Hitler in Persia or Afghanistan. India was regarded as potentially part of Japan's Greater East Asian Co-Prosperity Sphere. A "Free India" radio station was installed in Saigon, which encouraged the natives of the subcontinent to rise against their aggressors while the British were weak and fully occupied elsewhere. "Indian Independence" transmitters were also set up in Bangkok and Singapore, as was an "Indian Muslim Station." The Japanese formed the "Indian National Army," with Subhas Chandra Bose as its leader. Numerous leaflets were dropped on British Indian Army troops calling on them to join the Japanese and help liberate their mother country. One gaudy leaflet showed two Indians chasing a caricature of a British soldier surrounded by his shattered equipment and tattered flag. Another anti-British leaflet declared that the Japanese army had "exterminated the diabolical British power from all parts of East Asia," and it was now time to free India for the Indians.

All this was for the benefit of the Asiatics. For the Americans, and their Australian and New Zealand allies, the leaflets and radio transmissions took another form, aimed primarily at dividing them from one another. The Americans were accused of intending to make Australia into the 49th state of the union. Pornographic leaflets were distributed to Australian troops showing Australian girls in the sexual embraces of drunken G.I.s or Tommies while their boy friends were hacking their way through the jungles of Borneo. The Australians and New Zealanders were told that the British had always made them fight Britain's battles. Their soldiers were now fighting far from home on the shores of North Africa, while the bulk of the British army was safe in its island home.

For the remaining American forces in the Pacific who had been thrown back so brusquely after Pearl Harbor, the Japanese engaged the services of a half-Japanese woman, Iva Ikuko Toguri, who had lived all her life in America, where she had obtained a degree in geology from UCLA. Affectionately known to the G.I.s as "Tokyo Rose," she used to deliver 15-minute broadcasts daily, of a sentimental nature, appealing to their natural disposition to become homesick, and describing the native land some of them would never see again. She offered excellent swing music together with husky-voiced sex talk. (After the war she was tried by the Americans and sentenced to ten years in prison and a $10,000 fine.)

Another propaganda device used on short-wave radio was the prisoner-of-war broadcast. Allied prisoners were brought before the microphone, through which they sent messages to their families at home. Statements with their names and addresses were read over the air, and the eager listeners in America and Australia were assured that their men folk were alive and well. Some of the POWs described how well they were treated, the amenities in the camps, the fresh fruit and vegetables, tobacco, sugar . . . one camp had its own bakery. The messages were ingeniously sandwiched between news items of indeterminate length, so that the relatives had to listen to the whole program in the hope of hearing the prisoner's voice.

Technically efficient as was the vast radio network, it suffered from the broadcaster's faulty pronunciation and knowledge of foreign languages. The Japanese in wartime evidently had difficulty finding good translators. Such phrases as, "With the exception of one Japanese soldier dead, all the rest were in the best of spirits," or "The remaining British planes took to their heels," or "Japanese men look furious, but they are sweet inside," made the listener smile rather than tremble. Another curious statement from Batavia in March 1943 announced that "Britain is worried by the scarcity of silk. The British government therefore contemplates taming all the silkworms of Liberia . . . . but first they must be domesticated."

A more serious Japanese shortcoming at the beginning of the war was their faulty assessment of the American character and institutions. Knowing that the American people preferred peace to war, commerce to fighting, the Japanese assumed that they were all hostile to their leaders, Roosevelt and his government, who had prepared them for war. They underestimated the effect of the Pearl Harbor attack, which they seriously believed the American people would regard as a defensive act forced on Japan by "Roosevelt and his clique." In fact, that single action at Pearl Harbor on December 7, 1941, provided the Allies with a propaganda weapon which all the skill of the Japanese propagandists could not counter—"the stab in the back." The Japanese were also unwise enough to suppose that because a large section of Congress and the Republican Party hated Roosevelt's domestic policy, they hated his foreign policy too. In other broadcasts to America they boasted that Japan's spiritual strength rendered her soldiers capable of superhuman feats, while the American high standard of living produced physical and moral weakness. This, they contended, was confirmed by the American retreats in the first six months of the Pacific war. It would be better therefore to make peace and recognize the Greater East Asia Co-Prosperity Sphere.

Another hindrance to effective propaganda was the Japanese censorship system, by which in wartime the military high command monopolized the news. The Board of Information was made subject to direct control by the army and navy. At one stage military censorship was actually imposed on news obtained from the Foreign Office from its own sources. The Domei press agency was continually being ordered by the military authorities to emit a greater flow of stories and photographs to uplift morale —a demand which was made irrespective of the war situation or the amount of news available. The army and navy did not improve matters by being at loggerheads and maintaining separate organizations for their respective propaganda. When the army announced a victory, the navy felt it must do so too. So suspicious was the army of the navy that it had its own shipyards, cargo ships, and even cargo submarines; while the navy,

(Below) In early 1945, Tokyo newspapers were claiming military victories while the Japanese defense of the Pacific was cracking. The Allied blockade had cut Japan's supplies of raw materials and the American air force had stepped up its bombing raids. General MacArthur had pushed ahead in the Philippines and the British were driving the Japanese out of Burma. Propagandists in Tokyo had promulgated the Great East Asia Co-Prosperity Sphere as a harmonious league of Asian nations led by Japan. Americans rephrased the slogan "Asia for the Asians" as "Asia for the Japanese." Late in the war, American cartoons mirrored confidence in the collapse of Japan's empire.

(Top) As the Allies piled up victories in the Pacific, American cartoonists indulged in a bit of muscle-flexing. Such cartoons bolstered the public's confidence that America would win the Pacific war. (Bottom) Japanese home propaganda was based on false reports of military successes even as Japan's hegemony in the Pacific was crumbling.

MASTERLY UNDERSTATEMENT.

not to be outdone, had its own motor corps for land transport. The two services even maintained separate weather stations. After Guadalcanal, they argued fiercely as to whether Australia should be attacked directly from the sea (the navy argument), or over land through New Guinea (the army argument). The result was that the great Australian continent, where invasion might have succeeded in 1942, was never attacked at all.

Nevertheless, as long as Japan was winning, these weaknesses could be overcome. During the first six months, she had nothing but victories to show. Although the high command exaggerated their scope, it was telling the broad truth; Japanese propaganda was effective both at home and abroad, in raising morale and creating confidence in the government's ability to win the war. After each new victory, the "singing trees" at a thousand locations throughout the Co-Prosperity Sphere blared out the "*Kaigum,*" the navy march.

The turning point came in May 1942, when the run of victories was halted at the battle of the Coral Sea off the north Australian coast. Here, the advancing Japanese were surprised to find a much revived American navy, which harried them north, inflicting more losses than it sustained. This was followed a month later by the more decisive battle of Midway, in which the Americans sank four Japanese aircraft carriers—hitherto the principal instrument of Japan's expansion. Seven months later, when the American marines ejected the Japanese forces from Guadalcanal in the Solomons, Japan had reached the limit of her conquests. Thereafter, it was to be a slow but steady Japanese retreat westwards and northwards for three years, across the great watery spaces she had so precipitately invested.

In spite of these portentous events, the Japanese high command refused to entertain even the suspicion of a defeat. The prime minister himself, General Tojo, announced to the Diet on May 27, 1942, that in the Coral Sea engagement, the Japanese navy had completely annihilated the American Pacific fleet. Yet only a month later at Midway that same fleet sank four Japanese aircraft carriers and a number of ancillary craft. The Japanese aircraft carriers' dominion of the Pacific was over, but their leaders refused to admit it, even to themselves. On the obduracy of these men, a significant comment is made by Rear Admiral Matsushima in his book *The False Song of Victory*, published after the war. He reports that when news of the Midway battle was coming in, he was present in Tokyo at a naval press-briefing conference. The sinking of four Japanese aircraft carriers made a terrible impression. He notes the chief of the press section saying, "The most important thing is to keep it quiet. If ever a part of the truth becomes known, it will be difficult to control the situation." Matsushima adds, "No one spoke. These people were not trained to defeat. Everyone sat silent with arms folded. Thus, the naval press section fooled a nation."

If these setbacks could be concealed from the Japanese people, the daring and spectacular air raid by General Doolittle and his B-25s on Tokyo on April 18, 1942, could not be. It gave a galvanizing shock to the Japanese, who had been brought up for centuries to believe that their homeland was inviolable. The newspapers naturally belittled it, presenting Doolittle and his men as "demons who carry out indiscriminate bombing attacks on innocent civilians and noncombatants." As a proof of Tokyo's excellent air-defense system, a wing and an undercarriage of a shot-down B-25 were put on show. Six months later, three of the captured Doolittle airmen were executed. This was a foolish and hypocritical act by the authors of the Pearl Harbor attack, for it stimulated violent feelings of revenge in the Americans. It was now that the image of "the Japanese ape," in film and cartoon, became popular in the United States.

After the Coral Sea and Midway battles, the Americans undertook the arduous and bloody road of "island hopping" up the reaches of the western Pacific, gradually forcing the Japanese garrisons out of the Solomons, the Martials, the Carolines, until in mid-1944 they reached the Marianas, where the great strategic prize of Saipan awaited them. On the edge of the Asiatic continental shelf, Saipan was little more than 1,500 miles from Tokyo. From there, American heavy bombers would at last have a first-class land base from which to bomb the Japanese homeland (Doolittle's raid had been carried out from aircraft carriers). After another big battle of aircraft carriers off the Marianas, the Americans successfully stormed the heavily defended island. The propaganda value of the Saipan victory was immense. Not only had the Japanese people been led to believe that Saipan was impregnable, but from here the Americans could broadcast to Japan on the medium-wave band, which the Japanese were equipped to receive. Until now, owing to the vast distances, only short-wave broadcasting of American propaganda had been possible; but it had proved of little value, because all short-wave sets had been confiscated by the police. The fall of Saipan was such a blow to Japan that it led to the resignation of General Tojo's government. As Japan now lost one strategic foothold after another in the Pacific, the militarists were forced to reverse their previous claims that these places were of great strategic importance. They now said they were valueless to the Americans. This was bad propaganda, both for home consumption and the occupied territories.

Perhaps the greatest American propaganda triumph in the Pacific war was the dropping of leaflets from the air. The first of these landed on Japanese troops during the South Seas battles of 1942. In those days the Japanese high command regarded them without undue apprehension, particularly as they suffered from an early defect of all American propaganda to Japan; they were badly translated, into a Japanese which a Japanese literary man called "as archaic as Chaucer." Their illustrations, too, were unlikely to impress the Japanese soldiery. One showed a Japanese at his meal with his chopsticks placed on either side of the plate, like the Western knife and fork; whereas the Japanese lay them parallel at the base of the plate. Some pictures showed the kimono with the left side covering the right; the Japanese wear it right over left. These are small points, but they modified any credibility in the propaganda. The same could be said of the

(Top) A cartoon by Cargill from the Flint (Michigan) Journal. *In early 1944, Japan still hoped to maintain control of her empire, but the massive loss of air power was a sign that it was beginning to decline. (Bottom) Propaganda for Asian villagers was crude and simple. This sign promised that the Allies would liberate Asians from the Japanese invaders.*

(Below and opposite page) The American bombing raid on Tokyo led by Lieutenant Colonel James Doolittle on April 18, 1942, came as a psychological shock to the Japanese, who were brought up to believe that their homeland was impenetrable. The newspapers pictured Doolittle's men as demons who "carried out an inhuman, insatiable, indiscriminate bombing attack on the sly." As retaliation, the captured flyers were executed. Americans felt that the executions had violated the rules of warfare. President Roosevelt referred to the "barbarous execution by the Japanese government." Cartoons by Edwin Marcus and Sy Moyer portrayed the enemy as a barbarian, a familiar propaganda device used by all belligerents.

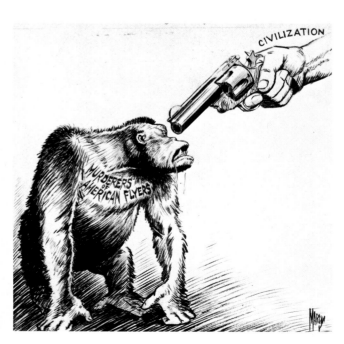

early broadcast propaganda, in which the American accent of the announcer or commentator was unmistakable. Like the British at the beginning of the war, the American propagandists had a lot to learn.

As they moved closer to the Japanese archipelago, these misunderstandings of custom and language were gradually eliminated; and the leaflets, particularly those announcing the list of places to be bombed, and which rained down in millions on the principal cities, were eagerly read by the civilian population. The Japanese were strictly forbidden to possess any of these leaflets, and were instructed, when they found them, to hand them over to the police. But when the "advance notice" of the bombing began, few people obeyed. Families read them aloud at night by concealed candlelight.

As the Americans advanced inexorably northwards, the Japanese propagandists seem to have lost their heads. They began inventing a series of nonexistent battles, as at Bougainville, in which the Americans were said to have suffered a devastating defeat. In 1942, when General MacArthur was ejecting the Japanese from Guadalcanal, they described him as "now a nervous wreck in Canberra." When in October 1943 an American task force attacked Formosa, the Japanese radio reported that seven American aircraft carriers had been sunk. In fact, two American cruisers had been damaged. As island after island was wrested from them, the militarists furnished lies, half-truths, and the suppression of truth, to such an extent that almost no announcement could be acepted at its face value. In his book *The Lost War,* the Japanese writer Masuo Kato says, "Japan was hopelessly beaten in psychological warfare, not because of any particular adroitness on the part of the Allies, but because the Allies based their propaganda on truth—whereas Japan was unwilling to deal in truth, almost from the outset."

In the last stages of the war, the Japanese propagandists fell back on "atrocity stories" in the Northcliffe manner, to whip up patriotic fervor. They said that if the Americans won, they would exterminate the entire male population of Japan and carry off all the women as paramours. All that was left for any self-respecting Japanese to do was to die for his country. After the bloody Okinawa fighting, many people in Tokyo firmly believed that every female there had been raped by at least one G. I.

A last piece of propaganda which was more effective was the public exhibition in the center of Tokyo of a B-29 bomber, which had been brought down over the city. Beside the great airplane was placed the little Japanese fighter which had shot it out of the sky. This showed how vulnerable was "America's brute force" to an individual fact of courage. The pilot of the fighter described to the press how, when he had climbed above the American giant, he had pumped his machine-gun bullets into it. He felt very small, he said, "like a peanut on a platter." Thousands flocked to admire his feat. Finally the kamikaze or suicide planes were introduced to whip up public morale and induce a spirit of imitation. Loaded with bombs and torpedoes,

(Top) A Japanese suicide plane starts its dive toward a U.S. warship in the Western Pacific. Kamikaze pilots were told that the salvation of Japan depended on them and that it was an honor to die for the Emperor. (Bottom) A painting which idealized the young Japanese air cadets who were ready to rush forth and defend the homeland.

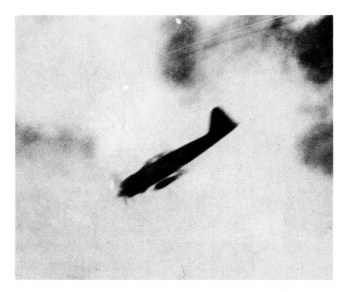

their pilots would deliberately crash them and themselves into the deck or sides of American vessels.

Similar sacrifices, if not as extreme, were demanded from the whole people; and for a time they gave of their best. Even when it was clear to them that Japan was losing, most Japanese had become so indoctrinated with the concept of *kokutai* that they clung to the belief that "God's country" could not possibly lose a war. Japan *must* be invincible, and they were told that "the decisive battle which is to destroy America is yet to be fought." But at this moment the Japanese navy, which alone could fight that battle, had virtually ceased to exist. In desperation, the leaders persuaded the people that voluntary self-deprivation was a hidden resevoir of strength. To go without food—and the supply situation was becoming hopeless—was to demonstrate one's powers of resistance. Radio Tokyo told citizens that "the strength is raised by the victory of the spirit." In the air-raid shelters as the bombs rained down they were told, and they believed, that calisthenics could make hungry men vigorous again.

Some people may see great virtue in the Japanese stoicism, as the defeats piled up and ship after ship, aircraft carrier after aircraft carrier, the only lines of defense, sank. People may well admire the Japanese concern over how to appear dignified in the eyes of the world, how not to lose face, when things are going badly. Right up to the end, Japanese sailors were instructed that if they had to abandon ship, they must man the lifeboats with the utmost decorum, or they would become the laughing stock of the world. "The Americans," they were told, "will make movies of you, and show them in New York."

By the beginning of 1945, everyone realized that the loss of territory was more serious than the official communiqués admitted. Toward the end, Domei took the daring and unprecedented step of carrying out an opinion poll. A fair proportion of the voters, while still intensely patriotic, expressed dissatisfaction with the misinformation or lack of information from official sources; they asked that more facts about the war be made public.

The approaching end became clear with the Potsdam Declaration of 1945. This was withheld from the Japanese people by their rulers; but they were told about it in the leaflets dropped in millions by American airplanes all over the home islands. From the Allied demand for unconditional surrender to be followed immediately by military occupation of their islands, they learned the extent of the disaster. The disillusion with their leaders was complete.

Then came the two atom bombs, followed by the final and most decisive propaganda campaign of the war, which saved perhaps hundreds of thousands of lives. In July 1945 the Japanese government had informed Washington through the neutrals that it was prepared to discuss peace terms. This would involve bargaining; and in order to secure a good position, the Japanese leaders decided not to inform their people of the negotiations. The Office of War Information therefore informed them in its own way. At dawn on August 14, 1945, American aircraft dropped some 3 million leaflets on Tokyo and the principal Japanese cities, announcing that the Japanese government had asked for talks. This effectively countered the objections by the powerful die-hard element in the Japanese cabinet who wanted to refuse the American terms and go on fighting. Peace would have come finally, it is true, but only after much more bloodshed. After the war, Japanese officials admitted that once their people knew that peace was being discussed, the government had no alternative but to accept the American terms. As an American State Department official later put it, "This one leaflet operation alone probably repaid the entire cost of OWI throughout the whole war."

Few propagandists can have had such difficult problems to face as had the Japanese in World War II. They were hamstrung and frequently misled by conflicting directives from the prime minister's office, the army headquarters, the navy headquarters. They were restricted on all sides by stringent censorship regulations, by red tape and official refusal to face facts. Had they been allowed, they might have turned the slogan "Asia for the Asians" to good account; for the Japanese success in the early days of the war in the occupied countries was due almost exclusively to this Asian racial appeal, the call to rid the Pacific of the European whites who had no business there, and to develop the great empty spaces of Australia, for example, with the native peoples of Oceania. They had a trump card in their hands, but they proved incapable of playing it. Any advantage that accrued from it was abrogated by the harsh nature of their rule. Unaccustomed to dominion over other nations, as rulers they proved inflexible and illiberal. When they made concessions to their new subjects, these were patently tactical, to be withdrawn when the war was won. Thus, they granted independence to Burma, on the periphery of their new empire and therefore harder to control, or to the Filipinos, who were the most advanced and numerous, but withheld it from Indonesia (although originally promised), and from Malaya, both of which their navy could dominate.

Another reason for their failure as colonizers was their inability to replace the flow of material goods provided by the Anglo-Americans during the latter's suzerainty. This was especially evident in the Philippines, whose upper classes were accustomed to American automobiles, refrigerators, and all those other mechanical devices which are regarded throughout the world as the symbols of civilization. When the Japanese failed to provide these, the natives soon lost confidence in all the Japanese talk of the Co-Prosperity Sphere.

The Allies were quick to realize this, and in their propaganda to the occupied territories they told the natives they were now living in a "Co-Poverty Sphere." Their constant theme was that all the Asian aspirations to independence were being thwarted as the Japanese destroyed the existing well-balanced economy, and turned the area into "Asia for the Japanese." So Japan fell as her allies had, one three months before, the other two years before. The famous Berlin-Rome-Tokyo axis had lasted a little

(Top) Propaganda leaflets such as this one were dropped on Japan at the rate of one million daily. The message stressed peace with honor, even under terms of unconditional surrender. The leaflet included quotes from President Truman's VE-day speech on surrender. (Bottom) A leaflet interpreting Roosevelt's "Four Freedoms" to the Japanese.

(Top) The second atomic bomb was dropped on Nagasaki in August 1945. The devastating blast prompted Japan's surrender but cost tens of thousands of lives. (Bottom) A panoramic view of Hiroshima after the atomic explosion. Within moments the entire city was razed. The destruction caused by the atomic bombs was unprecented in the history of mankind.

over five years. There were similarities between the Axis powers, between East and West, such as the insistence on military indoctrination, and the Japanese belief, as in Germany, that she was a country with a destiny; and that war pays. But fascism or Nazism in the European sense did not develop in Japan. There were no party organizations which virtually ran the country and tightly controled the propaganda media. No demagogue of the Hitler-Mussolini variety emerged; there was no undue concentration of power in the hands of one individual. The Japanese military leaders shared responsibility, argued fiercely with one another, and governed by compromise among themselves. They never promised their people a short war, as the Nazis did. On the contrary, they always said it was impossible to foresee its end. Their early victories were interpreted not as having an immediate, decisive effect but rather a future, cumulative one, in a struggle which could last a hundred years. It lasted exactly three years and four months.

Issued to commemorate the Conscription Law, effective
June 1, 1941/Manchukuo/Artist unknown.

*Co-Prosperity Sphere solidarity, c. 1943/
Japanese magazine cover/Artist unknown.*

*(Top) Issued in commemoration of the 2600th anniversary
of the birth of the Japanese Empire, 1940/Manchukuo/
Artist unknown. (Bottom) Issued for the 10th anniversary
of the creation of Manchukuo, 1942/Japan/Artist unknown.*

RISE
OF
ASIA

Japan proclaims her role as Asia's leader,
c. 1943/Japanese leaflet/Artist unknown.

Propaganda against the Allies, c. 1943/
Japan/M. Tsurui Hodoobu.

"The Story of Tank Commander Nishizumi," c. 1942/
Japanese film poster for occupied Indonesia/Artist unknown.

"National Savings Bond Drive," no date/Japan/
Artist unknown.

"Towards a Scientific Japan. Exhibition of
Inventions," no date/Japan/Artist unknown.

"Zip up your lips," no date/Japan/
Artist unknown.

Japanese sex leaflets were amusing but ineffectual, no date/Japan/Artist unknown.

*Australians fighting on New Guinea received
such leaflets, no date/Japan/Artist unknown.*

*Aussie women at home were said to be unfaithful,
no date/Japanese leaflet/Artist unknown.*

*The Japanese harped unsuccessfully on the infidelity
theme, no date / Japanese leaflet / Artist unknown.*

Commemorative issues, 1939-1945/
China/Artist unknown.

*Published by United China Relief, c. 1943/
USA/Martha Sawyers.*

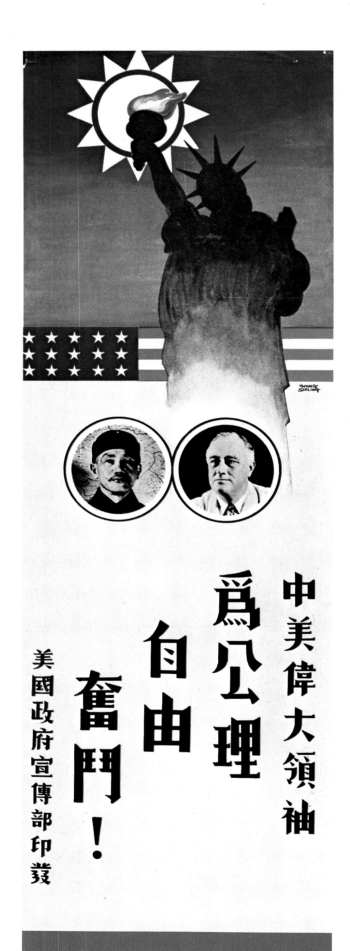

中美偉大領袖
爲公理
自由
奮鬥！
美國政府宣傳部印發

*Poster affirming U.S. support for Chiang Kai-shek,
c. 1942/USA for China/Wong Siuling.*

WINSTON S. CHURCHILL

FRANKLIN D. ROOSEVELT

JOSEPH STALIN

CHIANG KAI-SHEK

Chiang joins the Big Three in this poster, no date/England/Artist unknown.

An American aviator portrayed as a war god,
no date/USA poster for China/Artist unknown.

"The Indies must be free," 1945/Holland/
Nico Broekman.

Poster to strengthen resistance in the Philippines
c. 1943/USA/Artist unknown.

New Zealand was a U.S. ally in the Pacific, no
date/USA/Duco.

ASKARI WETU WASHINDA WAJAPANI
Smash the Japs!

African soldiers were recruited to fight Japan,
no date/England/Roland Davies.

INDIE MOET VRIJ !
WERKT EN VECHT ERVOOR!

"Work and fight to free the Indies," 1944/British
poster for the Dutch government/Pat Keely.

U.S. leaflets warned the Japanese of renewed might
after Germany's surrender, 1945/USA/Artist unknown.

ATTENTION AMERICAN SOLDIERS!

I CEASE RESISTANCE

THIS LEAFLET GUARANTEES HUMANE TREATMENT TO ANY JAPANESE DE-SIRING TO CEASE RESISTANCE. TAKE HIM IMMEDIATELY TO YOUR NEAREST COMMISSIONED OFFICER.

By Direction of the Commander in Chief.

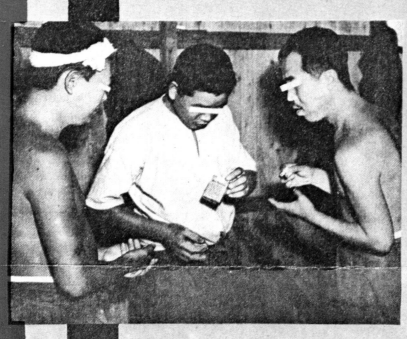

（し隠目の爲の護保族家の本日）

上の英文の内容は「この人は最早敵でな
く國際條約により生命・衣食住は勿論
醫療等が完全に保證さるべき者なりと
云ふ小意味が書かれて居る
左圖は既に當方に來て居られる諸君の
戰友の一部

17-J-1

Leaflets guaranteed humane treatment to Japanese who surrendered, c. 1945/USA/Artist unknown.

堅強壁壘

（三）

人人敵愾

（一）

制敵死命

（四）

步步設防

（二）

Japan's invasion of China on the "aggressive actions of the Chinese nationalists and on the underlying threat of the Comintern and Red imperialists." Like the German film *Feuertaufe,* it is a startling document justifying the invasion of one country by another. *Paradise in New Manchuria,* part of the China campaign propaganda, portrays this region as a rich economic area enjoying the benefits of Japanese administration.

Battles of Hawaii and the Malay Sea (1942) and *Battles on the Indian Ocean* (1942) were two fairly successful naval campaign films, but the credibility of the former was weakened by intercutting footage of battle scenes created with miniature models in the studio.

FILMOGRAPHY

The accompanying filmography consists of selected documentary or actuality films produced prior to and during World War II. Those produced during the 1930s show events that led up to the war. With a few exceptions, war-related documentaries made after 1945 are not included, even though they may appear to be based on authentic footage. Their points of view, so important for the study of documentary as propaganda, are not genuinely contemporary with the war. Nor are theatrical films (with one exception) included, although they are valuable for the wartime viewpoint and propaganda they contain. The films selected give the appearance of being factual and have the primary objective of informing rather than entertaining.

The selections, moreover, represent a small and perhaps unfair sampling of the thousands of films produced during the war. The larger, more powerful participants—Britain, the Soviet Union, Japan, the United States, and Germany—have received the greatest attention, but films from Italy, Canada, and China are also included. No effort has been made to include serial items like newsreels or screen magazines, produced in each of the major countries. Where possible the name of the director or producer is included, and a brief description of each film.

Many of the listed films are available for study in major film archives such as the National Archives and the Library of Congress in Washington, D.C.; the Museum of Modern Art in New York; the Imperial War Museum and the National Film Archive in London; and the Bundesarchiv in Koblenz, West Germany.

BRITAIN

Airscrew, Shell Oil. Arthur Elton, prod., Grahame Thorp, dir., 1940. An incentive film aimed at British industrial workers; illustrates the manufacture of metal airplane propellers.

Battle of the Books, Ministry of Information. Paul Rotha, prod., Jack Chambers, dir., 1941.

Cameramen at War, Realist Film Unit for the Ministry of Information. Len Lye, prod., 1944. A brief history of the work of top cameramen in combat.

The Curse of the Swastika, Pathé. Fred Watts, prod., 1940.

Dangerous Comment, Michael Balcon, prod., 1939.

The Dawn Guard, Ministry of Information. John Boulting, prod., Ray Boulting, dir., 1941.

Desert Victory, Army Film and Photograph Unit and the RAF Film Production Unit. David MacDonald, prod., Roy Boulting, dir., 1943. The British 8th Army campaign against Rommel's Afrika Korps, from El Alamein to Tripoli.

A Diary of Timothy, Crown Film Unit, Basil Wright, prod., Humphrey Jennings, dir., E. M. Forster, script, 1945. The story of a boy born into war and the conditions in which he and other children could expect to grow up.

Dustbin Parade, Ministries of Supply and Information. John Taylor, prod., John Halas and Joy Batchelor, animators; 1942.

The Eighty Days, Crown Film Unit. Humphrey Jennings, prod. and dir., Edward R. Murrow, commentary, 1944.

Fires Were Started, Crown Film Unit. Ian Dalrymple, prod., Humphrey Jennings, dir. and script, 1943. The excitement, tension, and suspense of civil defense during the London blitz.

The First Days, Government Post Office Film Unit. Alberto Cavalcanti, prod.; Harry Watt, dir, 1939. Interprets the atmosphere of London during September 1939, emphasizing calm determination, a sense of unity, and common purpose.

From the Four Corners, Denham and Pinewood for the Ministry of Information. A. Havelock-Allen, prod. and dir., 1941.

Germany Calling, Spectator Productions. Charles Ridley, prod., 1941. Excerpts from *Triumph of the Will* and other films of the Nuremberg rallies reedited to the tune of "Doing the Lambeth Walk."

The Heart of Britain, Government Post Office Film Unit for the Ministry of Information. Humphrey Jennings, dir., 1941.

Hitler Listens, Army Kinema Korps, 1944.

Kill or Be Killed, Ministry of Information for the War Office. Len Lye, dir., 1942. An instruction film for unarmed combat.

The Lion Has Wings. Royal Treasury. Alexander Korda, prod., 1940. The courage of the RAF pitted against great odds.

Listen to Britain, Crown Film Unit. Ian Dalrymple, prod., Humphrey Jennings and Stuart McAllister, dir., 1942.

London Can Take It, Crown Film Unit. Harry Watt and Humphrey Jennings, dir., 1940. The dignity of Londoners during one night in the first London blitz.

Men of the Lightship, Crown Film Unit. Alberto Cavalcanti, prod., David MacDonald, dir., 1940. Reconstructs the German attack on an unarmed lightship, whose survivors must struggle to reach land.

A New Fire Bomb, Shell Film Unit for the Ministries of Home Security and Information. Edgar Anstey, prod., Napier Beu, dir., 1942.

Newspaper Train, Realist for the Ministry of Information. 1941.

The Next of Kin, Ealing Studios for the Directorate of Army Kinematography. Michael Balcon, prod., Thorold Dickinson, dir., 1942.

Night Shift, Ministries of Supply and Information. Paul Rotha, prod., Jack Chambers, dir., 1942. The night shift of women workers in an ordnance factory.

Ordinary People, Crown Film Unit for the Ministry of Information. J. B. Holmes and Jack Lee, dir., 1941.

The Rape of Czechoslovakia, Paul Rotha. Frank H. Cox, prod., Jiri Weiss, dir., 1939. The German takeover of Czechoslovakia.

Salute to the Red Army, Newsreel Association for the Ministry of Information. Raymond Perris, compilation, 1943.

The Silent Village, Crown Film Unit in cooperation with the Czech Ministry of Foreign Affairs and the South Wales Miners Federation. Humphrey Jennings, dir. A memorial to the people of Lidice in the setting of a South Wales mining village.

A Soviet Village, Ministry of Information. Paul Rotha, prod., Jack Chamber, supervisor, 1944.

Spring Offensive, Government Post Office Film Unit. Alberto Gavalcanti, prod., Humphrey Jennings, dir., 1940. British farmers supply food for the homefront and for soldiers abroad.

Squadron 992, Government Post Office Film Unit for the RAF. Albert Cavalcanti, prod., Harry Watt, dir., 1940. The dramatic reconstruction of the Firth of Forth raid in the early weeks of the war; describes the defensive role of the balloon barrage.

Target for Tonight, Crown Film Unit. Ian Dalrymple, prod., Harry Watt, dir. and script, 1942. A dramatization of the courage of a British bombing crew during a raid over Germany as seen through the eyes of the men involved; shows the origin, planning, execution, and completion of a bombing run.

These Are the Men, Strand Film for the Ministry of Information. Donald Taylor, prod., Alan Osbiston, dir., Dylan Thomas, script, 1943. Sequences of *Triumph of the Will* with a propagandistic commentary.

They Also Serve, Realist Film Unit for the Ministry of Information. Ruby Grierson, dir., 1940. The role of British housewives during the war.

The True Story of Lili Marlene, Crown Film Unit. Humphrey Jennings, dir., 1944.

Tunisian Victory, Ministry of Information (Anglo-American production), 1944. The logistics of landing in darkness during the Tunisian campaign.

V-1: The Robot Bomb, Crown Film Unit, 1944.

Wales, Green Mountain, Black Mountain. Strand for the Ministry of Information. Donald Taylor, prod., John Eldridge, dir., Dylan Thomas, commentary; 1942.

We Sail at Midnight, Ministry of Information. Julian Spiro, dir., 1941. The operation of the lend-lease arrangement in supplying essential tools to a British tank factory.

Western Approaches, Crown Film Unit. Ian Dalrymple, prod., Pat Jackson, dir., 1944. U-boat drama, including a torpedoed crew, rescue, and the destruction of a submarine.

Words and Actions, British Commercial Gas Association. Edgar Anstey, prod., Max Anderson, dir., 1943.

World of Plenty, Ministry of Information. Paul Rotha, prod., dir., 1943. The effects of war on the distribution and consumption of food and the responsibility of the government to ensure the nation's nutrition.

Yellow Caesar, Ealing Studios Ltd. Michael Balcon, prod., Alberto Cavalcanti, dir., 1941. A devastating carciature of Mussolini.

Yesterday is Over Your Shoulder, Ministry of Information. Deham and Pinewood Production Co. Thorold Dicikson, prod. and dir., 1940.

CANADA

Action Stations, Canadian National Film Board. Joris Ivens, dir., 1943.

Churchill's Island, War Film Production Activities. John Grierson, dir., 1941. The overall plan for the defense of Britain, from individual action to total strategy.

Food—Weapon of Conquest, War Film Production Activities, 1942.

This is Blitz, War Film Production Activities. John Grierson, dir., 1942.

The Thousand Days, B. E. Norrish Inc. and Associated Screen Studios. Gordon Sparling, dir., 1943.

World in Action, Canadian National Film Board. John Grierson and Stuart Legg, prod. and dir. A monthly series reporting on all warfronts and the domestic scene.

CHINA

Dr. Bethune, Yehan Film Group. Wu Yin Lsien, photography; 1939. Portrays the Canadian doctor Norman Bethune with guerilla fighters of the border region.

North China is Ours, Northwest Film Co., 1939. The progress of the war against the Japanese in northwest China by the United Front; also, officers of the 8th Route (Communist) Army amid Kuomintang opponents.

Suiyuan Mongol Front, Northwest Film Co., 1935.

Yenan and the 8th Route Army, Yenan Film Group. Yuan Mu-jih, dir., 1939.

DENMARK

The Grain is in Danger, Hagen Hasselbalch, dir., 1944. The invasion of Denmark by the corn weevil serves as an allegory of the German occupation.

Your Freedom is at Stake, Theodore Christensen, dir.

FRANCE

La Bataille du Rail (Battle of the Rails), Cooperative Générale du Cinéma Francais. René Clement, dir. and script, c. 1945. Railroad sabotage by the resistance during the German occupation of France.

Journal de la Résistance (Journal of the Resistance), Le Comité du Libération du Cinéma Francais, 1944.

La Tragédie de Mers-el-Kebir, Service Cinématographique de la Marine Francaise. Jean Antoine, commentary, 1940. Made under the German occupation.

Une et Indivisible (One and Indivisible), L'Office Francais d'Information Cinématographique, 1944.

GERMANY

Adolph Hitlers Bauten (Adolf Hitler's Public Works), UFA. Walter Hege, dir., 1938.

Bauten im Neuen Deutschland (Building in the New Germany), Boehmer Film, 1939.

Das Buch der Deutschen (The Germans' Book), Tolirag Film, 1938.

Bückebürg, Reichspropagandaleitung (RPL), 1935.

Deutsche Panzer (German Panzer), UFA. Walter Ruttman, dir., 1941.

Deutschland Erwacht (Germany Awakes), NSDAP, 1933. The Nazi movement up to 1933.

Dr. Todt—Berufung und Werk (Dr. Todt—Vocation and Work), Hauptamt für Technik der NSDAP, 1935.

Einsatz der Jugend (Youth in Action), Gunther Boehnert, dir., 1939.

Englische Krankheit (The English Sickness), UFA. Kurt Stefan, dir., 1939.

Der Ewige Jude (The Eternal Jew), DFG. Fritz Hippler, dir., Dr. E. Taubert, idea and commentary, 1940. The Nazi view of the "Jewish Question."

Feldzug im Polen (Campaign in Poland), DFG and Deutsche Wochenschau. Fritz Hippler, dir., 1940. A terrifying account of the Nazi blitzkreig in Poland with an emphasis on ground operations.

Feuertaufe (Baptism of Fire), Tobis, for the Reich Air Force Ministry. Hans Bertram, dir., 1940. The German victory over Poland through the use of air power coordinated with ground forces.

Der Führer Schenkt den Juden Eine Stadt (The Führer Gives the Jews a Town), Aktualia, Psag, for the Ministry of Propaganda and the SS. Kurt Gerron, dir., 1944.

German Entry into Austria, 1938.

Gestern und Heute (Yesterday and Today), Reichspropagandaleitung (RPL) der NSDAP. Hans Weidemann, dir., 1938.

Herr Roosevelt Plaudert (Mr. Roosevelt Chats), 1943.

Hitlers Flug über Deutschland (Hitler's Flight over Germany), NSDAP, Munich, 1932. One of the first party films; Hitler's flights over Germany during the election campaign of 1932.

Jud Süss (Jew Süss), Ministry of Propaganda. Viet Harlan, dir., 1940. An anti-Semitic feature film starring Werner Kraus.

Kampfgeschwader Lutzow (Fighter Squadron Lutzow), 1941.

Mussolini in Deutschland (Mussolini in Germany), Fox-Tonende Wochenschau, 1937.

Olympiad: Fest der Volker, Fest der Schönheit (Olympia: Festival of the People, Festival of Beauty), Leni Riefenstahl, prod. and dir., 1938. The 1936 Olympic Games in Berlin.

Rundfunk im Krieg (Radio in War), Lex-Film Berlin, for the Ministry of Propaganda, 1944.

Rund um die Freiheitsstatue (Round about the Freedom Statue), Deutsche Wochenschau GmbH, for the Ministry of Propaganda, 1942.

Sieg des Glaubens (Victory of Faith), NSDAP, Leni Riefenstahl, dir., 1933. The 1933 Nazi party rally at Nuremberg.

Sieg im Westen (Victory in the West), Filmabteilung des Propagandaminsterium. Fritz Hippler, prod., Svend Nolan, dir., 1941. Germany's defeat of France.

Soldaten von Morgen (Soldiers of Tomorrow), Deutsche Film GmbH. Alfred Weidenmann, dir. and script, 1941.

Das Sowjetparadies (The Soviet Paradise), Reichspropagandaleitung (RPL). Friedrich Albat, dir., 1943.

Supreme Court Trial of the Anti-Hitler Plotters, 1944. A film of the trial of those accused of conspiracy in the attempted assassination of Adolf Hitler on July 20, 1944.

Tag der Freiheit (Day of Freedom), Reichsparteitagfilm, Berlin. Leni Riefenstahl, dir., 1935. A tribute to the Wehrmacht.

Triumph des Willens (Triumph of the Will), NSDAP. Leni Riefenstahl, prod. and dir., 1935. A spectacular account of the 1934 Nazi party rally at Nuremberg.

Unser Führer des Reiches Wiedergeburt (Our Führer of the Reich's Rebirth), NSDAP, 1934. An election film.

ITALY

Battle of the Ionian Sea, 1940. The Italian air and naval campaign against the British in the Ionian Sea and Mediterranean areas.

The First Blow Against the British Empire, 1940. The Italian campaign against the British in Somaliland and France.

Four Days of Battle, Instituto Nazionale LUCE, 1940. The Italian invasion of France.

Path of Heroes, c. 1936. The campaign in Ethiopia.

JAPAN

Battles of Hawaii and the Malay Sea (also called *War at Sea*), Toho Productions, 1942. Documentarylike style, but contains reenacted scenes and battles staged with models.

Battles on the Indian Ocean (also called *Gochin*), 1942. Filmed during a Japanese submarine cruise mission.

The Capture of Burma, 1943.

Dawn of Freedom, Toho Productions, 1942. The Philippines under United States rule; shows the conquest by Japan and the benefits of sharing in the Great East Asian Co-Prosperity Sphere.

Hammer Blows Against China, 1937. Newsreel reports of Japanese forces in China.

Japan Advancing to the North, 1934. The Japanese forces in China.

Japan in Time of Emergency, Japanese War Ministry and the Osaka Mainichi Newspaper Publishing Co., 1933. A film about the military and spiritual strength of the Japanese people; criticizes Western culture in Japanese society.

Malaya Taken, 1943.

Occupation of Sumatra, 1943.

Paradise of New Manchuria, no date. Manchuria as a beautiful, rich agriculture region with industry, modern cities, and a prosperous citizenry enjoying the benefits of work, education, and leisure.

Reconstructed China and Cooperation, North China Film Co., 1939.

To Establish a New Order in East Asia, Manchurian Motion Picture Assn., 1939.

Victory Song of the Orient, Sampaguita Pictures Inc., 1942. The Japanese conquest of the Philippines.

Why Defend China?, International Cinema Assn. of Japan, 1938. Blames Japan's invasion of China on the "aggressive action" of the Chinese Nationalists and on the underlying threat by the Comintern and "Red imperialism."

NETHERLANDS

The Last Shot, Ministry of Information. John Ferno, dir. and photography, no date.

POLAND

Battle of Lenino, Polish Army Military Film Unit, 1943.

Tale of a City: Warsaw, Polish Film Unit in Great Britain, 1944.

SOVIET UNION

The Battle for the Ukraine, Central Newsreel Studios. Alexander Dovzhenko, supervisor, Julia Solntseva and L. Bodik, dir.

The Battle of Vitebsk, Central Documentary Film Studio, 1944. With a staggering loss of human life, a Russian offensive liberates Vitebsk, a city held by the Germans for more than three years.

Berlin, Central Newsreel Studio. Yuli Raizman and Y. Svilova, dir., 1945. The campaign for Berlin, its surrender and occupation.

A Day of War, Central Newsreel Studio. Mikhail Slutsky, dir., 1942. Footage from all fronts as photographed on a single day—June 13, 1942.

The Defeat of Japan, Documentary Film Studio. Alexander Zarkhi and Josef Heifitz, dir., 1945.

The Defeat of the German Armies Near Moscow, Leonid Varlamov and Ilya Kopalin, dir., 1942. The role of civilians in the defense of the city, the battle outside Moscow, and the Red offensive which captured enemy-held towns. Released through Republic Pictures in the United States as *Moscow Strikes Back*, narrated by Edward G. Robinson.

Defense of Moscow, Central Newsreel Studio, Artkino, 1941. Serves as an example to the world of Soviet resistance to the German armies, whose forces are routed.

Estonian Earth, V. Byelayev, dir., 1940.

The Fight for our Soviet Ukraine, Central and Ukranian Newsreel Studios. Alexander Dovzhenko, Supervisor; Yulia Solntseva and Yakov Avdeyenko, dir., 1943. A tranquil agricultural region is invaded by the German armies.

Komsomols, Lydia Stepanova and Sergei Gurov, dir., 1943. The role of the Komsomols (Soviet Youth) in Russian history since 1918, including their role in the war.

Leningrad in Combat, Leningrad Studio. Roman Karmen et al., dir., 1942.

Liberated France, Documentary Film Studio. Sergei Yutkevich, editor; 1944. Allied footage on the liberation of France, recut by the Russians.

Liberation, Kiev Studio. Alexander Dovzhenko, dir.; Yulia Solntseva, co-dir., 1940. Conditions in the Western Ukraine and Western Byelorussia in September 1939, when Red troops moved up following the German attack on Poland.

The Liberation of Czechoslovakia, Ilya Kopalin and Pera Atasheva, dir., 1944. Reconstructs Czech history as an independent nation and its fate under Nazi occupation.

Mannerheim Line, V. Belayev, dir., 1940. The winter war against Finland.

Men of the Black Sea, 1942. Russian naval and ground operations against the Germans in the Black Sea region.

Our Russian Front, Russian War Relief Fund Inc., Artkino. Joris Ivens and Lewis Milestone, prod., Walter Huston, commentator, 1941. A compilation based on Soviet combat footage.

The People's Avengers, Central Newsreel Studios. V. Belayev, dir., 1943.

The Red Army, 1940.

Red Tanks, Lenfilm Studio, Artkino. Z. Drapkin and R. Maiman, dir. and writers; 1944. A staged film in which a daring Soviet tank corps rallies to the defense of the nation and thwarts the enemy.

The Siege of Leningrad, Lenin Newsreel Studios, 1942. A picture of life in the surrounded city of Leningrad; the underlying theme is Soviet determination for survival.

Stalingrad, Central Newsreel Studios. Leonid Varlamov, editor; Smirnov, Music, 1943. From the German air attacks and close fighting within the city to Field Marshall von Paulus' surrender of German forces on January 31, 1943.

To the Danube, Central and Ukranian Newsreel Studios, Poselsky and I. Kopalin, dir., 1940.

Toward an Armistice with Finland, Central Documentary Studio. Yuli Raizman, dir., 1944. Soviet-Finnish relations, 1939–44.

Ukraine in Flames, Central Newsreel and Kiev Studios. Alexander Dovzhenko and Yulia Solntseva, dir., 1945. The 1944 Soviet offensive in the Ukraine.

UNITED STATES

Action at Anguar. Signal Corps, 1945. The invasion and capture of Anguar Island by the 81st "Wildcat" Infantry Division in its first battle.

America's Hidden Weapon, Warner Bros. for the Office of War Information. William McGann, dir., 1944. Farmers and victory gardeners supply increased agricultural needs.

Appointment in Tokyo, Signal Corps in cooperation with the Army Air Force and the Department of the Navy, 1945. The war against Japan (1942–45) from the Japanese capture of Corregidor to Japan's surrender.

Army-Navy Screen Magazine, Signal Corps. Leonard Spiegelglass, prod., 1943–45. Entertainment and war news with a magazine format, designed for the serviceman.

Attack: The Battle for New Britain, Signal Corps, 1944. Explains the strategy of the New Britain campaign and comments on jungle life.

At the Front in North Africa, Signal Corps. Darryl F. Zanuck, prod., 1943. Covers the Allied landing in Algeria through the defeat of the Germans and Italians in Tunisia.

Autobiography of a Jeep, Office of War Information. Joseph Krumgold, prod. and dir., 1943. The story of the design, manufacture, and use of the jeep, humorously told from the jeep's point of view.

The Battle for the Marianas, Warner Bros. for the Marine Corps, 1943. A campaign documentary.

The Battle of Midway, Department of the Navy. John Ford, dir., 1942. The first American naval victory in the Pacific; centers on the island attack and the rescue of downed flyers.

Baptism of Fire, War Department, 1943. An acted film which recreates the apprehension of a soldier's first combat experience; shows how fears and anxieties are channeled into murderous aggressive instincts.

Bomber, Office of Emergency Management. Carl Sandburg, script, 1941. Details the usefulness and effectiveness of the B-26 medium bomber.

Brought to Action, Office of Strategic Services with the Department of the Navy, 1944. The Seventh Fleet on guard in the Gulf of Leyte in the Philippines.

Challenge to Democracy, War Relocation Authority, 1943. The forced relocation and internment of Japanese-Americans.

China Strikes Back, Frontier Films. Jay Jeyda, Irving Lerner, and Sydney Myers, 1937. The Red Army campaign against the Japanese in Shenshi.

Conquest by the Clock, RKO-Pathé. Slavko Vorkapich, dir., 1943. The importance of time in the production of war goods.

Crisis, Herbert Kline and Alexander Hamid, 1939. The fifth column in the Sudetenland; warning in America of things to come; Nazi violence against Czechs and German democrats.

The Cummington Story, Office of War Information. Irving Lerner, prod.; Helen Grayson and Larry Madison, dir. and script; Aaron Copland, music. An acted film depicting the accepting of war refugees in a New England town.

Dangerous Pennies, Office of Price Administration, 1945.

December 7, Office of Strategic Services. John Ford, prod., Gregg Toland, dir., 1942. A staged film intercut with documentary footage.

The Enemy Japan—Dream of Empire, Signal Corps, 1945. The Japanese expansion during the 1930s and World War II. Shows the use of occupied countries for the supply of raw materials.

The Enemy Japan—The Land, March of Time for the Department of the Navy, 1943. Joseph Grew, former U.S. Ambassador to Japan, describes Japanese land, agriculture, and industry.

The Enemy Japan—The People, March of Time for the Department of the Navy, 1943. Grew describes the effect of Shintoism and the samurai code on the Japanese psychology.

The Fighting Lady, Department of the Navy. Louis de Rochemont, prod. Photographed under the supervision of Edward Steichen, 1944. The gradual fusion of raw recruits and a new ship into a formidable fighting unit. Shows the attack on Truk Island in the battle of the Philippine Sea.

The Fleet That Came to Stay, Department of the Navy, 1945. The story of the kamikaze attacks during the invasion of Okinawa and the role of the U.S. fleet in the invasion.

The Four Hundred Million, Contemporary Historians, Inc., Joris Ivens, dir. and script, 1938. The aggression of the Japanese Imperial Army against China.

Der Führer's Face, Walt Disney, 1943. Donald Duck is exposed to Nazi terror in this cartoon film.

Fury in the Pacific, Department of the Navy, 1945. The story of the landings on Pelelieu and Augur in the Palaus.

Fellow Americans, Office of Emergency Management. Garson Kanin, dir. James Stewart, narrator, 1942. The bombing of Pearl Harbor as if it had happened to four typical American cities.

Gas Racket, Office of Price Administration, 1943. Dramatization of the sale of counterfeit and stolen gasoline ration stamps to gasoline dealers.

The Grain That Built a Hemisphere, Walt Disney for the Coordinator of Inter-American Affairs, 1943. An animated story of the cultivation of corn in the Americas.

Hands, Signal Corps for the Department of the Treasury, 1944. A war bond promotion trailer.

Here is Germany, War Department, Frank Capra, prod., 1945. Made for the American occupation troops, the film reviews the history of Germany.

How Good is a Gun?, Signal Corps, 1944. An incentive film for munitions workers.

How Strong is the Enemy?, Office of Strategic Services, 1944. Estimates the industrial and military strengths of the Axis powers.

Inside Nazi Germany, March of Time, 1938. The first detailed news report on German politics shown in American movie theaters.

Is Your Trip Necessary?, War Activities Committee of the Motion Picture Industry, 1943. Asks citizens to restrict travel to make more transportation available for the military.

Japanese Behavior, Office of Strategic Services, 1945. Psychology and living habits of the Japanese people.

Japanese Relocation, Office of War Information, 1943. The forced relocation and internment of Japanese and Japanese-Americans in the U.S.

Just for Remembrance, Signal Corps for the Department of the Treasury, 1944. War bond promotion.

Justice, Department of the Treasury, 1944. War bond promotion.

Know Your Ally Britain, Army Signal Corps. Anthony Veiller, dir., 1943.

Know Your Enemy Japan, War Department. Direction begun by Joris Ivens and completed by Frank Capra, 1945. An analysis of the Japanese psyche and a capsule view of Japan's history, with an emphasis on totalitarian and aggressive behavior.

Last Stronghold, RKO-Pathé, 1940. A newsreel compilation which reviews events since 1914.

A Letter from Bataan. Paramount Pictures. William H. Pine, dir., c. 1943. Relates the nightblindness of a soldier in Bataan to the need to conserve food.

Let There Be Light, Signal Corps. John Huston, dir., 1946. The treatment and rehabilitation of servicemen psychologically disturbed by their war experiences; shows how they can return to the mainstream of American life.

The Liberation of Rome, Signal Corps with the cooperation of the British Services Film Unit, 1944. The U.S. and British campaign against the Germans from the landing in Sicily to the fall of Rome.

Lights Out in Europe, Herbert Kline, 1940. The Nazi attack on Poland; shows the capture of the Polish corridor and attacks on civilians.

The Memphis Belle, Army Air Force First Motion Picture Unit. William Wyler, dir., 1944. The story of a B-17 Flying Fortress on a mission over Wilhelmshaven, Germany.

Mission to Moscow, Warner Bros. Michael Curtiz, dir., 1943. Based on the book by Joseph E. Davies, U.S. Ambassador to the Soviet Union from 1936 to 1938; dramatizes the need for strengthening the U.S. alliance with the Soviet Union in the fight against German militarism and fascism.

Mr. and Mrs. America, Department of the Treasury, c. 1943. The price of war in men's lives; an appeal for financial support.

Mud and Soldiers, Marine Corps, 1943. A Japanese war feature film reedited to explain military strategy.

My Japan, Department of the Treasury, 1943. Designed to stimulate the purchase of war bonds; uses captured film to illustrate Japan's determination.

Nazi Concentration Camps, U.S. Counsel for the Prosecution of Axis Criminality, 1945. Documentary footage shot by Allied cameramen showing conditions in concentration camps at the time of liberation; used as evidence at the war crimes trials.

The Nazi Plan, U.S. Counsel for the Prosecution of Axis Criminality, 1945. A film history of the Nazi party, assembled for the war crimes trials.

The Negro Soldier, War Department, 1944. The black man's contribution to American life and culture and the participation of black soldiers in World War II.

The New Spirit, Walt Disney for the Department of the Treasury, 1942. An animated film about taxes and the war effort as explained by Donald Duck.

News Review No. 1, United Films/OWI, 1943. Worldwide wartime activities, December 1941—February 1943.

News Review No. 2, United Films/OWI. Helen Van Dongen, editor, 1943. Report on war events from all fronts.

Out of the Frying Pan Into the Firing Line, Walt Disney, 1943. A cartoon in which Minnie Mouse promotes the saving of fat scraps.

The Ramparts We Watch, March of Time. Louis de

Rochemont, dir., 1940. Through the experience of a small American town, the film reenacts the U.S. entry into World War I, drawing parallels to another approaching war. Concludes with German footage of the attack on Poland.

The Rear Gunner, Army Air Forces in cooperation with Warner Bros. Gordon Hollingshead, prod., Ray Enright, dir., 1943. Dramatization of the training and experience of a rear gunner.

Reason and Emotion, Walt Disney for the Coordinator of Inter-American Affairs, 1943. An animated film illustrating the duality of the human personality, with application to the conflict between democracy and fascism.

Remember These Faces, Department of the Treasury, 1945. War bond promotion.

Report from the Aleutians, Army Signal Corps. John Huston, dir., 1944. The U.S. Army Air Force campaign against the Japanese in the Aleutian chain; shows camp life among an isolated bomber squadron and concludes with the successful attack on Kiska.

Resisting Enemy Interrogation, Army Air Forces, 1944. A Hollywood-style training film illustrating how even the most innocent conversation between American airmen and their German captors can lead to disaster.

Le Retour (*The Return*), United Films (Franco-American production). Henri Cartier-Bresson and Richard Banks. The return of French prisoners from Nazi concentration camps.

Ring of Steel, Office of Emergency Management, Phil Martin, prod., Garson Kanin, dir., Spencer Tracy, commentary, 1942. A tribute to the American soldiers who have protected the United States since 1776.

Russians at War, Office of War Information. Helen Van Dongen, 1943. Behind the lines with the Soviets.

The Russian People, Helen Van Dongen and Joris Ivens, 1942. A compilation of Soviet war newsreels.

Safeguarding Military Information, War Department, 1941. Careless talk about military movements results in disaster.

A Salute to France, United Films. Jean Renoir, dir. Maxwell Anderson and others, 1945. Staged and documentary footage; French, British, and American soldiers discuss their experiences during war.

San Pietro, Signal Corps. John Huston, dir. and script, 1944. The cost in American lives to take an Italian mountain village from its German defenders.

Siege, Julien Bryan, 1939. The Nazi attack on Warsaw as filmed from the rooftops; shows the killing and destruction as well as the reaction of the refugees.

Silence, Signal Corps for the Department of the Treasury, 1944. War bond promotion.

The Stilwell Road, Signal Corps (Anglo-American production), 1945. The construction of a road linking Allied

forces in Burma and China. Retreat through the Burmese jungles and efforts to supply China by air and at the same time recapture Burma to set up bases.

Story of Big Ben, Pathé News for the Naval Bureau of Aeronautics, 1944. A tribute to shipyard workers.

Story of a Transport, Coast Guard, 1945. The transportation of the luxury liner *USS Manhattan* into a torpedo ship, the *Wakefield*.

Subject Germany, Signal Corps, 1945.

Target for Today, Signal Corps for the Army Air Force. William Keighley, dir., 1944. Explains the plans and purposes of the daylight precision bombing of Germany. Traces the development of the mission down to groups and squadrons.

This is the Philippines, Signal Corps, 1945. Philippine culture and geography, and the Japanese capture.

Thunderbolts, Army Air Force. Directed by William Wyler, 1945. The air war over Italy.

To the Shores of Iwo Jima, Warner Bros. for the Department of the Navy, 1945. Coordinated combat operations recorded on film to illustrate the cost of war.

Toscanini: Hymn of the Nations, Office of War Information. Irving Lerner, prod., Alexander Hamid, dir., 1945.

The Town, Office of War Information. Joseph Krumgold, prod., Joseph von Sternberg, dir., 1944. Shows the European traditions found in an average midwestern American town, with its eclectic architecture, mixed population, and many religions.

Troop Train, Office of War Information, 1943. The transportation of an armed division by rail as an object lesson to civilians who might complain about the difficulties of travel.

The True Glory, Signal Corps and the British Ministry of Information. Carol Reed and Garson Kanin, dir., 1945. D-Day, the Allied landing in France, and the victorious campaign in the West; features the men who fought the battles.

Two Down and One to Go, War Department. Frank Capra, dir., 1945. The army's point system of discharges to be followed after the defeat of Germany. Made for soldiers in Europe who believed they would soon be on their way home.

The War 1941–44, United Films. Worldwide war activities.

War Town, Office of War Information, 1943. The problems created by wartime industries for housing, education, medical care, etc. in Mobile, Alabama.

"Why We Fight" Series, War Department, 1943–44.

Prelude to War, Frank Capra, dir., 1942. The international events of the 1930s and the development of fascism, with a view to explaining the causes of World War II, particularly why the U.S. was fighting.

The Nazis Strike, Frank Capra and Anatole Litvak, dir., 1943. Shows the German advance toward the countries of Eastern Europe emphasizing propaganda, terror tactics, and strategy.

Divide and Conquer, Frank Capra and Anatole Litvak, dir., 1943. The German drive through western and northern Europe; the fall of Holland, Denmark, Norway, and France.

The Battle of Britain, Frank Capra, dir., 1943. Britain's resistance to and defeat of the German Luftwaffe.

The Battle of Russia, Anatole Litvak, dir., 1943. Russian history from the point of view that the Russians, who challenge the "invincibility" of the German forces, have always defeated and expelled the invading enmy.

The Battle of China, 1944. China's resistance to the Japanese invasion.

War Comes to America, Frank Capra, dir., 1944. The achievements and ideals of American society at stake in the war against fascism; shows the shift in public opinion from isolationism to support for entry into the war.

Why We're Here, War Department, 1944. An explanation of the Burma campaign.

With the Marines at Tarawa, Warner Bros. for the U.S. Marine Corps, 1944. Shows the heavy toll of American lives involved in the capture of Japanese-held Tarawa.

World at War, Office of the Coordinator of Government Films. Samuel Spewack, prod., 1943. Compilation of newsreels and captured footage showing world events, 1931–1942, with an underlying pattern of fascist aggression "inevitably leading to the attack on Pearl Harbor and the Western hemisphere."

The World in Flames, Paramount News, 1940. A documentation of events which set the stage for war. Argues the necessity for the U.S. to arm in defense of the democratic way of life.

Yalta Conference, Signal Corps, 1945.

You John Jones, MGM for the War Activities Committee of the Motion Picture Industry, 1942.

Notes on Color Plates
By Victor Margolin

CHAPTER ONE: GERMANY

(Page 41) Among the faces on this election poster are Hitler (modestly placed in the upper right-hand corner), Einstein (below Hitler), Mussolini (lower left), the world heavyweight champion Max Schmeling (next to Mussolini), and Hindenburg (center). Though Hitler lost the 1932 presidential election to Hindenburg, who won with 53 percent of the vote, he was asked to become chancellor of Germany in January 1933.

(Page 42) "Germans must choose between the bankruptors of the past and the men of the future." Goebbels is said to have had a hand in the design of this poster. Heinrich Hoffman, who did the photomontage, was Hitler's personal photographer.

(Page 44) Hitler was portrayed in this painting as a new messiah. The black raven of German mythology emanating rays of light is the satanic obverse of the white dove which symbolizes the Holy Ghost in medieval religious paintings.

(Page 45 Top, left) Einstein left Germany in 1933, the year he was forced to resign from the Prussian Academy of Sciences. Philip Lenard, a Nobel Prize physicist who had earlier scientific disagreements with Einstein, took advantage of his favorable position in the Nazi hierarchy to write in the *Völkischer Beobachter*, "The most important example of the dangerous influence of Jewish circles on the study of nature has been provided by Herr Einstein with his mathematically botched-up theories consisting of some ancient knowledge and a few arbitrary additions." The building off which the great scientist is being swept is the Einstein Tower in Berlin, designed by Eric Mendelsohn.

(Page 48 Top, right) The octopus was frequently used in wartime propaganda as an image of the aggressor. A French cartoon from the "Phony War" period shows Hitler as the octopus. Churchill as an octopus also appears in a German occupation poster for France.

(Page 52) Hitler's pose in this painted-over photographic portrait imitates a tradition of ruler portraits dating back to the Renaissance.

(Page 53 Top, right) This poster publicized a street collection for youth hostels organized by the *Verband Deutscher Jugendherbergen* (Association of German Youth Hostels).

(Page 53 Bottom, left) The *"Kraft durch Freude"* (Strength through Joy) organization was created to program the leisure time of German workers. Holidays, evening classes, and amateur cultural activities were planned, as well as massive sports and gymnastic events.

(Page 54) Hitler initiated a giant propaganda campaign to produce and sell a low-priced "People's Car." Over 300,000 Germans, under a gigantic layaway plan, started saving 5 marks a week (original cost: 990 marks, about $396). All told $67,000,000 was collected but the public never saw a single Volkswagen. The 300-odd prototypes found their way to the German General Staff. The first civilian Volkswagens were produced in 1945, after the war.

(Page 56 Top, right) Traveling exhibitions were considered an important means of propaganda by the Nazis. A major anti-Semitic exhibit was *"Der Ewige Jude"* (The Eternal Jew).

(Page 58) Though the SS under Himmler was originally formed as a security force, the Waffen-SS was introduced in 1940. Waffen-SS soldiers supplemented the Wehrmacht troops on both the Western and the Eastern fronts, and were guilty of some of the worst atrocities of the war.

(Page 60 Bottom, right) Posters such as this one, made from an academic painting of the Führer, were hung on the walls of offices and schoolrooms throughout Germany.

(Page 61 Bottom) One of a series of wall newspapers for use in offices and schools. Flechtner designed at least four other posters for the series, which probably began in 1938 and continued until at least 1943. Mjölnir and Hohlwein, among other artists, also did designs.

(Page 62 Top, left) The two lightning bolts form a V, the victory sign which the Germans co-opted from the Allies. The slain dragon as an image of defeated Bolshevism was also used on other posters. (See page 202, Bottom, right)

(Page 62 Top, right) *Feind hört mit* (The enemy is listening). was the German equivalent of Britain's "Careless Talk Costs Lives" and the United States' "Loose Lips Sink Ships." German "careless talk" posters always showed the hulking shadow of a spy in the background; the British took a lighter approach, using cartoons and puns. All the belligerent countries had posters to portray the "careless talk" theme.

(Page 62 Bottom, left) The legal category *Volksschädling* (enemy of the people) also comprised the *Feindhörer* (enemy listener) or *Schwarzhörer* (black listener)—people who listened to enemy broadcasts. After the German setback at Stalingrad, many people risked severe punishment by tuning in BBC broadcasts.

CHAPTER TWO: ITALY

(Page 90 Top, right) These stamps show Mussolini's preoccupation with Italian youth from birth to the time they were old enough to join the army.

(Page 93 Top, left) The Fascist fighter chips away single-handed at the Russian bear. Mussolini's braggadocio inflated Italy's role in combatting the Soviet Union. Italian volunteer legions, along with troops from France, Scandinavia, Belgium, Holland and other occupied countries helped bolster the beleaguered Waffen-SS troops on the Eastern front. (See Waffen-SS recruiting poster, page 93, Bottom, right.) But their presence was hardly influential.

(Page 93 Top, right) The wolf, symbolizing Italy, has fiercely ripped the British flag to shreds while suckling Romulus and Remus with kindness and love. This image of extremes suited the Italian temperament.

(Page 96) Like Mjölnir and other cartoonists, Boccasile used the black American soldier as an image of cultural barbarism, which he contrasted with the white marble Venus de Milo, an image of European classical purity on which a value of two dollars was placed.

(Page 99 Top, left) Goffredo Mameli (1827–1849) was an Italian patriot who fought with Garibaldi and died in the war of 1848–49. He was a poet and his song *"Fratelli d'Italia"* became a popular song of the independence movement. Mameli is used in this poster to establish a continuity between Garibaldi's "red shirts" and Mussolini's soldiers, to whose helmets are attached the wings of Hermes.

(Page 99 Top, right) Italian workers began going to Germany in 1940. At first they were attracted by the pay and working conditions, but they were treated as members of an inferior race. When they acted counter to Nazi discipline, they were severely punished; many were sent to concentration camps.

(Page 100) The Todt Organization was responsible for public-works projects in Germany. After Mussolini fell from power, the organization employed Italians on construction projects within Italy.

(Page 103) The "liberator" was also depicted as an agent of destruction in a German poster for occupied Holland (p. 201).

CHAPTER THREE: ENGLAND

(Page 125) Fougasse believed that humor would work better on beleaguered Britons than stern exhortations. For Londoners on the run, he decided that simple images and phrases which could be absorbed at a glance would be most effective.

(Page 128) Posters by Games and other War Office designers were displayed in canteens, barrack rooms, medical huts, and other areas where soldiers congregated. Games, who was given a free hand with his designs, strove to elevate the graphic taste of the soldiers by his use of surrealist imagery, photomontage, and other techniques.

(Page 129) This poster was designed for the Ministry of Information's anti-VD campaign of 1943–44.

(Page 131) This poster symbolically depicted the Nazis as opponents of Christian values. The size of the cross in relation to the swastika affirmed that Christianity would triumph.

(Page 133) The hammer and sickle and the Star of David were used to imply Britain's domination by Bolsheviks and Jews.

(Page 136 Top) This curious piece of propaganda is drawn in the style of a Persian miniature. Roosevelt and Stalin, led by Churchill on a white steed, are chasing Hitler, Tojo, and Mussolini, who has been knocked off his horse by an arrow from Churchill's bow. The artist's calligraphic signature is next to the right foot of Roosevelt's horse.

(Page 136 Bottom) Sevek's streamlined style is reminiscent of Cassandre's posters of the 1920s and 1930s. The muscle-flexing giant signifies renewed British confidence after five years of hardship.

CHAPTER FOUR: UNITED STATES

(Page 165) This song was made famous by Spike Jones and his City Slickers.

(Page 170 Top) Shahn's poster refers to the forcible recruitment of French laborers to work in German factories.

(Page 173 Top, left) The face of Uncle Sam is that of the artist himself. The poster was published on September 6, 1944, three months after D-Day, and reflects the new confidence of the United States after a string of European victories.

(Page 173 Bottom) Rockwell's poster was issued soon after Bataan and Corregidor fell to the Japanese in the spring of 1942. It reflects the desperation of that period, when the United States was losing the war in the Pacific.

(Page 174 Top, right) Gaydos won second prize in the Museum of Modern Art's "United Hemisphere" Poster Competition in 1942. Each entry was to use one of twelve slogans expressing a new sense of unity in the hemisphere.

(Page 174 Bottom, right) Grohe's poster was used in factories but workers were uncertain whether the soldier was American or German, in spite of the German helmet. An Iron Cross on the helmet might have made the identity clearer but the poster's message, nevertheless, was not well defined. American designers had to learn that strong graphics were not necessarily as persuasive as more illustrative posters which hit closer to home.

CHAPTER FIVE: OCCUPIED EUROPE

(Page 193) The Rexist party was founded in Belgium by Léon Degrelle in 1935. René Magritte, the surrealist painter, reacted to the Fascist tone of Degrelle's propaganda by showing his image reflected in the mirror as Hitler. The poster was published by the Committee of Antifascist Intellectuals.

(Page 195 Top, right) The spirit of Pétain guides the collaborationist troops.

(Page 195 Bottom, left) The mother and child were common images on wartime posters. This poster shows them as victims of the ravages of war. A Greek War Relief poster (page 206 Bottom, left) showed them as symbols of courage and endurance. On a Canadian poster (page 169) they represented sacred values which the enemy would attack.

(Page 196 Top, right) The Germans used the specter of a Bolshevist onslaught to induce French workers to come to Germany.

(Page 199) The W. A. (*Wehrafdeling*, lit. defense division) was a paramilitary organization used by the Dutch occupation government as an auxiliary police force. The *Zwaarte Soldat* (*Black Soldier*) was the official W. A. publication.

(Page 202 Top, left) "Tout va très bien, Madame la Marquise" is the opening line of a popular French song. A servant first assures his mistress that all is well before proceeding to recount a long list of problems. The implication of this poster is that Churchill was offering the Europeans false hopes.

(Page 205 Top, left) The hand giving the V sign also looks like a dove of peace. The newspapers in the foreground—*Vrij!* (*Free*) and *La Libre Belgique* (*Free Belgium*)—were the leading resistance news sheets.

CHAPTER SIX: SOVIET UNION

(Page 225) This early anti-German poster shows the Russian worker struggling against a German aristocrat. The definition of the conflict in class terms, which reflects the influence of the Civil War, was later deemphasized. Russian wartime propaganda was based on loyalty to the nation rather than the party. The use of symbolism and the limited color range of red, black, and white typified Russian posters of the 1920s and early 1930s.

(Page 226 Bottom, right) The job of Russian propagandists in the winter of 1941 was to shore up the people's confidence that they would eventually repel the Germans. The huge hands and pincers of the Red Army express this confidence after the counteroffensive which shattered Hitler's plan to surround and capture Moscow.

(Page 227) The Russians, more than any other of Germany's adversaries, made Goebbels a prime target of their propaganda. Efimov drew him as Mickey Mouse with a swastika tail, Lebedev likened him to a braying donkey (page 238), and the Kukriniksi ridiculed him in numerous cartoons.

(Page 228 Bottom, right) As a parallel to the Soviet Army's winter counteroffensive in 1941–42 Ivanov and Burova's poster recalls the French defeat in the War of 1812. The figure in the background is Mikhail Kutuzov, the commander-in-chief of the Russian Army which compelled Napoleon and his troops to retreat from Moscow.

(Page 234 Top) To inspire the fighting forces, Russian propagandists recalled the exploits of the country's great military heroes. On the far left is Alexander Nevsky, who turned back the Teutonic Knights in 1242. Alexander Suvorov, in the center, helped defeat the Turks in the Russo-Turkish War of 1787–91, and Vasily Chapayev, on the right, led a Bolshevik division against Kolchak's anti-Bolshevik forces in the Civil War. He was killed in action in 1919.

(Page 235) The appeal to patriotic feelings for the motherland made Toidze's poster one of the most popular of the war. Stalin, in his "Holy Russia" speech of November 6, 1941, aroused his people's national pride by recalling the spirit of Russia's national heroes; generals like Donskoi, Suvorov, and Kutuzov, as well as eminent cultural figures such as Pushkin and Tolstoy. This appeal to the deepest feelings of the Russian people was more effective in bolstering their courage than any political rhetoric could have been.

(Page 239) When this cartoon appeared, the Russians had gained the offensive and could joke about Hitler's military strategy.

(Page 240) Ivanov's heroic figures typified the social realist style which dominated Soviet wartime posters. Although cartoons and caricatures were also used, the experimental graphics of the 1920s—the work of Rodchenko, Lissitzky, the Stenbergs, Prusakov, and Klutsis—had absolutely no influence on the visual style of the war years.

CHAPTER SEVEN: JAPAN

(Page 268 Top, left) Kimisaburo Yoshimura's *The Story of Tank Commander Nishizumi* (1940), which reflected the Japanese prewar humanist ideal, was one of Japan's greatest war films. It was excellent propaganda for the occupied countries because of its hero, a Japanese officer who was shown fraternizing with his men and aiding a Chinese woman and her child.

(Page 270 Top) The Japanese used a "divide and conquer" approach in their leaflet propaganda to Australian troops fighting on New Guinea and Papua. The Aussies were told that their women back home were succumbing to the advances of American and British soldiers while they were hacking their way through the New Guinea jungle.

(Page 273) The artist used the style of Milton Caniff, whose comic-strip characters "Terry and the Pirates" fought the Japanese throughout the war.

(Page 275) As a propaganda move to promote the Allied presence in China, Chiang Kai-shek was elevated to the status of The Big Three—Churchill, Roosevelt, and Stalin.

(Page 276) "Door gods" were small Chinese posters displaying figures from the Chinese pantheon. Rural families put them on their walls and changed them each lunar New Year. The China Division of the Office of War Information produced "door gods" for the Chinese peasantry which portrayed American aviators and preached Allied cooperation.

(Page 277) This poster appealed to the Dutch people to help break Japan's grip on the East Indies (See also page 279, Top, right).

(Page 279 Bottom, left) This leaflet, intended for Japanese troops and civilians, warned that the vast amount of Allied weaponry and manpower concentrated in Europe would be transferred to Asia. Japan's military leaders were blamed for the country's difficulties.

(Page 280) The original leaflet used the words "I Surrender" instead of "I Cease Resistance." It was unsuccessful because surrender was humiliating to the Japanese soldier. The wording on the second version avoided the stigma of surrender and had better results.

Bibliography

Altmann, John. "Movies' Role in Hitler's Conquest of German Youth." *Hollywood Quarterly*, v. 3, no. 4: 1949.

Anderson, Joseph and Donald Richie. *The Japanese Film: Art and Industry*. New York, Grove Press, 1960.

The Arts Inquiry. *The Factual Film*. London, Oxford University Press, 1947.

Auckland, R. G. *Aerial Propaganda Over Great Britain*. Sandridge, St. Albans, n.d.

Balcon, Michael, Ernest Lindgren and others. *Twenty Years of British Film, 1925–1945*. London, Falcoln Press, 1947.

Barnouw, Eric. *The Golden Web; 1933–1953 (A History of Broadcasting in the United States, v. 2)*. New York, Oxford University Press, 1966–1968.

Bartlett, F. C. *Political Propaganda*. Cambridge, Cambridge University Press, 1940.

Bellanger, Co. *La Presse Clandestine*. Paris, Armand Colin, 1961.

Blobner, Helmut and Herbert Holba. "Jackboot Cinema." *Films and Filming*, v. 3, Dec. 1962: 12–20.

Boelcke, Willi A., ed. *The Secret Conferences of Dr. Goebbels: The Nazi Propaganda War 1939–43*. New York, Dutton, 1970.

Bosmajian, Haig A. "The Role of the Political Poster in Hitler's Rise to Power." *Print*, May 1966: 28–31.

Bourget, Pierre and Charles Lacratelle. *Sur les Murs de Paris, 1940–1944*. Paris, Hachette, 1959.

Bramsted, Ernest K. *Goebbels and National Socialist Propaganda, 1925–1945*. Michigan State University Press, 1965.

Brenner, Hildegard. *Die Kunstpolitik des Nationalsocialismus*. Hamburg, Rowohlt, 1963.

Briggs, Asa. *The Birth of Broadcasting: The History of Broadcasting in the United Kingdom*. London, Oxford University Press, 1961–65 (v. 2).

Burden, Hamilton T. *The Nuremberg Party Rallies, 1923–39*. New York, Praeger, 1967.

Cannistraro, Philip. "*Il Cinema Italiano sotto il Fascismo*." *Storia Contemporanea*, anno 3, no. 3, 1972.

———. "The Organization of Totalitarian Culture: Cultural Policy and the Mass Media in Fascist Italy." Ph.D. Dissertation, 1971. (University Microfilms)

Capra, Frank. *The Name above the Title: an Autobiography*. New York, Macmillan, 1971.

Carroll, Wallace. *Persuade or Perish*. Boston, Houghton Mifflin, 1948.

Causton, Bernard. "Art in Germany under the Nazis." *London Studio*, v. 12, Nov. 1936: 235–46.

Childs, Harwood, ed. *Propaganda and Dictatorship*. Princeton, N.J., Princeton University Press, 1936.

Childs, Harwood and John B. Whitton. *Propaganda by Short Wave*, New York, Arno Press, 1972.

Cole, J. A. *Lord Haw-Haw and William Joyce*. New York, Farrar, Straus & Giroux, 1964.

Courade, Francois and Pierre Cadars. *The Nazi Cinema: A History*. New York, Pitman, 1974.

Daskal, V. "Adventures in Art under Hitler." *Horizon*, v. 9, March 1944: 192–204.

Delmer, Sefton. *Black Boomerang*. New York, Viking Press, 1962.

de Mendelssohn, Peter. *Japan's Political Warfare*. New York, Arno Press, 1972.

Dickinson, Thorold and Catherine de la Roche. *Soviet Cinema*. London, Falcoln Press, 1948.

Dougherty, William E. and Morris Janowitz. *Psychological Warfare Casebook*. Published for the Johns Hopkins University and Johns Hopkins Press, 1958.

Dryer, Sherman. *Radio in Wartime*. New York, Greenberg, 1942.

Farago, Ladislas, ed. *German Psychological Warfare*. New York, Arno Press, 1972.

Fehl, Philipp. "A Stylistic Analysis of Some Propaganda Posters of World War II." M. A. Thesis (unpublished), Stanford University, 1948.

Field, John C. W. *Aerial Propaganda Leaflets*. Sutton Coldfield, England; Francis Field Ltd., n.d.

Fielding, Raymond. *The American Newsreel, 1911–1967*. Norman, Okla., Oklahoma University Press, 1972.

Fraser, Lindley. *Propaganda*. New York, Oxford University Press, 1957.

Furhammar, Leif and Folke Isaksson. *Politics and Film*. New York, Praeger, 1971.

Games, Abraham. *Over My Shoulder*. New York, Macmillan, 1960.

Gec, ed. *La Caricatura Internazionale durante la Seconda Guerra Mondiale*. Novara, Istituto Geografico de Agostini, 1971.

George, Alexander. *Propaganda Analysis: A Study of Inferences Made From Nazi Propaganda in World War II*. Evanston, Ill., Row, Peterson, 1959.

Goebbels, Joseph. *The Goebbels Diaries 1942–1943*. Edited and translated by Louis P. Lochner. Garden City, N.Y., Doubleday, 1948.

Grunberger, Richard. *The 12-Year Reich: A Social History of Nazi Germany 1933–45*. New York, Holt, Rinehart, & Winston, 1971.

Hadamovsky, Eugen. *Propaganda and National Power: The Organization of Public Opinion for National Politics*. New York, Arno Press, 1972.

Hale, Oron J. *The Captive Press in the Third Reich*. Princeton, N.J., Princeton University Press, 1964.

Hardy, Forsyth, ed. *Grierson on Documentary*. London, Faber & Faber, 1966.

Heiber, Helmut. *Goebbels: A Bibliography.* New York, Hawthorne, 1972.

Henslow, Miles. *The Miracle of Radio: The Story of Radio's Decisive Contribution to Victory.* London, Evans, 1946.

Higham, Charles and Jack Greenberg. *Hollywood in the Forties.* New York, Zwemmer/Barnes, 1968.

Hoffman, Hilmar and Peter Kress. "German Cinema of the Nazi Period." *Film Library Quarterly*, v. 5, no. 2, spring 1972.

Hitler, Adolf. *Mein Kampf.* New York, Stackpole, 1939.

Hovland, C. I., A. Lumsdaine, and F. D. Sheffield. *Experiments in Mass Communication.* New York, Wiley, 1965.

Howe, Ellic. *Studies in Psychological Warfare During World War II.* London, Rider & Co., 1972.

Hull, David. *Film in the Third Reich: A Study of the German Cinema 1933–1945.* Berkeley, University of California Press, 1969.

International Propaganda/Communications: Selections from *The Public Opinion Quarterly.* New York, Arno Press, 1972.

Jarratt, Vernon. *The Italian Cinema.* London, Falcon Press, 1951.

Kirby, Edward M. and Jack W. Harris. *Star-Spangled Radio.* Chicago, Ziff-Davis, 1948.

Knight, Arthur. *The Liveliest Art: A Panoramic History of the Movies.* New York, New American Library, 1957.

Konlechner, Peter and Peter Kubelka, eds. *Propaganda and Counter Propaganda in Films of 1933–45.*

Krabbe, Henning ed. *Voices from Britain: Broadcast History, 1939–1945.* London, Allen & Unwin, 1947.

Kracauer, Siegfried. *From Caligari to Hitler: A Psychological History of the German Film.* Princeton, N.J., Princeton University Press, 1947.

Kris, Ernst, Hans Speier, and others. *German Radio Propaganda: A Report on Home Broadcasts During the War.* London, Oxford University Press, 1944.

Lavine, Harold and James Wechsler. *War Propaganda and the United States.* New York, Arno Press, 1972.

Lean, Tangye. *Voices in the Darkness: The Story of the European Radio War.* London, Secker & Warburg, 1943.

Lee, Alfred McClung and Elizabeth Briant Lee. *The Fine Art of Propaganda: A Study of Father Coughlin's Speeches.* New York, Harcourt, Brace & Co., 1939.

Lehmann-Haupt, Hellmut. *Art under a Dictatorship.* New York, Oxford University Press, 1954.

Leprohon, Pierre. *The Italian Cinema.* New York, Praeger, 1972.

Lerner, Daniel, ed. *Propaganda in War and Crisis: Materials for American Policy.* New York, Stewart, 1951.

Lerner, Daniel. *Sykewar—Psychological Warfare Against Germany.* Cambridge, Mass., MIT Press, 1974.

Leyda, Jay. *Films Beget Films: A Study of the Compilation Film.* New York, Hill and Wang, 1971.

——. *Kino: A History of the Russian and Soviet Film.* New York: Macmillan, 1960.

Linebarger, Paul M. A. *Psychological Warfare.* New York, Arno Press, 1972.

Lockhart, Sir R. H. Bruce. *Comes the Reckoning.* New York, Arno Press, 1972.

Low, David. *Autobiography.* New York, Simon and Schuster, 1957.

Malerba, Luigi and Carmine Siniscalo, eds. *Fifty Years of Italian Cinema.* Rome, Edizioni d'Arte, 1954.

Mandell, Richard. *The Nazi Olympics.* New York, Macmillan, 1971.

Manvell, Roger and Heinrich Frankel. *Dr. Goebbels.* New York, Pyramid Books, 1961.

——. *Films and the Second World War.* Cranbury, N.J., A. S. Barnes, 1974.

—— and Heinrich Frankel. *The German Cinema.* New York, Praeger, 1971.

Marcorelles, Louis. "The Nazi Cinema." *Sight and Sound*, v. 25, no. 4, autumn 1955.

Margolin, Leo. *Paper Bullets.* New York, Froben Press, 1946.

Meo, Lucy D. *Japan's Radio War on Australia, 1941–1945.* New York, Cambridge University Press, 1968.

Merton, Robert K. with Marjorie Fiske and Alberta Curtis. *Mass Persuasion: The Social Psychology of a War Bond Drive.* New York & London, Harper, 1946.

Millo, Stelio. "*Appunti sul Fumetto Fascista.*" *Linus*, v. 2, no. 10, January 1966.

Moltmann, Günter. Goebbels' speech on total war, Feb. 18, 1943. In Holborn, Hajo, ed. *Republic to Reich: The Making of the Nazi Revolution.*

Mosse, George L. *Nazi Culture: Intellectual, Cultural and Social Life in the Third Reich.* New York, Grosset and Dunlap, 1966.

Nishimoto, Mitoji. *The Development of Educational Broadcasting in Japan.* Rutland, Vt., Charles E. Tuttle, 1969.

Padover, Saul K. *Experiment in Germany: The Story of an American Intelligence Officer.* New York, Duell, Sloan and Pearce, 1946.

Priestley, J. B. *All England Listened: The Wartime Broadcasts of J. B. Priestley.* New York, Chilmark, 1967.

Rolo, Charles. *Radio Goes to War.* New York, Putnam, 1942.

Rosengarten, F. *The Italian Anti-Fascist Press, 1919–1945.*

Rotha, Paul in collaboration with Sinclair Road and Richard Griffith. *Documentary Film.* London, Faber and Faber, 1952.

—— and Richard Griffith. *The Film Till Now: A Survey of*

World Cinema. New York, Humanities Press,

Rotter, V. "The War in Posters." *Art and Industry*, v. 39, Sept. 1945: 66–79.

Sadoul, Georges. *Le Cinéma pendant la Guerre, 1939–1945.* Paris, Denoel, 1954.

———. *French Film.* London, Falcon Press, 1953.

Sauberli, Harry. "Hollywood and World War II: A Survey of Themes of Hollywood Films about the War 1940–45." M. A. Dissertation, 1967.

Schockel, Erwin. *Das Politische Plakat: Eine Psychologische Betrachtung.* Munich, 1938.

Selz, Peter. "John Heartfield's Photomontages." *Massachusetts Review*, winter 1963: 306–336.

Seth, Ronald. *The Truth Benders.* London, L. Frewin, 1969.

Siepmann, Charles A. *Radio in Wartime.* New York, Oxford University Press, 1942.

Speer, Albert. *Inside the Third Reich: Memoirs.* New York, Macmillan, 1970.

Stedman, Raymond William. *The Serials: Suspense and Drama by Installment.* Norman, Okla., University of Oklahoma Press, 1971.

Stoetzer, Carlos. *Postage Stamps as Propaganda.* Washington, D.C., Public Affairs Press, 1953.

Tannenbaum, Edward R. *The Fascist Experience: Italian Society and Culture, 1922–1945.* New York, Basic Books, 1972.

Watt, Harry. *Don't Look at the Camera.* New York, St. Martin's Press, 1974.

White, John Baker. *The Big Lie.* London, Evans Bros., 1956.

Williams, L. N. and M. *Forged Stamps of Two World Wars.* London, 1954.

Wollenberg, H. H. *Fifty Years of German Film.* London, Falcon Press, 1948.

Wulf, Joseph. *Kunst und Kultur im Dritten Reich*, 4 v. Gütersloh, Sigbert Mohn Verlag, 1963–64.

Wykes, Alan. *Goebbels.* New York, Ballantine, 1973.

———. *The Nuremberg Rallies.* New York, Ballantine, 1970.

Zeman, Z. A. B. *Nazi Propaganda.* London, Oxford University Press, 1964.

Index

Abetz, Otto, 179, 180
Action de la Gueux (newspaper), 191
Africa, 35-36, 37
Agitation, 211
Alexander Nevsky (film), 214, 219
Alfieri, 71
Allan, Jay, 139
All Japanese Songster's Association, 249
Alsace, France, 185
Alsace-Lorraine, 179
Amanauny, Emilien, 191
America First Committee, 141, 151
American Committee for the Struggle against War, 211
American Crusaders, 141
The American League against War and Fascism, 211
American League for Peace and Democracy, 216
L'Amerique en Guerre, 147
Amicucci, Ermano, 85
Amman, Max, 28
Anders, General, 222
Der Angriff, 13
L'Annonce faite à Marie (Claudel), 183
Anti-Semitism
    Fascist Italy, promulgation of, 84
    Nazi dissemination of, 33
    Pound, Ezra, and, 88
    United States and, 142
    in Vichy France, 184
Araki, General Sadao, 246, 247
Architecture (Nazi Germany), 26
Arditi, 67
Army-Navy Screen Magazine, 158
Art
    expressionism and Nazis, 24-25
    in Fascist Italy, 72
    Nazi, 25
    see also Murals
Asia for the Asians, 263
Australia, 254, 256
Austria, Anschluss with, 27
Avantguardisti, 73

Badoglio, Pietro, 88
Balbo, Italo, 69
Balfour, Michael, 285
Balilla, 70, 72, 74
Balilla (radio), 80
Baptism of Fire, 32, 34
Bar-le-Duc, France, 185
Battle for the Ukraine (film), 219
Battle of Britain, 86

Battle of Britain (film), 158
Battle of Cape Matapan, 86
The Battle of China (film), 158
Battle of Orel (film), 219
The Battle of Russia (film), 158
Battle of the Coral Sea, 258
Batton, Barton, Durstine and Osborn, 141
BBC, 188, 284
    Allied propaganda, and, 37-38
    propaganda role, 109
Beaverbrook, Lord, 218
Befehlszentrale, 26
Belgium
    clandestine press in, 190
    New Order and, 184
    resistance to Nazi Germany in, 185-86
Bennett, Rex, 151
Berlin (film), 219
Berryman, Clifford, 150
Beware of the British Serpent, 141
Big lie, 142, 143, 287-88
Bird, Cyril Kenneth, 119
Black propaganda
    British use of
        at Cherbourg, France, 115
        letters home, 114-15
    defined, 111
    Office of Strategic Services (U.S.), 144
    PWD/SHAEF production of, 287
    secret radio transmitters, use of, 112-14
    Soldatensender, 114
Black Record (Vansittart), 111
Blökzijl, Max (Lying Max), 184
Blood Business, the, 141
Blutfahne, 18
Boccasile, Gino, 81, 87
Bolshevism, 36-37, 188
Book burning, 30
Bose, Subhas Chandra, 256
Boy Scouts, 22
Bracken, Brendan, 110
Brecker, Arno, 26
Die Brennessel, 28
British Council, 108
British Psychological Warfare Department, 144
Bruce-Lockhart, Sir Peter, 108, 109, 110
Bruntz, George C., 290
Bund deutscher Madchen, 22
Bureau of Thought Supervision (Japan), 242
Burma, 263

Cabinet Information Bureau (Japan), 242

Campaign Division (MOI) (Gr. Br.), 116
Capra, Frank, 152
Careless talk posters, 119
Carroll, Wallace, 286
Cartoons, 118-19, 150, 152
Cathedral of light, 16-18
Catholic church and Fascist Italian government, 71
    on *Balilla* girls, 74
    on use of religious terminology, 76
    and youth education, 74
Catholic Youth, 22
Cavalcanti, 119
Chakotin, Serge, 212
Chamberlain, Neville, 108, 188
Chapayev, Vasily, 218
Chaplin, Charles, 29, 151
Chartres, France, 185
Cherbourg, France, 115
Childs, Marquis, 141
China, 243-44
Christian Front, the, 141
Churchill, Winston, 33, 108, 110, 188, 192, 284, 285, 288
Chut (newspaper), 190
Ciano, Count Galeazzo, 82
Cinema   *See* Films
Claudel, Paul, 183
Colonel Britton, 186
Comes the Reckoning (Bruce-Lockhart), 110
Comic strips, 72-73
Comintern Congress, 1928, 216
Committee of Public Information (U.S.), 139
Communist Party of California, 216
Compassionate leave, 114
Confessions of a Nazi Spy (film), 151-52
Conversations on Fascist Culture, 72
Cooper, Duff, 108, 109-10
Il Corriere dei Piccoli, 72
Corriere della Sera (newspaper), 71
Corwin, Norman, 148
Council of People's Commisars, 217
Coventrizzare, 86
Coward, Noel, 118
Credere, Obbedire, Combattere (film), 80
Creel, George, 139
Crewe House, 107
Croce, Benedetto, 72
Crossman, Richard H. S., 285, 287
Czechoslovakia, 186

Dalton, Dr. Hugh, 108

Danish Agricultural Pest Commission, 192
D'Annunzio, Gabriele, 67, 72
Davis, Elmer, 144-45
Déat, Marcel, 180
The Defeat of the German Armies before Moscow (film), 219
Defense film organization (China), 242
De Gaulle, Charles, 284
Degenerate art, 25
Degrelle, 184
Delmer, Sefton, 113
Denisovsky, 218
Denmark, 34, 192
Department of Agitation and Propaganda (U.S.S.R.), 211-12
Department of Propaganda to Enemy Countries (Gr. Br.), 108
Der Angriff, 13
Der Führer's Face (film), 152
Der Stürmer, 12, 20
Desert Victory (film), 118
Die Brennessel, 28
Die Kunst im Dritten Reich, 25
La Difensa della Razza, 84
Disney, Walt, 152
Divide and Conquer (film), 158
Documentary films
    Soviet Union, use of, 219
    United States, use of, 152
Domei, 248-49, 257
Donald Duck, 152
Donovan, Colonel William O., 144
Doolittle, General James, 258-59
Dopolavoro, 76-77
Duce, the   *See* Mussolini, Benito
Duke of Windsor, 29
Dunkirk, 181
Dutch Nazi Party, 184

Ebert, Friedrich, 107
Eckart, Dietrich, 28
Eden, Anthony, 33-34
Efimov, 218
Ein Arzt sucht seinen Weg (Kunkel), 30
Eisenhower, General Dwight D., 146, 284
Eisenstein, Sergei, 214, 219
Enciclopedia Italiana, 69
Ente Italiano Audizione Radiofonica, 80
Ente Radio Rurale (Italy), 81
Ethiopia, 84
    Italian invasion of, 81
Evening Standard, 119
Evocatio, 283

Exhibitions
    in Fascist Italy
        Mostra della Rivoluzione Fascista, 81
        use of, 81
Exhibitions Division (MOI), (Gr. Br.), 116
Expressionist art, 24-25

Facta, 69
Falcon Fighters (film), 252
Falling Leaf, 32, 180
Fall of the City (MacLeish), 283
The False Song of Victory (Matsushima), 258
Fanck, Arnold, 250
Fasces, 69
Fasci di combattimento, 69-70
Fasci Femminili, 73
Fascism
    D'Annunzio, Gabriele, role of, 67
    Japanese propaganda favoring, 250
    symbol for, 69-70
    violence, role of, 69
Fascist Italy
    ancient Rome, identification with, 70
    anti-British propaganda, 85
    anti-Semitism, promulgation of, 84
    entrance into war, 86-87
    France, relationship with, 86
    Great Britain, relationship with, 84-85
    Mussolini, Benito, fall of, 88
    Nazi Germany and, 87, 88
    propaganda in U.S. compared to Germany, 88
    U.S., relationship with, 86
    women in, 73-74
    work, attitude in, 85
    youth organizations in, 71-73
Fascistizzare, 69
Fascist Party (Gr. Br.), 108
Feldzug im Polen (film), 34
Ferdonnet, 32, 180
Ferrara, Italy, 69
Fifth Column Fear (film), 252
Film
    anti-Bolshevik, 36-37
    China, use of, 242
    in Fascist Italy
        Battle of the Grain, 77
        Credere, Obbedire, Combattere, 80
        I ragazzi di Mussolini, 77-80
        Luciano Serra Pilota, 80
        Scipio Africanus, 80
        The Siege of Alcazar, 80

Il Sole, 77
L'Uomo della Croce, 80
    use of, 77-80
German-Japanese venture, 250
Goebbels, Joseph, and, 19
in Great Britain, 116-18
    Desert Victory, 118
    In Which We Serve, 118
    The Life and Death of Colonel Blimp, 118
    London Can Take It, 118
    Men of the Lightship, 118
    San Demetrio London, 118
    Spring Offensive, 118
    Target for Tonight, 118
    They Also Serve, 118
    Yellow Caesar, 119
in Japan, 250-52
    Falcon Fighters, 252
    Fifth Column Fear, 252
    Five Scouts, 250
    International Smuggling Game, 252
    The Last Days of the British Empire, 252
    Miracle Worker, 252
    Most Beautifully, 252
    The Opium War, 252
    A Record of Love, 252
    Torpedo Squadrons Move Out, 252
    Volunteers of Death, 252
    You're Being Aimed At, 252
in Nazi Germany, 19-21
    Jüd Süss, 20
    Olympia, 19-20
    A Pass in Promise, 21
    Triumph of Will, 19
resistance, use of, 191-92
    in Denmark, 192
    Pontcarvel, 191-92
    Les Visiteurs du Soir, 192
in Soviet Union
    Alexander Nevsky, 219
    documentaries, 219
    Girl No. 217, 219
    Secretary of the District Committee, 219
    Turksib, 212
    Zoya, 219
in United States, 150-58
    The Battle of Britain, 158
    The Battle of China, 158
    The Battle of Russia, 158
    Confessions of a Nazi Spy, 151-52
    Divide and Conquer, 158

documentary films, 152
Der Führer's Face, 152
The Great Dictator, 151
March of Time, 152
The Moon is Down, 151
Mrs. Miniver, 151
The Nazi Strike (1943), 152-58
North Star, 152
Prelude to War (1942), 152
Secret Service in Darkest Africa, 151
serials, 151
Two Down, One to Go, 158
War Comes to America, 158
"Why We Fight," 152
in Vichy France, 182
La Libre Amérique, 183
youth, indoctrination through, 21
Film distributors, 152
Finland, 211
Fireside chats, 148
Fitzpatrick, Daniel, 150
Fiume, Italy, 67
Five Scouts (film), 250
Foro Mussolini, 70
Fougasse See Bird, Cyril Kenneth
Fox Movietone, 152
France
see also Vichy France
during Phony War, 32-33
Fascist Italy, relationship with, 86
May-June crisis of 1940, 180
New Order, role in, 181-84
1936-1939 Nazi propaganda against, 179
resistance in
films, use of, 191-92
Saar plebiscite, handling of, 27
surrender to Germany, 34
United States propaganda and
L'Amérique en Guerre, role, 147
leaflets, role, 147
see also Vichy France
Free India (radio), 256
Free Yugoslavia (radio), 216
French Resistance, 184
Fresco painting, 25
Fronterlebnis, 29
Frontpost (newspaper), 147, 290
Der Führer's Face (film), 152
Funk, Walter, 181

Games, Abram, 119
Garbo, Greta, 29
Garibaldi, Guiseppe, 87

Gentile, Giovanni, 71, 72
German-American Bund, 142
German-Americans, 142-43
German Social Democrats, 107
Germany See Nazi Germany
Germany Calling (film), 118
Gestapo, 184
Giese, Hans-Joachim, 32
Giolitti, 69
Giornale dei Balilla, 72
Giornalino del Fanciullo, 80-81
Giovanni Fascisti, 73
Giovanni Italiane, 73
Giovinezza, 71
Giraudoux, Jean, 180
Girl No. 217 (film), 219
Goebbels, Joseph, 11, 29, 30, 31, 37, 188, 192
activities of, 1939-1940, 34
activities of, 1941-1942, 35-36
cinema role of, 19
death of, 40
end of war years activities, 38-40
führer legend, creation of, 13-16, 34-35
German-Japanese film venture, 250
Iron Curtain, use of term, 183
Katyn incident and, 38-40
Night of the Long Knives, presentation of, 16
Officer's Plot of July 20, 1944, role in, 40
Olympic Games, presentation of, 20
as political propagandist, 12-16
propaganda against France, 180
propaganda and truth, 18-19
radio, use of, 26
Soldatensender, on, 114
Spanish Civil War and, 179
Total War speech, 36
unconditional surrender declaration and, 117
Goering, Hermann, 37
Gold vs. work, 85
Goose step, 82
Grandi, Count, 85
Gray propaganda, 287
Great Britain
Allied propaganda by BBC, 37-38
Fascist Italy, and
as pre-war enemy, 84-85
propaganda against, 85
France, and
destruction of fleet at Mers-el-Kabir, 182

during Phony War, 180
Japan, and
propaganda against, 249
World War I attitude toward, 243
Nazi Germany, and
during Phony War, 32-33
relationship with, 31
Press Censorship Department, 116
propaganda
against Fascist Italy, 87
delivered to Germany in World War I, 107
home use, World War I, 107
up to World War II, 108
United States, and, 142
The Great Dictator (film), 151
The Greater East Asia Co-Prosperity Sphere, 252-55
The Great Patriotic War, 217
Grossdeutsche Reich, 181
Gruppi Universitari Fascisti, 72
Guadalcanal island, 258
Guernica (Picasso), 283
Gurfein, Murray I., 285

Hakko Ichiu, 246
Halifax, Lord, 119
Harmsworth, Alfred, II, 107
Harris, Air Marshal Francis, 110
Heimatroman, 30
Herz, Martin F., 285, 290
Hitler, Adolph, 11, 37-38, 288
on Churchill, 33
declaration of Russian victory, 112
on Fascist Italy slogans, 82
French policy, 1936-1939, 179
Führer legend, 34-35
Goebbels, J., creation of legend by, 13-16
as military propagandist, 12
Mussolini, meeting with, 82-84
Night of the Long Knives, role, 16
Officer's Plot of July 20, 1944, 40
on propaganda, role, 180
radio, use of, 26
Spanish Civil War and, 179
Hitler ist der Sieg, 40
Hitlerites, 222
Hitler Youth, 22
Hohlwein, Ludwig, 24
Holland
clandestine press in, 191
New Order and, 184
resistance to Nazi Germany in, 185

Hollywood
    films for propaganda purposes, 150-58
    Nazis, representation of, in, 151
    see also Films in U.S.
Holy Russia speech (Stalin), 217
Homosexuality, 21-22
Horst Wessel Lied, 18
House of Orange, 185
Huss, Jan, 186
Huston, John, 152

Il Corriere dei Piccoli, 72
Il Messaggero (newspaper), 71
Il passo Romano, 82
Il Sole (film), 77
Il Tempo, 86
Il Tevere, 74
India, 256
Indian National Army, 256
Indonesia, 253, 254, 263
Information films   *See* Documentary
    films
Inghilterre e Italia nel' 900 (Smith), 86
Inspectorate for Radio Broadcasting
    (Italy), 80
Instituto Nazionale Fascista di Cultura, 72
International Smuggling Game (film),
    252
Interventionists, 144
In Which We Serve (film), 118
I Raggazi di Mussolini, 77-80
Ireland, 33
Iron Curtain, 183
Isolationism
    Coughlin, Father, role, 141
    Roosevelt, Franklin D., and, 139-140
    World War I propaganda influence on,
        139
Italian Academy, 72
Italy   *See* Fascist Italy
Itami, Mansaka, 250

Jackson, C. D., 285
Japan
    Australia and, 254, 256
    censorship system, 257-58
    failure as colonizer, 263
    films, production of, 250-52
    German-Japanese Cultural agreement,
        250
    India, relationship with, 256
    Indonesia and, 253, 254
    industrial emergence, 243

Malaya and, 253
    patriotic weeks, use of, 249
    Pearl Harbor attack, 257
    Philippines and, 253
    Potsdam Declaration of 1945 and, 262
    propaganda
        internal difficulties, 263
        pre-World War II attitude toward,
            242
    radio
        prisoner-of-war broadcasts, 256-57
        use of, 254
    religion, political structure of, 246
    Sino-Japanese conflict, 243-44
    United States propaganda and, 152
Japanese-Americans, 148
Jaroslavski, 222
Jenning, Humphrey, 118
Jewish Bolshevism, 179
Jew Süss (film), 182
Jimmu, 246
Johst, Hanns, 29
Joyce, William (Lord Haw Haw), 33
Jüd Süss, 20
Jugs, 109
Jünger, Ernst, 21

Kadaver factory, 107
Kamikaze pilot, 260, 261
Kato, Masuo, 260
Katyn incident, 38-40
Knight, Eric, 152
Kodo, 253
Kokuhonsha association, 246
Kokutai, 246
Kosmodemyanskaya, Zoya, 219
Kraft durch Freude, 76
Krylov, Porfiri, 218
Kuhn, Fritz, 142
Kukriniski, the, 218
Kunkel, 30
Die Kunst im Dritten Reich, 25
Kuprinov, Mikhail, 218

L'Annonce faite à Marie (Claudel), 183
La Difensa della Razza, 84
La Libre Amérique (film), 183
La Libre Belgique (newspaper), 190
L'Amérique en Guerre, 147
La Nave (D'Annunzio), 67
Lasswell, Harold, 110, 116, 284
The Last Days of the British Empire
    (film), 252
Laval, Pierre, 184, 188

Leaflet bomb, 146
Leaflets
    Great Britain, use of, 110
    Nazi Germany, use of, 32-33
    Phony War, use of, 180
    PWD/SHAEF use of, 285-86
    safe conduct passes, 147
    United States, use of, 146-47, 259-60
Lebedev, 218
Lectura Duci, 77
Légion Volontaire Française, 183
Le Monde du Travail (newspaper), 190
Lenin, Nikolai, 211, 212
Leninist (radio station), 33
Les inconnus dans la maison (film), 182
Le Soir (newspaper), 141
Le Soir Volé (newspaper), 191
Les Visiteurs du Soir (film), 192
Letters as black propaganda, 114
Leva Fascista, 73
La Libre Amérique (film), 183
La Libre Belgique (newspaper), 190
Libyan campaign, 108-9
The Life and Death of Colonel Blimp
    (film), 118
Lightships, 118
Lindbergh, Charles, 141
Litvak, Anatole, 152
Lloyd George, David, 107
London Can Take It (film), 118
Lord Haw Haw, 33
The Lost War (Kato), 260
Low, David, 109, 118-19
LUCE   *See* L'Unione Cinematografica
    Edcutiva
Luciano Serra Pilota (film), 80
L'Unione Cinematografica Educativa,
    77-80
L'Uomo della Croce (film), 80
Luzzio, Allesandro, 85
Lying Max, (Max Blockzijl), 184

MacArthur, General Douglas, 260
McClure, Robert A., 285
MacLeish, Archibald, 283
Main Political Education Committee of
    the Republic (U.S.S.R.), 212
Malaya, 253, 263
Mamelli, Goffredo, 69
Mann, Thomas, 29
Ma Perkins, 150
March of Time (films), 152
Marconi, Guglielmo, 72
Mariana Islands, 259

Martin, David Stone, 150
Masaryk, Thomas, 186
Mass demonstrations
    Goebbels, Joseph, use of, 16
    Speer, Albert, role, 16-18
Mass production, 158
Matsushima, Rear Admiral, 258
Mauldin, Bill, 150
Mayakovsky, 212
Megret, Maurio, 184
Mein Kampf (Hitler), 12, 82
Men of the Lightship (film), 118
Il Messaggero (newspaper), 71
Midway island, 258
Milan, Italy, 77
Miniature magazine, 110
Ministry for Popular Enlightenment and
    Propaganda, 11
Ministry of Information (Gr. Br.), 108,
    109, 180
    Campaigns Division, 116
    Exhibitions Division, 116
    Publication Division, 116
    World War II propaganda function,
    115-16
Ministry of Popular Culture (Italy), 71
Miracle Worker (film), 252
Miranuma, Baron, 246
Mix, Tom, 151
Mjolnir, 24
MOI   *See* Ministry of Information
    (Gr. Br.)
Monroe, James, 146
Monte Cassino, 147
The Moon is Down (film), 151
Moor, 219
Mosley, Sir Oswald, 108
Most Beautifully (film), 252
Mostra della Rivoluzione Fascista
    (exhibit), 81
Motion Picture Law of 1920 (Germany),
    19
Motion pictures   *See* Film
Mrs. Miniver (film), 151
Murals, 25-26
Murrow, Edward R., 111
Mussert, Anton, 184
Mussolini, Benito
    declaration of war against U.S., 111-12
    Hitler, meeting with, 82
    on female youth, 74
    on film as propaganda, 77
    on the Italian Empire, 81
    slogans, coining of, 81

Spanish Civil War and, 179
use of piazza, 67

Nachrichten für die Truppe, 287
Nana (film), 21
National and Patriotic Association of
    Publicists, 249
National Socialism   *See* Nazi Party
La Nave (D'Annunzio), 67
Nazi Art, 25
Nazi Germany
    Africa, expulsion from, 35-36
    Allied propaganda, effect of, 37-38
    architecture in, 26
    book burning in, 30
    as defenders of Western civilization, 36
    French policy, 1936-1939, 179, 180
    German-Americans, influence of, 142-43
    German-Japanese cultural agreement,
        250
    Great Britain, and
        propaganda from, 107
        relationship with, 31
    homosexuality in, 21-22
    literature in, 29
    New Order and France, role in 181-84
    newspapers in, 28-29
    propaganda, use of, 11-40
    propaganda compared to Fascist Italy,
        88
    propaganda strategy, 288
    PWD/SHAEF campaign against,
        284-90
    radio, use of, 26-27, 28
    resistance against in occupied coun-
        tries, 184-88
    Riefenstahl, Leni, presentation of,
        19-20
    sculpture in, 26
    Soviet Union, and
        invasion of, 35-37
        1941 declaration of victory, 87
        occupation of territory, 224
        pact of friendship, 216-17
        prisoner of war propaganda, 222-24
        relationship with, 30-31
        Stalingrad, explanation of, 36
        traditional feelings, 37
        war attitude of, 222
    Spanish Civil War, role in, 179
    theater in, 29
    United States, and
        prewar relationship, 141-42
        propaganda

leaflets, role of, 147
    Sternebanner, 147
    Vichy France, relationship with, 182
    V sign, adoption of, 186
Nazi Party, 22
The Nazi Strike (film), 152-53
Nazi-Soviet pact of August 1939, 141
Netherlands *See* Holland
Nevsky, Alexander, 218
New Deal (U.S.), 148
The New Earth (film), 250
New Order, the, and
    Belgium, 184
    France, 181-84
    Holland, 184
    Norway, 184
Newspapers *See* Press, the
Newsreels
    Baptism of Fire, 32
    in Nazi Germany, 32
    United States, uses of, 152, 158
The Night of the Long Knives, 16
1928 Comintern Congress, 216
Nitti, 69
Nippon Demp, 249
Non abbiamo bisogno, 74
Normandy, invasion of, 38
North Africa, 35-36, 37
Northcliffe, Lord, 11, 107
North Star (film), 152
Norway, 34
    Allied report on, 188
    New Order and, 184
Nuremburg, Germany, 16
Nuremburg Rally, 1934, 19-20

The Oath of the People (film), 250
Office of Facts and Figures (Gr. Br.), 174
Office of Strategic Services (U.S.),
    144, 284
Office of War Information (U.S.), 144,
    146, 150, 262-63, 284
Officers' Plot of July 20, 1944, 40
Ohm Krüger (film), 182
Olympia (film), 19-20
Olympic Games (Berlin), 19-20
Ondine (Giraudoux), 180
The Opium War (film), 252
The Oppenheim Family (1939), 214
Orlemanski Stanislas, 222
OSS, 144, 284
Osservatore Romano, (newspaper) 74
Owens, Jessie, 20
OWI, 144, 146, 150, 262-63, 284

Pact of Steel, 84
Padover, Saul K., 285
Paintings   *See* Art; Pictorial art;
    Murals
Paley, William S., 285
Panay (ship), 152
Partridge, Bernard, 119
A Pass in Promise (film), 21
Passierschein leaflet, 286
Il Passo Romano, 82
Patriotic week, 249
Pavolini, 71
Pearl Harbor, 148
Pease, Lute, 150
Perkins, Ma, 150
Petain, Marshal Henri, 182, 188
Philippines, the, 253
Phony War, 32, 180
Picasso, Pablo, 283
Piccole Italiane, 73
Pictorial art, 24-25
Pi Pao, 242
Pirandello, Luigi, 72
Pope,
Plank, Josef, 28
Platz, Franz Josef, 30
Plays *See* Theater
Poland
    clandestine press in, 190
    Katyn incident, 38-40
    partitioning of, 217
    resistance to Nazi Germany in, 185
Political Bureau of the All Union Com-
    munist Party, 217
Political cartoons, 118-19
Political Warfare Executive, 109-284
Pontcarvel (film), 191-92
Pope Pius XI, 74
Popolo d'Italia (newspaper), 71
Popular Front, the, 179
Postage stamps, use of,
    by Fascist Italy, 70
    by Nazi Germany, 24
    by Soviet Union, 217
Posters
    Careless talk posters, 119
    China, 242
    Fascist Italy, 81
    France, 181-82
    Great Britain, 119
    Japan, 242
    Nazi use of, 22-24
    resistance, 188
    Soviet Union, 212, 218-19

Tass window posters, 219
    United States, 150
    Potsdam Declaration of 1945, 262
Pound, Ezra, 88
Prelude to War (film), 152
Press, the
    clandestine press
        Action de la Gueux, 191
        Chut (Belgium), 190
        Le Groupe de la rue de Lille, 191
        information in, 191
        in occupied countries, 190-91
        La Libre Belgique, 190
        Le Monde du Travail, 190
        Le Soir Volé, 191
    in Fascist Italy, 70-71
    in Nazi Germany
        control of, 28-29
        Die Brennessel, 28
        Sprachregelungen, 28-29
        Völkischer Beobachter, 28
    Japan
        Domei, 248-49
        management of, 248-49
Press Censorship Department (Gr. Br.),
    116
Press Decree of 1924, 70-71
Priestley, J. B., 116
Professor Mamlock (film), 214
Propaganda
    black, 111
    Cold War, use of, 283
    credibility, role of, 287
    democracies and, 142-43
    Great Britain, World War I, 107-19
    Hollywood and, 150-51
    Italy, 70-88
    Japan, use of, 243-64
    mass demonstration, 16-18
    Nazi Germany, use of, 11-40
    postage stamps as, 24
    posters
        in Fascist Italy, use of, 81
        Great Britain, use of, 119
        Nazi Germany, use of, 22-24
        United States, use of, 150
    Pound, Ezra, role, 88
    process of, 284
    PWD/SHAEF, strategy of truth,
        286-89
    resistance, use of, 190-92
    strategy of, 283-84
    theater as
        Fascist Italy, use of, 77

    in Nazi Germany, 29-30
    truth and, 18-19
    United States, use of, 139-58
    white, 111
    word of mouth, 116
Propaganda railway train, 219
Propaganda squads, 242
Psychological warfare
    campaign against Germany, 283-90
    PWD/SHAEF campaign against Nazi
        Germany, 284-90
Psychological warfare departments
    British Psychological Warfare
        department, 144
    Office of Strategic Services (U.S.),
        144
    Office of War Information (U.S.), 144
Psychological Warfare Division/
    Supreme Headquarters Allied
    Expeditionary Force
        See PWD/SHAEF
Publications Division (MOI) (Gr. Br.),
    116
Puccini, Giacomo, 72
PWD/SHAEF, 283-84
    obedience training strategy, 285
    organization of, 284-85
    propaganda
        factualism and indirection, 289-90
        policy against Nazi Germany, 284-90
    strategy of truth, 286-89
PWE, 109, 284

Quisling, Vidkun, 183, 184

Radio
    in Fascist Italy
        Ethiopia invasion, role, 81
    Great Britain, use of, 37-38, 110-11
    in Japan
        prisoner-of-war broadcasts, 256-57
        use of, 248, 254
    in Nazi Germany
        Anschluss with Austria, role, 27
        foreign broadcasting, 28, 33
        radio warden, role, 27
        Saar plebiscite, role, 27
        use of, 26-27
    resistance, role, 190, 192
    secret radio transmitter, use of, 112-14
    in Soviet Union, post-Revolution, use
        of, 212
    in United States
        fireside chats, 148

"This is War", 148-50
 use of, 148-50
Radio warden, 27
RAF, 86-87
Rallies See Mass demonstration
The Rape of the Masses (Chakotin), 212
A Record of Love (film), 252
Regime Fascista (newspaper), 71
Reich Chamber of Culture, 30
Reich Motion Picture Law, 19
Reichswasserleiche, 21
Reich Theater Chamber, 29
Religion
 Japan, role in political structure of, 246
 Soviet Union and, 214-16
  attitude after 1941, 222
Resistance
 Allied propaganda and, 188-89
 in Belgium, 185
 cinema, use of, 191-92
 clandestine press, role in, 190-91
 in Czechoslovakia, 186
 in Holland, 185
 in Poland, 185
 posters, use of, 188
 radio, use of, 190-92
 in Vichy France, 184-85
 V sign, use of, 186
Ridley, Charles, 118
Riefenstahl, Leni, 19, 20, 118
Ritter, Karl, 21
Rockwell, Norman, 150
Roetter, Charles, 33
Rogerson, Sydney, 119
Rome, ancient, 70
Roosevelt, Franklin, 110, 288
 fireside chats, 148
 isolationism and, 139-40
Rost, 212
Royal Air Force, 86-87
Russia See Soviet Union
Rust, Dr., 21

The Saar—the Way to Understanding is
 Clear, 27
Saar plebiscite, 27
Safe conduct passes, 147
Saipan, 259
San Demetrio London (film), 118
Scarface (film), 77
Schunzel, 29
Schweitzer, Hans, 24
Scipio Africanus (film), 80
Scotland, 33

Scottish transmitter, 33
Sculpture, 26
 in Nazi Germany, 26
Second Rome, 70
Secretary of the District Committee
 (film), 219
Secret Service in Darkest Africa (film),
 151
Seine-et-Oise, France, 185
Seppla, 28
Serials (film), 151
Seth, Ronald, 147
Seyss-Inquart, 185
Shahn, Ben, 150
Shaw, George Bernard, 29
Sherwood, Robert E., 144
Sicilian invasion, 146
The Siege of Alcazar, 80
Siege of Leningrad (film), 219
Sieg im Westen (film), 34
Silver Shirts, the, 141
Sino-Japanese conflict, 243-44
Slogans, 81-82
Smith, Dennis Mack, 86
Social Justice (magazine), 141
Söderbaum, Kristina, 20, 21
Sokolov, Nikolai, 218
Sokolov-Skaya, 218
Soldatensender, 114
Soldatensender West, 287
Il Sole (film), 77
Solomon Islands, 258
Sondermeldungen, 37
Sons of the She-Wolf, 72
Soviet Department of Church Affairs,
 222
Soviet Union
 communications media, use of, 211
 Department of Agitation and
  Propaganda, 211-12
 felons, use of, 219
 film, use of, 212-13
 Finland, invasion of, 211
 Katyn incident, 38-40
 Nazi Germany, and
  invasion of, 35-37
  occupation of territory, 224
  pact of friendship, 216-17
  propaganda to prisoners of war,
   222-24
  relationship to, 30-31
  Stalingrad, explanation of defeat, 36
  traditional feelings, 37
  Vichy France and, 183

 war attitude toward, 222
 postage stamps, use of, 217
 posters, use of, 212, 218-19
 propaganda railway train, 219
 radio, use of, 212
 religion in
  attitude after 1941, 222
  propaganda against, 214-16
 United States
  films and, 152
  relation with, 216
Spain, 179
Spanish Civil War, 179
Speer, Albert, 16-18, 26, 82
Sports (Italy), 73, 76-77
Spracheregelungen, 28-29
Spring Offensive (film), 118
Squadristi, 69-70
SS (Schutzstaffel), 184
Stalin, Joseph, 31, 211, 216, 217, 224
Stalingrad (U.S.S.R.), 36
Stamps See Postage Stamps
Standing Directive for Psychological
  Warfare, 286-87, 289
State Publicity Corporation (U.S.S.R.),
 212
Stefani, 80
Sternebanner (newspaper), 147
Streicher, Julius, 20
Der Stürmer (newspaper), 12, 20
Suvorov, 218

Talmedge, R. H., 119
Target for Tonight (film), 118
Tass window posters, 219
Il Tempo (newspaper), 86
Il Tevere (newspaper), 74
Textbooks, 72
Theater
 China, use of, 241-42
 Fascist Party (Italy), use of, 77
 in Nazi Germany, 29-30
Theater Law of 1934, 29
They Also Serve (film), 118
The Third Reich See Nazi Germany
Third Rome, 70
This is London (Murrow), 111
This is War (radio series), 148-50
Thompson, Dorothy, 144
Thorak, Josef, 26
Thought war, 242
Tito, Marshal, 216
Todt Organization, 88
Toguri, Iva Ikuko (Tokyo Rose), 256

Tojo, General, 246, 258
Tokyo Rose, 256
Torpedo Squadrons Move Out (Film),
    252
Toscanini, Arturo, 72
Total War (Goebbels), 36
Traitors and Patriots (film), 21
Travail! Famille! Patrie!, 183
Treaty of Locarno, 179
Treaty of Versailles, 179
Triumph of Will (film), 19-20, 118
The Truth Benders (Seth), 147
Tunisia, 37
Turati, 74
Turksib (film), 212
Two Down, One To Go (film), 158

UFA studio, 19
The Unconquerable Soul (exhibit), 116
Undersecretariat for Press and
        Propaganda (Italy), 71
L'Unione Cinematografica Educativa,
    77-80
Union of Soviet Socialist Republics
    See Soviet Union
Union of the Militant Godless, 214, 222
United Newsreels, 158
United States
    Fascist Italy, relationship with, 86
    film, use of, 150-58
    Japan, relationship with
        assessment of character, 257
        propaganda against, 249
    leaflets, use of, 146-47
    Nazi Germany and, 141
    propaganda, use of, 139-58
    Soviet Union, attitude toward, 216
L'Uono della Croce (film), 80
U.S.S.R.   *See* Soviet Union

V-1 and V-2 secret weapons, 38, 186

Valéry-Larbaud, 183
Vansittart, Lord, 111
Vargas, Jorge, 253
Vatican, the   *See* Catholic Church
VE (radio), 26
Velodrom d'Hiver episode, 184
Vichy France
    anti-Semitism in, 184
    film in, 182
    Germany, relationship with, 182
    resistance in, 184-85
    Soviet Union and, 183-84
    SS and Gestapo in, 184
    see also France
Victory gardens, 150
Vienna (film), 219
Viktoria, 186
Village in the Red Storm (film), 36-37
The Virgin's Association (Indonesia),
    254
Vittorio Emmanuele III, 81
Völkischer Beobachter, 12, 28, 112
Volunteers of Death (film), 252
Von Hindenburg, Paul, 16
Von Krosig, Schwerin, 19
Von Schieben, General, 115
Von Schirach, Baldur, 22
V sign, 186

War Comes to America (film), 158
War posters   *See* Posters
Watt, Harry, 118
What Is To Be Done? (Lenin), 211, 212
Whispering campaign, 38
White propaganda
    defined, 111
    Hitler, declaration of Russian Victory,
        112
    Murrow, Edward R., broadcast, 111
    Mussolini, declaration of war, 111-12
    Office of War Information (U.S.), 144

PWD/SHAEF production of, 287
Why We Fight Back (film), 152
Willy and Joe (cartoon), 150
Wilson, Woodrow, 139
Wings over Honolulu (film), 77
Wintershilfesspende, 35
    Hitler, relationship to, 18
Women (Fascist Italy), 73-74
Word of mouth propaganda, 116
Working class (Fascist Party, Italy),
    76-77
The World Congress against War, 211
World War I
    propaganda
        Great Britain, use of, 107
        United States, use of, 139

Yellow Caesar (film Cavalcanti), 119
You're Being Aimed At (film), 252
Youth
    indoctrination of, 246-47
        in Fascist Italy, 71-72
        in Japan, 246-47
        in Nazi Germany, 21, 22
Youth education in Fascist Italy
    radio, use of, 80-81
    Sons of the She-Wolf, 72
Youth organizations
    in Fascist Italy
        Avantaguardisti, 73
        Balilla, 72-73
        Giovanni Fascisti, 73
        Giovanni Italiane, 73
        Leve Fascisti, 73
        Piccole Italiane, 73

Zarianov, 214
Zoya (film), 219

Credits

P. 11, (Bottom, left) Library of Congress. P. 17, (Bottom, left) Library of Congress; (Top, right) Library of Congress; (Bottom, right) National Archives; (Middle, right) Library of Congress. P. 18, (Top and bottom) Library of Congress. P. 19, (Top) Library of Congress. P. 21, (Top) Library of Congress; (Middle and bottom) Museum of Modern Art Stills Library. P. 25, (Bottom) Library of Congress. P. 26, (Top, middle and bottom) Library of Congress. P. 27. (Top) Harris Lewine Collection. P. 28, Library of Congress. P. 29, Library of Congress. P. 31, (Top and bottom) Museum of Modern Art Stills Library. P. 32, Library of Congress. P. 33, (Bottom) Library of Congress. P. 35, (Bottom) Library of Congress. P. 36, Musée Royal. P. 37, (Top and bottom) Herb Friedman Collection. Pp. 38, 39, Richard Merkin Collection. P. 40, (Top) Richard Merkin Collection; (Middle) Library of Congress; (Bottom) National Archives; (Bottom, right) Library of Congress. P. 41, Library of Congress. P. 42, Library of Congress. P. 43, U.S. Army Historical Collection. P. 44, U.S. Army Historical Collection. P. 45, (Top, left) Library of Congress; (Top, right) Library of Congress; (Bottom, left) Library of Congress; (Bottom, right) Imperial War Museum. P. 46, (Top, left) Library of Congress; (Top, right) Bundesarchiv; (Bottom) Library of Congress. P. 48, (Top, left) Library of Congress; (Top, right) Library of Congress. P. 49, Library of Congress. P. 50, (Top, right) Library of Congress. P. 52, Bundesarchiv. P. 53, (Top, left) Library of Congress. P. 55, Library of Congress. P. 56, (Top, left) Library of Congress. P. 57, (Top, right) Library of Congress; (Bottom) Library of Congress. P. 58, (Top, left) Library of Congress. P. 58, Bundesarchiv. P. 59, Library of Congress. P. 60, (Top, left) Imperial War Museum; (Bottom, left) Library of Congress. P. 61, (Bottom) Imperial War Museum. P. 62, (Top, left) Musée Royal de l'Armée et d'Histoire Militaire; (Top, right) Bundesarchiv; (Bottom, left) Bundesarchiv. P. 64, Milton Cohen Collection. P. 67, National Archives. P. 71, Culver Pictures, Inc. P. 74, Culver Pictures, Inc. P. 75, (Top) National Archives; (Bottom) Museum of Modern Art Stills Library. Pp. 78, 79, (Entire spread) National Archives. P. 82, (Top) Milton Cohen Collection. P. 84, National Archives. P. 85, National Archives. P. 87, Library of Congress. P. 88, National Archives. P. 91, (Bottom, right) Milton Cohen Collection. P. 93, (Bottom, left) Library of Congress. P. 94, (Top, middle and bottom) Hoover Institution on War, Peace and Revolution. P. 95, Library of Congress. P. 98, (Top, left) Archivio Capitolino; (Top, right) Archivio Capitolino. P. 99, (Top, left) Archivio Capitolino; (Top, right) Archivio Capitolino. P. 100, Archivio Capitolino. P. 103, Archivio Capitolino. P. 104, Library of Congress. P. 107, (Top) National Archives. P. 112, (Top) Milton Cohen Collection; (Bottom) Herb Friedman Collection. P. 114, (Top) Imperial War Museum; (Bottom) Imperial War Museum. P. 115, (Top) Imperial War Museum; (Bottom) Imperial War Museum. P. 116, (Top and bottom) Imperial War Museum. P. 117, Museum of Modern Art Stills Library. P. 118, (All photos) Museum of Modern Art Stills Library. P. 120, Les Zeiger Collection. P. 121, Imperial War Museum. P. 122, (Top, left) Library of Congress; (Top, right) Library of Congress; (Bottom) Imperial War Museum. P. 123, Imperial War Museum. P. 124, (Top, left) Imperial War Museum; (Top, right) Imperial War Museum; (Bottom, left) Imperial War Museum. P. 125, (Top, left) Imperial War Museum; (Top, right) Imperial War Museum; (Bottom, left) Imperial War Museum; (Bottom, right) Imperial War Museum. P. 126, (Top, left) Imperial War Museum; (Top, right) Imperial War Museum. P. 127, (Top, left) Imperial War Museum; (Top, right) Imperial War Museum. P. 128, Imperial War Museum. P. 129, Imperial War Museum. P. 130, (Top, right) National Archives; (Bottom, left) National Archives; (Bottom, right) Imperial War Museum. P. 131, Imperial War Museum. P. 132, Library of Congress. P. 133, (Top and bottom) Milton Cohen Collection. P. 134, Library of Congress. P. 135, Richard Merkin Collection. P. 136, (Top) Library of Congress; (Bottom) Imperial War Museum. P. 139, (Top and middle) Library of Congress; (Bottom) Les Zeiger Collection. P. 140, (Top and bottom) Library of Congress. P. 141, (Top) Library of Congress; (Bottom) Culver Pictures, Inc. P. 142, (Middle) Library of Congress. P. 143, (Top and bottom) National Archives. P. 146, Herb Friedman Collection. P. 147, (Top and bottom) Les Zeiger Collection; (Middle) National Archives. P. 148, (Top and bottom) Les Zeiger Collection. P. 149, (Entire page) Les Zeiger Collection. P. 154, (Entire page) Culver Pictures, Inc. P. 156, (Second row, right) New York Public Library. P. 158, (Top) Les Zeiger Collection; (Middle and bottom) Museum of Modern Art Stills Library. P. 159, (Top and bottom) Museum of Modern Art Stills Library. P. 160, (Top) Museum of Modern Art Stills Library. P. 161, Library of Congress. P. 162, Richard Merkin Collection. P. 163, San Francisco Archive of Comic Art. P. 164, (Top, left) National Archives; (Top, right) National Archives; (Bottom, left) Library of Congress; (Bottom, right) Library of Congress. P. 165, Les Zeiger Collection. P. 166, (Bottom) San Francisco Archive of Comic Art. P. 167, (Top, left) San Francisco Archive of Comic Art; (Top, right) Library of Congress; (Bottom) Copyright © Esquire Magazine. P. 169, National Archives. P. 171, National Archives. P. 172, (Bottom, left) National Archives. P. 173, (Top, left) National Archives; (Top, right) National Archives; (Bottom) National Archives. P. 174, (Top, right) National Archives; (Bottom, left) National Archives; (Bottom, right) National Archives. P. 175, (Top, left) National Archives; (Top, right) National Archives; (Bottom, left) National Archives; (Bottom, right) National Archives. P. 183, Musée Royal de l'Armée et d'Histoire Militaire. P. 185, (Top) Musée Royal de l'Armée et d'Histoire Militaire; (Bottom) Bibliotheque Nationale de Documentation. P. 186, (Second row, left) National Archives; (Third row, left) Musée Royal de l'Armée et d'Histoire Militaire; (Third row, left) Peter Robbs Collection. P. 187, Museum of Modern Art Stills Library. P. 188, (Bottom) Peter Robbs Collection. P. 190, (Bottom) Library of Congress. P. 191, (Top and bottom) Musée de l'Armée et d'Histoire Militaire. P. 192, (Bottom, left and right) Museum of Modern Art Stills Library. P. 195, (Top, right) Musée des Deux Guerres Mondiales; (Bottom, left and right) Musée des Deux Guerres Mondiales. P. 196, (Top, left and right) Musée des Deux Guerres Mondiales. P. 197, (Top, left) Musée des Deux Guerres Mondiales; (Top, right) Musée des Deux Guerres Mondiales. P. 202, (Top, left and right) Musée Royal de l'Armée et d'Histoire Militaire; (Bottom, right) Musée Royal de l'Armee et d'Histoire Militaire; (Bottom, left) Library of Congress. P. 203, Musée des Deux Guerres Mondiales. P. 204, (Top, left) Musée des Deux Guerres Mondiales; (Top, right) Library of Congress. P. 205, (Top, left) Musée Royal de l'Armée et d'Histoire Militaire; (Top, right) Musée Royal de l'Armée et d'Histoire Militaire. P. 206, (Top, left) National Archives; (Bottom, left) National Archives; (Bottom, right) National Archives. P. 208, Hoover Institution on War, Peace and Revolution. P. 217, (Top and bottom) Library of Congress. P. 219, Library of Congress. P. 220, Library of Congress. P. 221, National Archives. P. 223, National Archives. P. 224, Imperial War Museum. P. 225, Imperial War Museum. P. 226, (Top, left) Imperial War Museum; (Top, right) Library of Congress. P. 227, (Top) Imperial War Museum; (Bottom, left) Imperial War Museum; (Bottom, right) Imperial War Museum. P. 229, Imperial War Museum. P. 230, Imperial War Museum. P. 231, Imperial War Museum. P. 232, Library of Congress. P. 233, (Top) Library of Congress; (Bottom) Library of Congress. P. 234, (Top and bottom) Imperial War Museum. P. 235, Library of Congress. P. 238, Victoria and Albert Museum. P. 240, Imperial War Museum. P. 243, (Top) Library of Congress. P. 244, (Top, right) Imperial War Museum. P. 249, (Top) Library of Congress; (Bottom) Library of Congress. P. 250, (Top and bottom) Museum of Modern Art Stills Library; P. 251, (Top and bottom) Museum of Modern Art Stills Library. P. 262, (Top) Wide World Photos, Inc. P. 263, (Bottom) Wide World Photos, Inc. P. 264, (Bottom) Wide World Photos, Inc. P. 266, (Top, right) Library of Congress. P. 267, (Top, left) Hoover Institution on War, Revolution and Peace; (Top, right) Library of Congress. P. 268, (Top, left) Library of Congress; (Bottom, left) Library of Congress. P. 269, Library of Congress. P. 270, (Top and bottom) Hoover Institution on War, Revolution and Peace. P. 271, Library of Congress. P. 274, National Archives. P. 275, National Archives. P. 276, Library of Congress. P. 278, (Top, left) Musée des Guerres Mondiales; (Top, right) Library of Congress. P. 279, (Top, left) Library of Congress; (Bottom) Library of Congress. P. 280, Library of Congress.

The text of this book was set in 12 point Bodoni Book,
named after Giambattista Bodoni (1740-1813).
Bodoni Book is a refined, delicate face
particularly appropriate for books and, as originally
set by the Linotype Company, is based on
a composite conception of the Bodoni manner.

PRODUCER AND ART DIRECTOR
Harris Lewine

DESIGNER
Seymour Chwast

COPYEDITOR
David Sachs

MECHANICALS
Rubin Pfeffer

COMPOSITION
Lino-Tech

PRINTER AND BINDER
Mohndruck